Iberian and Latin American Studies

The Poetics of Otherness in Antonio Machado's 'Proverbios y cantares'

The Poetics of Otherness in Antonio Machado's 'Proverbios y cantares'

Nicolás Fernández-Medina

UNIVERSITY OF WALES PRESS

CARDIFF

2011

www.uwp.co.uk

British Library CIP
A catalogue record for this book is available from the British Library.

ISBN 978–0–7083–2322–9

e-ISBN 978–0–7083–2323–6

.

Typeset by Columns Design Limited, Reading
Printed by CPI Antony Rowe, Chippenham, Wiltshire

Contents

Series Editors' Foreword

Over recent decades the traditional 'languages and literatures' model in Spanish departments in universities in the United Kingdom has been superceded by a contextual, interdisciplinary and 'area studies' approach to the study of the culture, history, society and politics of the Hispanic and Lusophone worlds – categories that extend far beyond the confines of the Iberian Peninsula, not only in Latin America but also to Spanish-speaking and Lusophone Africa.

In response to these dynamic trends in research priorities and curriculum development, this series is designed to present both disciplinary and interdisciplinary research within the general field of Iberian and Latin American Studies, particularly studies that explore all aspects of cultural production (inter alia literature, film, music, dance, sport) in Spanish, Portuguese, Basque, Catalan, Galician and indigenous languages of Latin America. The series also aims to publish research in the History and Politics of the Hispanic and Lusophone worlds, at the level of both the region and the nation-state, as well as on Cultural Studies that explore the shifting terrains of gender, sexual, racial and postcolonial identities in those same regions.

Acknowledgements

I would like to extend my sincerest appreciation to Professor Michael Predmore for reintroducing me to Antonio Machado's poetry during my graduate years at Stanford University. Professor Predmore's expert knowledge of nineteenth- and twentieth-century Spanish literature and history as well as our long discussions on Spanish poetry steered me toward the core ideas in this book. I am also very grateful to Armand F. Baker, who read several chapters of my manuscript and provided me with feedback and recommendations. In Spain, Jordi Doménech supplied me with excellent bibliographical references and guided me in locating several documents and articles concerning Machado's life and work. I must also express my indebtedness to my colleagues John Lipski, Sherry Roush, Bob Blue, Marie Speicher and Maria Truglio at The Pennsylvania State University for their feedback and comments on my manuscript. At the University of Wales Press, I would like to thank Sarah Lewis, the anonymous reviewers of my manuscript, and the series editors and copy-editors for all their support and professionalism. My deepest thankfulness goes to my wife, Kelli, and daughter, Beatriz.

Introduction

Beyond the Lyrical and Proverbial: Antonio Machado's Poetic Thinking

El pensamiento poético, que quiere ser creador, no realiza ecuaciones, sino diferencias esenciales, irreductibles; sólo en contacto con lo otro, real o aparente, puede ser fecundo.

Antonio Machado, *Juan de Mairena*

From his first book *Soledades* (1903) to *Campos de Castilla* (*CC*, 1912) and the first edition of *Poesías completas* (1917), and onwards to *Nuevas canciones* (*NC*, 1924) and the writings of the apocryphal Abel Martín and Juan de Mairena of the 1930s, Antonio Machado distilled his poetic thought into the sententious forms prevalent in Spanish folklore. Over the years, his poetry became more concise and conceptual, and it connected with the aphoristic tradition of what Mairena called *el saber popular*. As Mairena put it: 'Escribir para el pueblo es escribir para el hombre . . . Por eso yo no he pasado de folklorista, aprendiz, a mi modo, de saber popular' (1971a: p. 150). This often cited dictum illuminates one of the cornerstones of Machado's poetry: the poetic word is the privileged site for an open dialogue between the *yo* and the *tú*, and the *pueblo*'s knowledge, as expressed in its dynamic folklore, is the epistemological field of this dialogue. The many *rimas*, *canciones* and *parábolas* we find in Machado's works are a fine testament to this dialogue between the *yo* and *tú*, yet the ultimate succinct expression that speaks to its more meditative line of inquiry is best conceived in his 'Proverbios y cantares' (*PrCs*), the over one hundred and sixty, mostly four-verse octosyllabic folk-inspired poems spanning from 1909 to 1937.[1] It is Machado's fondness for poetic distillation in the *PrCs* that makes these poems so accessible and, oftentimes, so impossibly elusive. A handful of them, like the much-admired poem xxix in *CC* that brings to mind Machado's life-traveller, 'Caminante, son tus huellas el camino, y nada más' (famously made into a song by Joan Manuel Serrat in 1968), or poem viii in *NC*, the shortest of the collection, which states 'Hoy es siempre todavía', are referenced by readers now and again as examples of Machado's unique poetic-philosophical craft. However, we still do not have an accurate picture of how these *PrCs* contribute to one of the fundamental concerns of his *oeuvre*: the concept of Other.[2]

Ever since his first poems in *Soledades*, the subject of otherness (the quality or state of being other, and how the experience of difference can defy systems of classification, interpretation and social categorization) infused almost every aspect of Machado's writing. Over the years, he approached otherness not only as a way to transcend a philosophical tradition of solipsistic idealism (what he called 'el cantarse a sí mismo'), but also as a means to incorporate the rich complexities of social life into his work. In broad outline, otherness for Machado was almost always conceived through a poetic-philosophical praxis that attempted to understand how the self interacted with the world, and how the self experienced and learned from this complex interaction, rather than a question of power, domination, and repression that the concept 'other' often conjures up today (I am referring specifically to the postcolonial criticism of Homi K. Bhaba, Gayatri Spivak and the late Edward Said who have theorized 'otherness' in relation to socio-economic, cultural and political exploitation). How can one, Machado often asked himself, establish meaningful communication with an Other in the world? How can one engage 'un *otro* real', as his alter-ego Abel Martín referred to it, whose presence involves the self in a deeply ethical relationship? The *PrCs* offer revealing insights into these deceptively simple questions, and they are arguably Machado's most representative and least systematically studied poems on this subject.

Part of the difficulty surrounding the *PrCs* is their brevity. 'Antonio llega a condensar [su poesía] de tal modo', José Machado tells us, 'que le basta a veces cuatro palabras para decir algo esencial' (19). Understanding how these 'cuatro palabras' contribute to Machado's poetic-philosophical *Weltanschauung* in his *PrCs* has never been simple. To begin with, a great majority of the poems follow the Spanish folk tradition of *cantares* formally speaking (the *soleá, solearillas, redondillas*, etc.), but this tradition is displaced by a proverbial voice whose inspiration, tone, irony, wit and deep contemplative quality greys the lines of what exactly constitutes the lyrical and the proverbial. There are also a number of epigrammatic poems in the *PrCs*, but to label them as epigrams, aphorisms, or maxims diminishes their rich poetic character. Furthermore, to read them, as many have, as a random collection of poetic-philosophical odds and ends, or merely as a jumble of minor witty poems ('poemillas'), also blurs their symbolic allusions with the larger work. The poetry's elusiveness perhaps explains why the *PrCs* have never fully accommodated strict folklorist or philosophical interpretations, as we shall see, and it is this elusiveness that makes the *PrCs* such a dynamic part of Machado's poetry when it comes to his concept of Other.

The present book aims to illuminate the unique character of the *PrCs*. It proposes that the *PrCs* reveal a distinct poetics in Machado's poetry and thought that adds new depth to his concept of Other. My aim is to show how this poetics unfolds, how it reveals and conceals itself in the critical thinking of the aesthetic-philosophical fragment that Machado developed in his own unique way to express what Friedrich Schlegel called 'the impossibility and necessity of complete communication'. In a classic sense, the concept of fragment implies incompleteness and discontinuity. In postmodernist thinking, the fragment represents the demise of so-called metanarratives that attempt to impose any form of hegemony, telos, or sociopolitical holism to epistemology and the mechanisms of knowledge production (as Lyotard famously put it, 'I define postmodern as incredulity toward metanarratives') (xxxiv). The concept of 'whole', or any holistic world view for that matter, has become suspect within postmodernist criticism, and the fragment enacts the symbolic 'ruins' (the absence, the loss, the nostalgia for origins) of modernity's narratives of harmony and centredness.

These are not the meanings I intend specifically for the concept of fragment or fragment poem. The fragment, as I will conceive it, is related to the fragment that comes about in the early Romantic period and relies on such things as conciseness, indeterminacy, contradiction, irony, and self-reflexivity to examine everything from literary genres to the construction of subjectivity. Approaching the *PrCs* with this type of discursivity in mind, and taking as my examples the work of Friedrich Schlegel, G. A. Bécquer and Friedrich Nietzsche, it will become clear how Machado develops a certain type of 'fragment thinking' in his poetry to create an open work in which the poetic word engages an inner dialogue (a self-reflexivity of the poetry itself on what it says and is capable of saying), and a seemingly infinite dialogue with what lies beyond it (how we can interpret what is said in a multitude of ways). As Umberto Eco defined it in *The Open Work*, the 'open' work is 'a complete and *closed* form in its uniqueness as a balanced organic whole, while at the same time constituting an *open* product on account of its susceptibility to countless different interpretations which do not impinge on its unadulterable specificity' (p. 4).[3] Although postmodernist criticism has challenged Eco's concept of openness, its fundamental discussion on the varied ways it establishes 'works in movement' between addresser and addressee still holds today: the principle of ambiguity, point of view/reference, and the work's socio-aesthetic field of relations, to name a few. Eco is right to remind us that 'the "work in movement" is the possibility of numerous different personal interventions, but it is not an amorphous invitation to indiscriminate participation. The invitation offers the performer the opportunity for an oriented insertion into something which always remains the world intended by the author' (p. 19). The idea of 'openness' turns our attention to the complex dialectics between poetry and world and self and Other. In sum, Eco's open/closed definitions will merely be insinuated throughout the book, and I believe they are useful in appreciating how the poems' closedness (their inner dialogue and singularity) functions in relation to their openness (how they might suggest poetic-philosophical meanings within Machado's larger work and his concept of otherness). It is imperative, therefore, to consider the *PrCs* both internally, within the boundaries of the section, and externally, in relation to the larger work (including Machado's prose, letters, criticism, articles, apocryphal writings, and socio-historical milieu) to shed light on the poetry's open/closed relationship.

The fragment, then, undertakes two key functions in this book: firstly, it will serve as a conceptual tool to historically contextualize Machado's thinking on otherness (I will not advocate the 'purity' of the fragment genre in Machado, but rather show how certain aspects of the genre – its inherent scepticism and idea of infinity, for instance – offer him a framework through which to address those Romantic questions on subjectivity and objectivity that he considered foundational when it came to his idea of Other); and secondly, it aims to reveal how the *PrCs* enter into a dialogic relationship with the larger work.

Given the elusiveness of the *PrCs*, it is not surprising that they have been interpreted in a variety of ways and have given rise to divergent opinions on how they contribute to Machado's poetry and thought.

Tuñón de Lara, one of the first critics to pay any serious attention to these poems, demonstrated how they provided revealing insights into Machado's usage of Spanish folklore, yet he was unsure what to make of several of them because they were too abstract and indeterminate: 'En muchos de los cantares se observa ya algo característico de Machado: la ambivalencia del pensamiento: ¿Ironía? ¿Duda filosófica? ¿Pluralismo de exposición algo platoniano? De hecho las exégesis de esos poemas pueden tener un número casi ilimitado de facetas' (p. 111). When Sánchez Barbudo interpreted the *PrCs*, he underlined their philosophical relevance in examining Machado's concept of Other, noting how they touched upon themes like narcissism and the nature of subjectivity. Yet he believed that a good many of the poems were often too enigmatic (perhaps too personal to Machado) to transmit very much, lyrically speaking:

> A menudo son poemillas prosaicos; y a veces resultan en exceso enigmáticos, como si Machado hubiera tratado de ponerse a tono con los "vanguardistas" de la época buscando rarezas. En más de un caso el lector podría dudar si se encuentra en verdad ante un poema, o es que se trata en absoluto de un poema. (1967: pp. 352–69)

For J. M. Aguirre, the *PrCs* lack lyrical merit, while Giménez Caballero, Francisco J. Rabassó, and Fuente Ballesteros interpret the *PrCs* within the poetic tradition of Japanese haikus.[4] Dámaso Alonso, perhaps the most critical of all, considered the *PrCs* as 'poemas minúsculos, definidores, dogmáticos, condensación de turbias intuiciones puramente cerebrales, alejados de la experiencia viva' that confirmed Machado's lyrical exhaustion after the publication of the 1917 edition of *CC* (pp. 149–50). The 'exhaustion' argument continued with Eugenio de Nora and Bernard Sesé, the latter proposing that 'el aspecto algo heterogéneo [de *Nuevas canciones*] refleja también esa falta de unidad en la inspiración . . . La brevedad misma de la mayoría de los poemas revela esta dificultad de la capacidad creadora' (p. 457).[5]

It is thanks to Oreste Macrí, Emilio García Wiedemann and Melero Ruiz, whose analyses have uncovered a wealth of insights into the form and function of these poems (and in a sense, they have introduced the *PrCs* into more contemporary discussions of Machado's poetry), that we have been able to consider the *PrCs* within a broader critical framework. Oreste Macrí's readiness to look beyond strict definitions of what constitutes folklore and philosophy in the *PrCs* allows him to discern the oppositional tensions between poetry and philosophy that organize certain areas of Machado's work: 'El refranero machadiano, muy variado entre opuestos polos – lírico y filosófico –, encierra consideraciones condensadísimas y equilibradas entre "concepto" y ejemplo figurado' (p. 184). Emilio García Wiedemann has examined the unity and origins of the *PrCs*, and he has shown how Machado's work became more fragmented as it developed. What is of particular interest is how Wiedemann carefully documents the alterations to the numbering and arrangement of the poems in their various publications over the years, demonstrating Machado's concern with the order and presentation of the *PrCs*. Ultimately, his study refutes Gutiérrez-Girardot's finding that '[la] ordenación [de los *PrCs*] no parece obedecer a un hilo consecuente'.[6] For Melero Ruiz, the concept of universality is an essential part of the *proverbio* and *cantar*. The *proverbio* generalizes reason and knowledge, while the *cantar* harnesses the lyrical intensity of poetry and song, and for this reason the *proverbio*'s meditative tone and the *cantar*'s lyricism combine to produce 'un efecto de "gracia"': a poetry that is both lyrical and philosophical (pp. 325–41).

Machado's *PrCs*, perhaps like no other part of his work, demonstrate how his sententious poetry has bewildered and inspired readers over the years. There is little doubt that the folklorist appraisal of these poems has always retained a strong presence within critical scholarship. Our propensity has been to privilege the lyrical *cantar* over the gnomic and philosophical *proverbio*, and naturally so, many have argued, considering the poet's family of notable folklorists and his lifelong interest in the *copla*. As one might expect, the *cantar* is interpreted by way of the *cante hondo* (the deepest and most serious genre of flamenco), the Andalusian landscape, Machado's Sevillian roots, and the influence of his family, particularly his folklorist father Antonio Machado y Álvarez 'Demófilo'. This approach – indebted to the invaluable studies by Alvar, Aparicio, Arrebloa, Carvalho-Neto, Hecht, Romeralo and Urbano – has demonstrated that Machado's folklore had little to do with *fin de siglo* poetic fads or a familial responsibility per se, but rather it attempted to articulate Spain's intra-historical reality at a specific socio-historical point in time.[7]

This folklorist reading raises a few questions about how Machado's poetry has been interpreted. While there is no question that the *PrCs* reveal remarkable insights read in this manner, they are only half read, so to speak. What of the *proverbio*? What of its relationship with the *cantar*? How does the *proverbio* converse with the *cantar*? How does it advance, among other concerns, Machado's concept of Other, especially considering the various references to metaphysics and philosophy in the *PrCs*? Obviating the *proverbio*, or simply interpreting it as a minor gnomic inflection within the *cantar* genre, hinders a more cohesive appraisal of this part of his poetry. Machado spent years studying all types of maxims and proverbs, and they appear often in his poetry and prose mostly as a way to condense, rephrase or address a philosophical question with some type of 'valor poético'. Moreover, there is seldom a time when there is not some kind of extratextual framing in his use of proverbs. That is, he uses proverbial expressions to invoke a tradition of thinking (or, we might say, the fundamental problems that occupied a tradition of thinking) as a springboard for his own poetic meditations.

That said, defining the *cantar* also presents its own challenges. As a folk poetic genre, does it belong wholly to flamenco? And what differentiates it from, say, the *canción*? Using poems and biographical references mostly from *Los complementarios*, Manuel Alvar proposes that Machado's discovery of *canciones* in 1916 cleared the way for the sententious poems that would later appear in *NC* (1976: p. 128). When Alvar establishes the distinction between *cantares* and *canciones* – the basis that suggests '[que] al descubrir la poesía folklórica o tradicional, Antonio Machado se ha encontrado con canciones' – he does not return convincingly to the early poetry to follow through on how the *PrCs* establish a clear line of poetic thinking from 1909 to the 1930s.[8] Machado's fondness for sententious poetry appeared as early as 1907 with *Soledades. Galerías. Otros poemas* (*SGOP*) in poems like 'La glosa a Jorge Manrique' (LVIII) and the 'Consejos' (LVII) (and as I will show in chapter 2, his interest in the *copla* and *cantar* surfaced even earlier in the late 1890s). He was careful in distinguishing between *cantares* and *canciones*, and in *CC*, *NC*, and in several publications between 1909 and 1923 such as *La Lectura*, *Revista de Occidente* and *España*, the poems of the *PrCs* appear under titles containing *cantar* and never *canción*. In *NC*, as the title makes clear, *canciones* are a mainstay, but not in the *PrCs*. However, it must be said that the distinction *cantar–canción* is ambiguous, since both terms refer to the oral tradition of songs. As Joaquín Costa noted in his *Tratado de política* (1888) on Spanish folklore, 'canciones: Se han llamado también coplas, cantigas, cantilenas, cánticas, cantares, cuartetas, redondillas, quintillas, rimos [*sic*], etc., nombres los unos, no privativos de este linaje de composiciones, sino extensivos a géneros más amplios de nuestro Parnaso' (p. 54). When the *cantar* and *canción* are differentiated in critical scholarship, many times it is along geographical lines: the *cantar* conjures up Spain's southern regions of Andalusia (as in the *cante* flamenco), while the *canción* evokes the country's central and northern regions (as in the ancient *canción asturiana*). This differentiation is problematic since the *cantar* can be said to form part of a longer genealogy of songs beyond Andalusia and flamenco that harkens back to Spain's epic 'cantares de gesta' (Rosalía de Castro's *Cantares gallegos*, for instance, draw their inspiration from the old tradition of Galician-Portuguese *cancioneros*).[9] In his *PrCs*, Machado opted for the *cantar*, and in many cases did in fact refer to the flamenco tradition, yet as I will demonstrate in chapter 1, the *cantar* was hugely popular with late Romantic and folklorist poets at the turn of the century who used it as an ideal poetic medium to transmit a very 'modern' lyrical immediacy: a lyrical immediacy, in sum, indebted to the innovations of the German lieder that poets like Bécquer discovered in attempting to articulate the often ethereal boundaries between self and world.

The philosophical character of Machado's poetry has experienced renewed interest in recent years. There has been a concerted effort to forge a more intelligible image of the quiet, self-effacing poet of the 'torpe aliño indumentario' who spent years studying not only the wisdom of proverbialists, but also the works of Heraclitus, Plato, Aristotle, Leibniz, Kant, Nietzsche, Bergson and Scheler. Machado himself admitted that philosophy – defined in the Socratic tradition as the study of wisdom and truth – was a lifelong passion of his. During periods of his life, such as the bleak years after his wife Leonor's death in 1912, philosophy dominated his readings entirely. In a letter to Ortega y Gasset on 2 May 1913, he admits: 'He vuelto a mis lecturas filosóficas –únicas en verdad que me apasionan. Leo a Platón, a Leibniz, a Kant, a los grandes poetas del pensamiento' (2001b: p. 332). He also formally studied philosophy. As early as 1900 he had considered completing a degree in *Filosofía y Letras* in Madrid, but only followed through with it in 1915. Earlier, in 1911, he had travelled to Paris to attend Henri Bergson's lectures in the Collège de France. By 1918 he had obtained his degree. The following year he began a doctoral degree in philosophy, but never completed it.

In light of Machado's philosophical studies, readers have uncovered the complexity of discourses present in his more sententious poetry, including the *PrCs* (the *PrCs* in *NC* are dedicated to Ortega y Gasset, perhaps revealing the importance of philosophy in understanding his *proverbio* and *cantar*). This revisionist effort has revealed

Machado's indebtedness to Romanticism and its concern with self-hood and individuality in figures like Friedrich Schlegel and Bécquer, particularly in how poetry required a self-reflexive and ironic language to express the poet's world view. Machado's apocryphal Martín and Mairena, both sceptical of the capacity of language to convey the inner life or reality (and both captivated by the fragmented form), are imagined as late nineteenth-century thinkers who struggle with the Romantic philosophical tradition. Perhaps Ángel González said it best when he noted Machado's 'inequívocas raíces . . . en la más ortodoxa tradición romántica'. He adds, 'el intento de superar la tradición romántica lo llevó a cabo aprovechando, como punto de partida, el mismo impulso individualista que había movido a los románticos' (p. 35).[10] From this perspective, critics like Abellán, Belaunde Morerya, García-Bacca, Ribbans, Sesé and Zamora, to name a few, have demonstrated how the *PrCs* lend themselves to all types of philosophical analyses not only concerning questions of Romantic subjectivity, but also time, death, God and ontology.[11]

Gonzalo Sobejano's study 'La verdad en la poesía de Antonio Machado: de la rima al proverbio' has broadened our understanding of the *PrCs* within this revisionist scholarship by uncovering the relationship between Machado's early poetry (with a special emphasis on the *Soledades'* shorter poems and the *PrCs* of *CC* and *NC*) and Mairena's fragmentary prose. Sobejano reveals how Machado's poetry progressed towards more sententious forms over the years, and he demonstrates how his desire to distill his poetry to its very constitutive elements beyond the symbolist and *modernista* ornamentation of his early poetry evolved as his concept of Truth deepened. Confronting this capitalized Truth was a crucial turning point for Machado. It was analogous to a socio-philosophical 'awakening' that came about not only from his epistolary relationships with thinkers like Miguel de Unamuno that I will discuss in chapter 3, but from his experiences as a rural teacher in Soria, a provincial town where he witnessed Spain's ignorance and poverty and fully immersed himself in his philosophy books as a way to escape his solitude. All these factors converged in the *PrCs*:

> Agudizada esa búsqueda de Verdad a partir de 1909, la poesía epigramática de Machado viene a ser, al mismo tiempo que una manera de distanciarse del modernismo (para él, a fin de cuentas, insatisfactorio), una forma de entablar contacto con el tú esencial y salir del subjetivismo lírico hacia una objetividad anchurosamente

humana . . . La vocación hacia la expresión sentenciosa de ideas vividas
. . . atestigua su anhelo de la Verdad, por encima de la belleza, la
intensidad, la sugestión, o el esplendor imaginativo y sensorial. (p. 47)

Machado's idea of Truth takes form in how his poetry begins to
speak of the self in terms of the Other, or what he termed 'lo elemental
humano', a timeless communal bond between the *yo* and *tú*. A critical
point I adopt from Sobejano's study is that Machado's *PrCs* can be
considered part of a new poetic sensibility that appears in 1909.
(Before Sobejano, however, José Hierro had declared in the 'Prólogo'
to his 1968 *Antonio Machado: Antología poética* that the *proverbios, can-*
tares, and other sententious forms that began appearing after 1909
added 'una nueva dimensión' to Machado's poetry.) Although the
subject of otherness surfaced in other areas of his poetry and in other
texts throughout the years – *Los complementarios* and Mairena's
Sentencias, for instance – the *PrCs* represented a unique space in which
to develop a certain understanding of otherness. The appearance of
the *PrCs* in 1909 signals how far Machado had come in establishing a
more effective dialogue with the Other, and this dialogue leads him,
on the one hand, to the core dilemmas of Romantic subjectivity, and
on the other, to the folkloric forms and wisdom of the *proverbio* and
cantar. Lastly, Sobejano outlines some of the *PrCs*'s foundational
premises that I will develop more thoroughly in this book, such as the
poetry's symbolism, the didacticism and epistemology of the *proverbio*
and *cantar*, and the poetry's evolution from a more hermetic lyricism
'outward' toward the world of collective experience.

Before I move on, one final question remains: why consider only the
PrCs and not all of Machado's sententious poetry? To begin with, there
is something unique about the *PrCs* that sets them apart. Unlike
Machado's *rimas, canciones, epigramas, sátiras, apuntes* and *parábolas*, the
PrCs appeared consistently in his writings between 1909 and 1937, and
they share a symbolic context not found as readily in the other shorter
poems (in a few cases Machado combined his *epigramas, sátiras,*
apuntes, and *parábolas* with his *PrCs*, such as those poems that appeared
in *La Lectura* under the title 'Cantares, proverbios, sátiras y epigramas'
in 1913, and the 'Apuntes, parábolas, proverbios y cantares' in 1916).
Moreover, Machado continually rearranged and ordered his *PrCs* in
various publications, and they appear in everything from his published
poetry books to his personal papers. He laboured on his *PrCs* for
almost three decades, and the core theme of otherness, as well as the
poetry's meditative quality, most clearly spilled over into other areas of

his work (such as the writings of Martín and Mairena). At one point, Machado even considered writing a separate book dedicated to his *PrCs*. Shortly after Juan Ramón Jiménez praised the 1912 edition of *CC*, he thanked Juan Ramón in his *Nota biográfica* of 1913 stating: 'Preparo tres libros que pueden responder a los títulos siguientes: *Hombres de España, Apuntes de paisaje* [,] *Canciones y proverbios*' (2001b: p. 334). In a later version of the 'Nota biográfica', Machado provided more information on his plans to publish these volumes separately, and it is of note that he changes the original title *Canciones y proverbios* to *Cantares y proverbios*: 'Tengo casi terminados tres volúmenes *Hombres de España* [,] *Apuntes de paisaje* [,] *Cantares y proverbios*, que irán saliendo sucesivamente' (2001b: p. 347). Although these books were never published (the poems were included in the later publications of *CC* and the *Poesías completas*), there is little doubt that he not only was quite fond of his *PrCs*, but he considered them as a separate creative thread within his *oeuvre*. From his recently published notebooks *Colección Unicaja Manuscritos de los Hermanos Machado* (Málaga: 2005), we also know that he returned to these poems repeatedly during inspired moments, continually modifying and condensing them, as if to distill his poetic word to its most concrete meaning.[12] The poems provided a private space to add sudden thoughts, intuitions, and proverbial expressions that were constantly mulled over and slowly edited into publishable poems over the years. As never before, Machado's notebooks reveal the intertextuality and significance of the *PrCs* within his larger work. In fol. 105r of *Cuaderno 2*, for instance, poem VIII, which was jotted down in a flash of inspiration, is fragmented over time into three separate poems (ix, x, and xi) that appeared in the *PrCs* in *NC*. Poem VIII of *Cuaderno 2* reads:

> Sol en Libra. Mi ventana
> está abierta al cielo frío
> –¡oh rumor de agua lejana!–
> La tarde despierta al río.
> En el viejo caserío
> –¡anchas torres sin cigüeñas!–
> enmudece el son gregario,
> y en el campo solitario
> suena el agua entre las peñas.
> Como otra vez, mi atención
> está del agua cautiva;
> pero del agua en la viva
> roca de mi corazón.

Poem VIII as it appears in *NC* as poems ix, x and xi:

ix
Sol en Aries. Mi ventana
está abierta al aire frío
–¡Oh rumor de agua lejana!–.
La tarde despierta al río.

x
En el viejo caserío
–¡oh anchas torres con cigüeñas!–
enmudece el son gregario,
y en el campo solitario
suena el agua entre las peñas.

xi
Como otra vez, mi atención
está del agua cautiva;
pero del agua en la viva
roca de mi corazón.

It is worth considering how Machado reworks the original draft material in *Cuaderno 2* into poems ix, x and xi. Poem VIII of *Cuaderno 2* recreates an early autumn sun in Libra ('Sol en Libra'): the running distant brook and the old hamlet are enveloped by the cool autumn air. The storks, harbingers of fertility and prosperity, have migrated, adding to the sombreness of the afternoon ('–¡anchas torres sin cigüeñas!–'). The fields are bare and the hamlet's communal song has petered out. The gurgle of running water – a persistent reminder of time for Machado – returns to intensify the speaker's solitude and reveal the captive dreams inside his soul ('agua cautiva'). In poem ix of the *PrCs*, however, Machado altered the sun's position, which now appears in Aries ('Sol en Aries'), indicating an early spring atmosphere. It follows that the storks have returned to the hamlet ('–¡oh anchas torres con cigüeñas!–'), and the flowing water represents a more generative symbol of springtime regeneration. The pastoral scene in poems ix, x and xi is thus more uplifting and optimistic. By establishing independent – yet interdependent – pieces, the poems come across as more ruminative poetic revelations of the land and its people, and they proceed from an initial cosmic invocation (the constellations, the sun, the seasons), to an image of the hamlet (towers and fields), to the speaker's interiority (the heart). What remains constant in this progression from the outward cosmos to the speaker's interiority is the passage of time in the flowing water, which becomes more insistent in each poem: from a distant and almost imperceptible rumour in poem ix, it becomes an audible sound in poem x, and finally, it fully envelops the speaker's soul in poem xi. The speaker's solitude in poem VIII in *Cuaderno 2* is transformed into a yearning for springtime renewal in a poetic triptych in which continuity and discontinuity (the scenic and emotive progression from one poem to the next) are indispensable to reading the fragments within the whole. And clearly, these poems speak to Machado's larger work. Aside from alluding to core themes in *Soledades* like springtime rejuvenation (the symbolic month of April in 'Salmodias de abril') and the passage of time in water imagery, they also conjure up pastoral scenes elsewhere in his poetry.[13] In 'Orillas del Duero' (IX), for instance, the poem opens with the arrival of storks to a church's bell tower:

> Se ha asomado una cigüeña a lo alto del campanario.
> Girando en trono a la torre y al caserón solitario,
> ya las golondrinas chillan [. . .]
>   El Duero corre, terso y mudo, mansamente.
> El campo parece, más que joven, adolescente.
> Entre las hierbas alguna humilde flor ha nacido,
> azul o blanca. ¡Belleza del campo apenas florido,
> y mística primavera!

From this starting point, chapter 1 will introduce some of the critical and philosophical arguments that guide my reading of the *PrCs*. This chapter sets the book's tone and it is dedicated to three specific topics that converge in the *PrCs*: 1) Machado's idea of Other – its Romantic roots beginning with Kantian idealism – and its lyrical and philosophical implications in his work; 2) the concept of fragment and fragment poetry in the *PrCs*; and 3) the socio-historical foundations of the *proverbio* and *cantar* in the Spanish context and Machado's usage of these genres. Chapter 1 explores how the *PrCs* signify within what Machado referred to as his poetic 'metafísica'. As he explained it, 'todo poeta debe crearse una metafísica que no necesita exponer, pero que ha de hallarse implícita en su obra' (1971b: p. 148). Or put another way: 'Todo poeta [. . .] supone una metafísica; acaso cada poema debiera tener la suya – implícita – claro está – nunca explícita –, y el poeta tiene el deber de exponerla, por separado, en conceptos claros' (2001a: p. 363).

Chapter 2 will consider Machado's formative years from 1875 to 1903. The Machado family, his father Demófilo in particular, was instrumental in his early education. In his father's writings, which Machado knew well, it is possible to unearth five key lessons on folk poetry that reappear and structure the *PrCs*: polyphony, immediacy, indeterminacy, complexity, and sententiousness. Machado's years in the Krausist Institución Libre de Enseñanza were also important. In the Krausist *hombre* he was introduced to the moral and philosophical ideas of the collectivity that would influence his poetry and thought in later years. During his bohemian period in Madrid after 1892, Machado takes his first steps as a writer for the periodical *La Caricatura*, and through an analysis of some of these early writings we get a better sense of his dislike for Spain's late Romantic (and outmoded) literary scene. Folk poets like Enrique Paradas and Salvador Rueda, both proficient in *cantares*, exert a great influence on him during this time, and they demonstrate how folklore – and the *cantar* specifically – could not only tackle questions concerning poetic subjectivity, but it could also lead the way to a broader poetic renewal. Lastly, I analyse a handful of poems in *Soledades* and *SGOP* in this chapter to illustrate how the early poems foreshadow some of the themes and formal properties of the *PrCs*, and I show to what extent the *proverbio* and *cantar* appeared in Machado's work from the very beginning.

There is little doubt that the *proverbio* and *cantar* influenced Machado's thinking early on, well before he took pen to paper to write his first poems. The decisive years from 1903 to 1913, the genesis period of the *PrCs* that I will examine in chapter 3, demonstrate to what extent he returned to his formative years in search of poetic inspiration. As many readers have noted, Machado's poetry undergoes a shift from its early symbolist and *modernista* sensibility of the *Soledades* to a more socially conscious outlook in *CC*. His correspondence with Unamuno between 1903 and 1905 is critical in establishing a clearer picture of the socio-historical factors of this shift. Under Unamuno's unflagging guidance, Machado becomes more socially minded and begins to regard the Other as an essential part of his poetry. Through a number of poems, his evolving ethics and his distancing from symbolist and *modernista* poetry are shown to influence his concept of Other that surfaces in the first published *PrCs* in 1909. A critical revelation for Machado is the idea that recognizing the Other *as* Other (acknowledging otherness without imposing any ideological constraints or objectifying the Other) has to present itself prior to any normative ethical understanding.

As Machado's concept of Other evolved, it branched out into other spheres of inquiry. Chapter 4 will deal with how he examines God in the *PrCs* through the self–Other relation. Overall, his idea of God is very personal, complex and oftentimes not very clearly defined, but the *PrCs* offer us a clearer picture of his secular idea of God. In the *PrCs*, he imagines God, paradoxically, as being both present and absent from the world in that He is unknowable and eternal, yet through intersubjective engagement man can *feel* – and thus make present – some semblance of His divineness. This self–Other relation is shown to clear a path to a type of emancipative spiritual experience between the *yo* and *tú*. Through the indeterminacies and allusions in a number of poems in the *PrCs*, Machado will use Jesus as the symbolic cornerstone of his idea of a collective God.

If there is one obstacle to Machado's concept of otherness, at least in a practical sense, it is ignorance. There can be no meaningful dialogue between the *yo* and *tú* when ignorance is the rule of politics and government and threatens to undermine any socio-political reconciliation. For Machado, ignorance represents the greatest impediment to any practical intersubjective engagement in Spain, and any concept of Other that aspired to the highest social, political and ethical good had to confront the country's 'régimen de iniquidad'. When Machado refers to this 'régimen de iniquidad', he is actually alluding to how the Church and State had kept Spain's rural majority suffering in ignorance and poverty. In several *PrCs*, he uses the principle of Socratic ignorance to educate his reader about the country's 'régimen de iniquidad'. Chapter 5 will discuss this relationship between epistemology and otherness in Machado's *PrCs*, keeping in mind the transitions that changed Spain's socio-economic landscape during the first decades of the twentieth century.

Lastly, the conclusion will examine the unending inquiry of the *PrCs* in terms of Machado's concept of Other. What he presents to readers of his poems is not only a nuanced understanding of how Spain confronted Romantic problems of subjectivity and alterity in the early twentieth century, but also an open examination into the foundations of otherness that connects with more contemporary philosophers like Emmanuel Levinas.

I should like to end this introduction by noting that Machado's concept of Other is larger than any one book alone. So too are his *PrCs*, several of which were not included here mainly for reasons of space. What the reader will find in the following pages is an interpretation of the poetics of otherness in the *PrCs*, an interpretation that leaves room – as Machado, the sceptic of sceptics, always insisted – for ulterior readings and formulations. For many scholars, the Other in Machado's *oeuvre* (the *tú* or the *otro*) acts as a rhetorical device through which he examines himself; in other words, he addresses the *tú* or the *otro* as a way to converse with his other intimate self or selves on a much deeper level. This understanding of Machado's otherness as an inner dialogue is not only valid, but appears in various parts of his work. If anything, this inner alterity makes his concept of Other that much more complex and interesting. His famous soliloquy in 'Retrato' says it all:

> Converso con el hombre que siempre va conmigo
> –quien habla solo espera hablar a Dios un día–
> mi soliloquio es plática con este buen amigo
> que me enseñó el secreto de la filantropía.

My primary concern in this book, however, is to explain Machado's poetics of otherness as originating from concepts such as self, difference and collectivity, and how notions of self, no matter how poetically and philosophically intricate, depend on an Other, and Others, in the world.

Chapter 1

The Problem of Subjectivity: How to Know the Self and Other

The external appearance of things is only a symbol which is the task of the artist to interpret. Things have truth only in the artist; they only possess an inner truth.

Charles Morice, *La Littérature de tout à l'heure*

Machado returned to the concept of Other again and again over the years. He understood that the 'real' Other in the world often eluded comprehension, and it was in these moments of evasion when poetry could establish what Mairena called 'el diálogo amoroso en que se busca la comunión por el intelecto en verdades' (1971a: p. 67). Philosophy was also important because it provided concepts that could help 'el intelecto' define these common truths between self and Other, and it could provide a way to understand the significance of this dialogue in everyday life. Philosophy and poetry, then, like two complementary halves, were intertwined with the discovery of otherness. 'Sólo el pensamiento filosófico tiene alguna nobleza', Mairena declared, '[p]orque él se engendra, ya en el diálogo amoroso que supone la dignidad pensante de nuestro prójimo, ya en la pelea del hombre consigo mismo' (1971a: pp. 117–18). Likewise, 'hay hombres . . . que van de la poética a la filosofía; otros que van de la filosofía a la poética. Lo inevitable es ir de lo uno a lo otro' (1971a: p. 137). It is through Mairena's teachings that Machado's concept of Other has most often been explained, since he theorized extensively on the subject in his ironic and witty manner, yet Machado's *Proyecto de un discurso de ingreso en la academia española* of 1931 – a lecture he prepared for his induction into the Royal Spanish Academy – is one of his most revealing writings on the subject, and it condenses almost three decades' worth of his ideas on how poetry and philosophy explore concepts of self and Other.[1] Through the *Proyecto de un discurso*, it is possible to begin delimiting the so-called 'problem of subjectivity' (the difficulty of knowing the self and world) that occupied Machado for most of his life, and reveal to what extent it influenced the *PrCs*.

Kantian Metaphysics and the Need for Realness

From the *Proyecto de un discurso*'s initial question '¿Qué es la poesía?', Machado defines what he considers to be the crisis of contemporary lyric poetry, yet under his criticisms of Verlaine, Joyce and other poets, we find a more searching analysis of how Western philosophy from the Romantic age onwards had destabilized the very idea of objectivity. For Machado, a tradition of transcendental metaphysics that began with Immanuel Kant had set into motion a critique of objectivity in the nineteenth century that had slowly eroded the belief in a unified, homogeneous and individual object. 'Casi todo [el siglo XIX] milita contra el objeto', Machado contends, adding, 'Kant lo elimina en su ingente tautología, que esto significa la llamada *revolución copernicana*, que se le atribuye. Su análisis de la razón sólo revela la estructura ideal del sujeto cognoscente' (2001b: p. 693). Kant's Copernican revolution, broadly conceived, synthesized rationalism and empiricism into a coherent theory of experience and knowledge, and in his quest for a universally and scientifically valid basis of experience, he proposed that the subject, through an *a priori* understanding of space and time, was in fact the producer of experience. Although there is considerable debate on the ramifications of Kant's Copernican revolution, one of its most important insights was that the thing-in-itself – the *noumenon*, or object of inquiry – remained inaccessible as such to the subject. Thus, the forms of our thinking apprehend things as they appear, not as they intrinsically are.

Kant's philosophy appears often not only in Machado's *Proyecto de un discurso*, but throughout his poetry and prose, and it offered Machado a springboard from which to examine the foundations of nineteenth-century metaphysics and its theories of subjectivity and objectivity. In poem xxxix (*CC*) of the *PrCs*, for example, he describes Kant as both an innovator ('sabio profesor') and an anachronism ('y volar /otra vez, hacia Platón'):

Dicen que el ave divina,
trocada en pobre gallina,
por obra de las tijeras
de aquel sabio profesor
(fue Kant un esquilador
de las aves altaneras;
toda su filosofía.
un *sport* de cetrería),
dicen que quiere saltar
las tapias del corralón
y volar
otra vez, hacia Platón.
¡Hurra! ¡Sea!
¡Feliz será quien lo vea![2]

Machado refers to Kant's dove metaphor in the image of the 'ave divina' and various other references to birds and flight ('aves altaneras', '*sport* de cetrería', 'volar'). In the introduction to the 1787 edition to the *Critique of Pure Reason*, Kant explains how his philosophy differs from that of his predecessors such as Berkeley and Hume, and he discusses the relationship between metaphysics and knowledge by speculating that a dove (metaphysics) might think it could fly more easily without the impediment of air around it (experience of the world). 'The light dove', Kant explains, 'in free flight cutting through the air the resistance which it feels, could get the idea that it could do better in airless space' (p. 129). As Kant goes on to suggest, such a bird would, of course, discover that flying in a vacuum is impossible, and he refers to Plato's ideal Forms to explain his distrust of any metaphysics that ignored the role of experience in how we acquire knowledge of the world:

> Likewise, Plato abandoned the world of the senses because it posed so many hindrances for the understanding and dared to go beyond it on the wings of the ideas, in the empty space of pure understanding. He did not notice that he made no headway by his efforts, for he had no resistance, no support, as it were, by which he could stiffen himself, and to which he could apply his powers in order to get his understanding off the ground. (p. 129)[3]

For Machado, Kant's metaphysics also suffered in that it too failed to realize that the theory of pure reason (*a priori* understanding and the inaccessibility of the object) is problematized by our experience of the world. In the first four verses of the poem, Kant is imagined clipping the wings of the 'ave divina' and transforming it into a 'pobre

gallina'. As Machado interpreted it, 'Kant, con su crítica de la razón
teórica, corta las alas al pensar metafísico, mostrando la incapacidad
de la mente humana para toda construcción ideológica que no sea
mera estructuración y ordenamiento de la experiencia sensible'
(1971b: p. 218).[4] Kant not only transforms the 'ave divina' into a
'pobre gallina', but Kant himself is portrayed as wanting to 'volar /
otra vez, hacia Platón': in other words, he attempts, philosophically
speaking, a similar speculative flight into a vacuum as did Plato, and in
this light, the last verses of the poem can be interpreted in a much
more ironic manner: '¡Hurra! ¡Sea! / ¡Feliz será quien lo vea!' Kant's
pure reason is too restrictive and limiting, according to Machado, and
it represents the metaphysical dead end – the 'callejón sin salida' – that
he refers to in his *Proyecto de un discurso* when he alludes to solipsistic
thinking leaving little room for otherness beyond constructions of the
understanding. In poem IV of the *Apuntes, parábolas, proverbios y
cantares* published in *La Lectura* in 1916, he further criticized Kant's
philosophy, particularly its twelve *a priori* concepts termed 'categories'
by which the world is experienced and known. For Machado, these
ordered categories represented a privative and empty understanding:

> Sobre la blanca arena aparece un caimán,
> que muerde ahincadamente en el bronce de Kant.
> Tus formas, tus principios y tus categorías,
> redes que el mar escupe, enjutas y vacías.

Yet, ironically, what attracted Machado to Kant's dove metaphor was
precisely what urged the latter to include it in his first *Critique*: the
dangers of using metaphysical 'flights' to speculate about how the self
understands the world. And just as Kant censured Plato for his faith in
ideal Forms, Machado too censured Kant for his faith in transcendental idealism. Metaphorically speaking, the impossibility of these metaphysical 'flights' had definite didactic value, since in Machado's eyes
Kant's philosophy, like his dove, had attempted to fly into a speculative
beyond, and rather than expand our knowledge of reality and the
world, it had drastically limited it to subjective concepts: 'Kant nos da –
aunque en verdad de una manera equívoca – una limitación de lo real
al campo de lo fenoménico y categorías subjetivas' (1971b: p. 92). For
Machado, Kant's transcendental idealism, and its core idea that the
objects of experience are real but transcendentally ideal, regarded the
object through the veils of perception, cognition and categories, and
sidestepped the object's very essence there in the world and how it
affected us on a more intuitive and personal level. Mairena elaborates

on this point steering the discussion to the questions of otherness and objective reality, stating:

> Si nada es en sí más que yo mismo, ¿qué modo hay de no decretar la irrealidad absoluta de nuestro prójimo? Mi pensamiento borra y expulsa de la existencia – de una existencia en sí – en compañía de esos mismos bancos en que asentáis vuestras posaderas. La cuestión es grave. (1971a: p. 212)

Oftentimes Machado's readings of Kant are partial and overly critical. Only in 1914 does he begin mentioning Kant's broader philosophical *oeuvre* (conscious of the plural 'Críticas'), and even then he rarely refers to the *Critique of Practical Reason* or the *Critique of Judgment* until later on (and mostly in a fragmentary fashion through his alter-egos, who sometimes reveal, as in Mairena's case, his more low-brow Kant criticism: 'en leer y comprender a Kant se gasta mucho menos fósforo que en descifrar tonterías sutiles y en desenredar marañas de conceptos ñoños') (1971a: p. 70).[5] Indeed, his appreciation of Kant might have been rather different had he earlier spent more time on the *Critique of Judgment*, which addresses the 'incalculable gulf' between concepts of nature and freedom and confronts questions of sociability and universal communicability in aesthetic pleasure. Likewise, a better grasp of Kant's moral philosophy in the *Critique of Practical Reason* and *Metaphysics of Morals* would have been more illuminating in terms of the broader ethical implications of Kant's categorical imperative (the self–Other relation considered through the lens of the Kantian idea that every man is an end in himself). Yet Machado's readings of the German philosopher gravitated toward the topics of subjectivity/objectivity and transcendental idealism presented most thoroughly in the first *Critique*, which he had read several times and knew well thanks to Morente, Cassirer and Natorp.[6] We cannot underestimate how deeply Kant and the first *Critique* influenced Machado's poetry. 'Mi pensamiento está generalmente ocupado', he admitted as early as 1912, 'por lo que Kant llama *conflictos de las ideas transcendentes* y busco en la poesía alivio a esta ingrata faena' (2001b: p 346).

By 1912, Machado is thinking of the Other when he tackles these questions of transcendental idealism as this Other was conceived after Kant. This involved reassessing how the world – both poetically and philosophically – had become increasingly confined within theories of selfhood throughout the nineteenth century. Lacoue-Labarthe and Nancy have examined Kant's notion of subjectivity demonstrating how

significantly he affected Romantic ideals of self and set the groundwork for a complex and 'modern' subjectivity by auguring the non-
substantial representation of the subject:

> What is formed or constructed by the transcendental imagination is
> thus an object that may be grasped within the limits of a priori
> intuition but is nothing that can be thought under the concept of *eidos*
> or *Idea*, an originary and genuine form of reason itself . . . What results
> from this is a cognition within the limits of possible a priori
> experience, but such a cognition is incapable of restoring anything like
> the subject. (p. 31)

Robert Pippin has also mapped various philosophical theories of
subjectivity after Kant in an attempt to reconstruct the rise of the
so-called 'modern' nineteenth-century subject while taking into
account the sociopolitical implications of this project. For Pippin, it
was after Kant, and after the discoveries of transcendental idealism,
that 'a human subject is, rather, a meaning-*making* subject . . . a
self-conscious subject, in this active, self-determining relation to itself
in all experience as well as in all action'. Yet what is perhaps most
significant, particularly as it concerns Kantian reason, is that 'it is this
project – reason's examination of its own possibility and the attendant
controversies over the nature of the object of such a study and the right
implications to draw from it – that sets the agenda for an extraordinary
flurry of philosophical activity [in the nineteenth century]' (p. 30).
Machado is well aware of the 'controversies over the nature of the
object', to use Pippin's words, and they lead him in his *Proyecto de un
discurso* to defend the Other's 'realness' (physicality and feeling) and
show how this 'realness' might influence one's sense of self. Once
again, he returns to Kant noting that 'del hombre kantiano no
sabemos cómo sea el rostro, ni el carácter, ni el humor, ni sabemos
cómo siente, ni siquiera cómo piensa, sólo sabemos cuál es el rígido
esquema de su razón en el espejo de la ciencia fisicomatemática'
(2001b: p. 693). From this perspective, and given Machado's criticisms
of solipsistic thinking in the *Proyecto de un discurso*, Kant is conceived as
setting the stage for a cult of the self in which the *yo*, with the
appearance of Romantic subjectivity (Machado alludes in turn to
Fichte, Schelling and Hegel to establish the trajectory of his argument), had strayed into a type of social estrangement:

> Cuando el espíritu romántico desfallece como un atleta que agota su
> energía en la mera tensión de sus músculos, sólo se salva el culto al yo,
> a la pura intimidad del sujeto individual. Y una nueva fe, un tanto

perversa, se inserta en la fe romántica en la soledad del sujeto. Se piensa que lo individual humano, el yo propiamente dicho, el sí mismo es lo diferencial entre hombre y hombre y carece de formas de expresión genéricas. Razón y sentimiento son cosas de todos, instrumentos ómnibus que el poeta desdeña en su afán de cantarse a sí mismo, no responden a la íntima realidad psíquica. (2001b: p. 695)

Kant does not advocate a cult of the self or solipsism, and in his 'Refutation of Idealism', which appears in the first *Critique*, he took great pains to differentiate his ideas from Descartes' 'problematical' doubt and Berkeley's 'dogmatic' *esse est percipi* argument (p. 326). Yet Machado interpreted Kant's transcendental idealism as a pivotal discovery in a broader sociocultural progression toward what he claimed was an insular subjectivity: a concept of self in which the Other was inaccessible except through a type of rigid and schematic reason. The objectivity question for Machado, particularly as he examined it through the Kantian lens, had to do with the *limits* of reason when confronted with the Other in the world. It was through what these limits of reason revealed about the self that he approached Schopenhauer and Bergson as original philosophical voices. Although he recognizes the Kantian inflection in Schopenhauer's philosophy, he nevertheless admires the 'acephalic' potential of his theory of the will in revealing a new order of reality. Schopenhauer departed from Kant in the fundamental premise that the *noumenon* is knowable as volitional activity, and Machado reformulates this idea by alluding to the shortcomings of Kantian idealism as he understood them: 'Lo decisivo de Schopenhauer es su concepción del ser como voluntad en completo divorcio con todas las categorías del pensar. Aquí aparece ya desembozadamente la nueva fe del siglo, la nueva metafísica' (1971b: p. 218). Bergson's concept of time as fluid *durée* – a flowing consciousness of the here-and-nowness of experience – was just as significant for Machado as was his theory of intuition, which he explained to Valle-Inclán in 1916 as a form of revelation of concrete reality: 'Que la intuición – en el sentido bergsoniano de íntima revelación de la vida – sea lo esencial en la obra de arte y aun en la del filósofo, cosa es que no dudo' (2001b: p. 400). It was the *limits* of reason that had stripped the 'comunión humana' of its constitutive collective meaning, or what Machado explained in the *Proyecto de un discurso* as the 'sentido común' and the unifying 'sentimiento', and it follows that scepticism toward reason could bring about a new epistemological stance concerning the Other's 'realness':

Lo otro no existe: tal es la fe racional, la incurable creencia de la razón humana. Identidad = realidad, como si, a fin de cuentas, todo hubiera de ser, absoluta y necesariamente, *uno y lo mismo*. Pero lo otro no se deja eliminar; subsiste, persiste; es el hueso duro de roer en que la razón se deja los dientes. (1971a: p. 50)

Yet we must be very clear that Machado did not believe in the unproblematic recognition of materiality: that is, in the existence of a direct equivalence between reality and the representations and concepts we form of it in our minds. On the contrary, he spent years scrutinizing the problem, but he understood that the experience of the Other could not be confined to complex modes of representation. On this point, Roberto Murillo Zamora points out that:

[E]n Machado, la antinomia de la realidad y la apariencia no se señala para evitarla, sino para pensarla filosóficamente en toda su radicalidad . . . la antinomia de Machado roería las creencias básicas . . . Serían más bien los razonamientos, llevados a últimas consecuencias, los que aparecerían contradictorios, y estos razonamientos dependen de la metafísica, de la nada, de la heterogeneidad, y no de clasificaciones cruzadas en el interior del ente. (pp. 33–5)

By confronting lyric poetry's decline from the Romantic period to the 1930s in his *Proyecto de un discurso*, Machado reiterated what he had declared in some form since 1903: the self must recognize the Other in the concrete world of the 'comunión humana'. This act of recognition was crucial because it implied not only considering the dual realms of feeling ('sentimiento') and reason (the 'sentido común' of the collective) as integral parts of his life and work, but also allowed him to begin theorizing what a committed intersubjectivity would look like on a more sociopragmatic level. Machado's concern with the Kantian subject's physical 'rostro' (the fact that this subject is faceless) is revealing in this respect, since the concern with the face-to-face encounter points to the ethical imperative that arises from the Other's presence, and it brings to mind a type of Levinasian ethics in which, quite simply, physical presence (the face before me) makes the self aware of the 'infinity' of the Other.[7] Perhaps for this reason Martín's theory of objectivity demands 'un *otro* real' who could be recognized not through the complex categories of Kantian reason, but through something as irrational and physical as love. It is not surprising that Machado's preoccupation with objectivity is addressed in Martín's concept of love as an erotic yearning for otherness:

Que fue Abel Martín hombre mujeriego lo sabemos, y, acaso, también onanista; hombre, en suma, a quien la mujer inquieta y desazona, por presencia o ausencia. Y fue, sin duda, el amor a la mujer el que llevó a Abel Martín a formularse: ¿Cómo es posible el objeto erótico? (1953: pp. 12–13)

Machado reveals to what degree the object ('mujer', 'presencia o ausencia') can overwhelm reason (Martín's 'inquietud' and 'desazón') and open a reflective space in which we can question how we understand the world ('¿Cómo es posible el objeto erótico?'). The object, both present and absent, can transcend the limits of reason, and it is this grey area of meaning that is so compelling poetically speaking, especially in light of how poetry can reveal what Machado called 'la esencial heterogeneidad del ser', or the idea that what is Other is part of one's concept of self ('es precisamente amor la autorrevelación de la esencial heterogeneidad de la sustancia única') (1953: p. 15). Using the male/female duality as a simple metaphor for his argument, Machado proposes that self and Other are two sides of the same existential-ontological coin, and in moments of love, heeding the physical and often irrational nature of yearning, both long for recognition, communication, reciprocity and completion. In the end, the Other in the world, that 'hombre de carne y hueso', to use Unamuno's expression, affects one's subjectivity more deeply than Kant could have imagined (and on this point Mairena adds: 'Porque si nuestro prójimo no existe, mal podremos amarle') (1971a: p. 211). It remains clear that Kant's philosophy was an important source of inspiration for Machado in both determining his own concepts of subjectivity and objectivity, and in conceiving the Other beyond the confines of transcendental idealism. Without Kant's findings, it is doubtful he could have penetrated so deeply into the matter.

The Rise of Individualism

Through his Kant readings, Machado responded to how the Other was essentially desubstantiated through concepts of reason, a theme that traversed much of his poetry and prose from his first *PrCs* to Mairena's writings of the 1930s. In Mairena's words: '*Las tan desacreditadas cosas en sí. . . La cosa en sí ¡tan desacreditada!* [. . .] Asusta pensar hasta dónde puede llegar el descrédito' (1971a: p. 217). As several of his generational peers had done, Machado demonstrated a deep scepticism toward reason, and he explored the Romantic problem of subjectivity and its broader 'lyrical turn', which was still debated in Europe at the turn of the twentieth century. Broadly defined, this problem derived from the idea that if the ordinary world is in the end unknowable in and of itself, it follows that the phenomenal world, while clearly dependent on objective reality for what is given in experience, must represent, in some form, a place of the known, of truth and authenticity. As Charles B. Guignon explains it:

> Romanticism, far from providing an alternative to scientific objectification, simply turns reality over to the sciences once and for all and rests content with creating its own reality in imagination. Romanticism's final story is that we can let science have reality, because we have another reality – a special reality that is in here, within the self. Given this view of things, however, the self is not just the center of the universe. It is the universe. (p. 34)

The outcomes of this problem are indeed far-reaching, and in the past decade there have been numerous studies like those of McGann, Siskin and Henderson, to name a few, that have attempted to historicize the origins of this problem of subjectivity by revisiting Romantic concepts of identity and inwardness.[8] In retrospect, Machado was undertaking a very similar revisionist project because he believed that the problem of subjectivity had to be tackled at this essential level of inwardness. 'Porque el solipsimo podrá responder o no', as Mairena explains, 'a una realidad absoluta, ser o no verdadero; pero de absoluto no tiene pelo. Es la conclusión inevitable y perfectamente lógica de todo subjetivismo extremado' (1971a: p. 212). Machado was aware that Romantic self-referentiality offered the self new territory to develop the private realm of the imagination, which he conceived as an intense intuitive-poetic force, yet also a force that placed the self at the 'center of the universe', to use Guignon's expression. In *Jerusalem* (1804), for instance, Blake speaks of the inward 'Worlds of Thought' to conceive the imagination as an almost divine concept through which one could discover and construct subjectivity: 'I know of no other Christianity and of no other Gospel than the liberty both of body and mind to exercise the Divine Arts of Imagination' (p. 258). The self was an *active* self in this boundless world of the imagination, which was capable of generating a much deeper level of self-knowledge, and the concrete world beyond it was, in the words of Harold Bloom, 'dirt upon [one's] feet' (p. 115). Romantic poets and writers after Blake explored the creative possibilities of this infinite imagination. In his famous article 'Salon 1859' on the modern science of photography, Baudelaire discusses the inner realm of the imagination, and in his opinion, 'I consider it useless and tedious to represent what exists, because nothing that exists satisfies me [. . .] I prefer the monsters of my fancy to what is positively trivial' (p. 373). Baudelaire's 'monsters of fancy' represent that creative dynamism that considered the exterior world as a hindrance on one's imaginativeness. It was the realm of the intimate self, the secret realm of imaginative 'fancy', where the artist needed to look for inspiration and solace. The early Lukács of *Soul and Form* documented the heights to which Baudelaire's 'monsters of fancy' had risen in subsequent generations (the Parnassians, Symbolists, Decadentists, etc.) and he criticized how they had cultivated that 'morbidly intense inwardness of today's writers' (p. 47). In sum, Blake and Baudelaire legitimized the self as the 'center of the universe' in the imagination and they revolutionized nineteenth-century poetry.

What has been said so far provides only a general picture of a much broader sociocultural process of individuation during the nineteenth and early twentieth centuries in Europe, or what we could consider to be the individual's 'problem of self-grounding' that came with economic progress and increased industrialization.[9] The point is that the subject, in response to an increasingly secular and positivistic world, was often forced to retreat inward to find or construct some semblance of stable meaning. This Romantic legacy of inwardness for Machado – what he called 'lo individual humano', 'culto al yo', and 'cantarse a sí mismo' – had created an untenable individualism in the post-Kantian subject, and this individualism, problematized by the crisis of values and religious belief, is history's true motor of change, he believed. It is not by chance that Mairena's alter-ego Jorge Meneses speaks in historical materialist terms of how this rise of individualism had worked against concepts of collective identity in modern poetry:

La lírica moderna, desde el declive romántico hasta nuestros días (los del simbolismo) es acaso un lujo, un tanto abusivo, del hombre manchesteriano, del individualismo burgués, basado en la propiedad privada. El poeta exhibe su corazón con la jactancia del burgués enriquecido que ostenta sus palacios, sus coches, sus caballos y sus queridas. El corazón del poeta, tan rico en sonoridades, es casi un insulto a la afonía cordial de la masa, esclavizada por el trabajo mecánico. (1953: pp. 52–8)

There is, however, more to this rise of individualism that concerned Machado. Scientific approaches thrived in the second half of the nineteenth century, and Machado was also influenced by positivism and evolutionism. His experience with positivism, as I will demonstrate more at length in the following chapter, came primarily by way of his folklorist father Demófilo, who was one of the first proponents of positivism in Spain after breaking away from Krausist doctrine in the late 1870s. Darwin's evolutionism and Spencer's social philosophy made a lasting impression on Demófilo, chiefly through the scholarship of biologist Thomas Huxley and anthropologist Edward Tylor, both of whose work he had reviewed and translated. According to Demófilo, social life and science converged in folklore making it an ideal ground for scientific inquiries seeking to establish the foundations of universal social laws: 'El Folk-Lore . . . abarca, bajo un aspecto toda la vida y todas las ciencias, y es, a su vez, una faz o aspecto de todas ellas' (1887: p. 280). In Restoration Spain, this type of epistemological practice promised practical applications in Demófilo's opinion: in the proper hands, and with the right political impetus, it could open the way to a national project of *regeneracionismo*. As he stated it, 'el estudio de la literatura popular es camino de regeneración' (1884b: p. xx). Antonio Machado y Núñez, Machado's grandfather, was also familiar with evolutionism, and he had introduced Darwin's theories into the University of Seville in the 1880s and was responsible for establishing the journal *Revista Mensual de Filosofía, Literatura y Ciencias de Sevilla* dedicated to the dissemination of positivist and evolutionist theories in Spain.

Machado realized that the science of facts, in its uncompromising methodologies, allowed little room for such concepts as intuition or love. All unobservable phenomena were suspect. For this reason the French critic, historian and positivist Hippolyte Taine famously proposed that such things as vice and virtue could in fact be studied with the same scientific certitude as chemistry (Tatarkiewicz, p. 166). Machado rejected this positivist certitude believing it to be subservient to utilitarianism and, with time, his rejection of its methodologies (observation, limits, calculations, etc.) brought him back once again to the questions of subjectivity and objectivity:

El positivismo es una consecuencia agnóstica de la eliminación del objeto absoluto y del descrédito inevitable de la metafísica. A él acompaña una emoción de signo contrario, humana, demasiado humana, pero no menos subjetiva que la romántica: la del hombre como sujeto empírico de una vida sin trascendencia posible, mero accidente cósmico, efímero episodio en el ciego curso de la naturaleza. (2001b: p. 693)[10]

Spain's late nineteenth-century sociopolitical milieu did little to thwart the rise of the individualism Machado had alluded to in his *Proyecto de un discurso*. This period in Spain presented challenges on several fronts. Not only did the country lose the remnants of its empire in the Spanish–American War of 1898, but the failure of the 1868 revolution, coupled with Prime Minister Cánovas del Castillo's failed *turno político* and the increase in *caciquismo* and oligarchic rule after 1875, produced a sense of sociopolitical impasse for many Spaniards hoping for change and renewal. During this *fin de siglo* period, Ganivet had spoken of how a great gulf was opening up between what he determined was the nation's 'vida exterior' and its 'vida íntima'; this gulf underscored the sociopolitical incommunicability that he believed was stifling the individual:

> [S]i existe un medio de conseguir la verdadera fraternidad humana, éste no es el de unir a los hombres debajo de organizaciones artificiosas, sino el de afirmar la personalidad de cada uno y enlazar las ideas diferentes por la concordia y las opuestas por la tolerancia. Todo lo que no sea esto es tiranía, tiranía material que rebaja al hombre a la condición de esclavo y tiranía ideal que le convierte en hipócrita. (p. 128)

Given this state of affairs, Machado and his peers surveyed the Western philosophical tradition for new critical discourses with which to examine the origins of Spain's 'crisis del alma', as it came to be know. Unamuno had translated Marx, Hegel and Kierkegaard; Pío Baroja and Ángel Ganivet were knowledgeable of Nietzsche's and Schopenhauer's philosophy; Azorín was well-versed in Kropotkin's and Bakunin's social theories; and Manuel de la Revilla and José del Perojo had translated and disseminated parts of Kant's *Critiques* 'para defender la causa del criticismo [. . . y] para hacer valer la posición neokantiana en España [. . . que] quería ofrecer una alternativa al radical pensamiento de [los eruditos oficiales]' (Villacañas, pp. 18–20). At their disposal was not only the Krausist Institución Libre de Enseñanza and the teachings of many regenerationists and progressive liberals associated with it, but also journals like *La Emancipación*, *Revista Contemporánea* and *La España Moderna*, which introduced Engels, Lombroso, Marx, Renan, Mill, Taine and Karolenko, among others, into Spanish literary circles between 1875 and 1914. What furnished cohesion to this influx of new ideas for many intellectuals like Machado was precisely the problem of subjectivity and how it could shed new light on Spain's sociopolitical problems.

Between 1903 and 1907, as we shall see, Machado takes his first steps in articulating those questions on the self–Other relation that would reappear in the *PrCs*. They include the following: how is the Other knowable? How is knowledge of the Other constituted and circulated? And finally, how can the nineteenth-century's legacy of individualism be effectively overcome? The *PrCs* emerged as one way of taking up these questions from within the aesthetic and philosophical folds of the Romantic tradition. In terms of the underlying problem of subjectivity, Machado understood that the moment we adopt any type of system of thought, not only is the 'openness' of meaning in philosophy and art restricted, but knowledge of the Other – and the world more generally – is limited by the system itself. Regarded in this manner, systems of thought, as Adorno had lamented in his *Negative Dialectics*, 'are marks of an *a priori* conditional failure' because they close themselves off 'so that no doubts are raised as to the unimpeachable seamlessness, closure and acribia of the thought-product' (p. 33). The rigours of system-thinking allowed little room for criticism, discussion or disbelief, and for Machado this was unacceptable for the simple reason that it limited one's freedom and creativity:

> Se inventarán nuevos sistemas filosóficos en extremo ingeniosos, que vendrán, sobre todo, de Alemania, contra nosotros los escépticos o filósofos propiamente dichos. Porque el hombre es un animal extraño que necesita – según él – justificar su existencia con la posesión de alguna verdad absoluta . . . Contra esto . . . debéis estar absolutamente en guardia. (1971a: p. 114)

Machado was sceptical of system-thinking. What he proposed instead was a 'pensar poético' along the lines of the *PrCs* and Martín's and Mairena's fragmentary writings. He believed that the Neokantian movement, which was popular in early twentieth-century philosophy and had shaped the thinking of Ortega y Gasset, did not have to mean returning to grand systems of thought in the German idealist tradition. On the contrary, it could clear a path to an open method of critical inquiry into topics like epistemology and subjectivity. 'Pero la vuelta a Kant', he declared, 'no puede ser la resurrección del sistema, sino de un método de severo pensar sobre el estado actual del conocimiento' (1971b: p. 47). In the movement, irony and self-reflexivity of shorter poetic forms, it was possible to gain insight into otherness from different angles of entry without imposing any closure on the matter. The experience of the Other is, at its core, an *ongoing* experience that is never completed, never rounded off or whole, and by its very nature it transcends any system of thought. Such a proposition, I believe, was one of the ways Machado attempted to overcome 'lo individual humano' in his work in order to poetize some semblance of the inexhaustible 'comunión humana'.

Reading the Fragment, Reading the Whole: Poetry's Becoming

In order to appreciate how the *PrCs* convey the ideas presented in the preceding section, we must turn to Schlegel, Bécquer and Nietzsche to situate the fragment within the poetic and historical framework that Machado alludes to in the *proverbio* and *cantar*. It will become apparent that the fragment, its very genesis and evolution from the Romantic period onwards, is directly related to the problem of subjectivity that Machado examined in his work.

Friedrich Schlegel and the Jena group of German Romantics rediscovered the fragment's literary and metaphysical potential at the cusp of the eighteenth century. There were others before Schlegel who had developed the fragment with some success and had influenced him, such as François La Rochefoucauld (known mostly for his epigrams in *Réflexions, ou sentences et maximes morales* of 1665 that expressed, in a sometimes paradoxical manner, the European nobility's pessimism and disenchantment with life), Blaise Pascal (the *Pensées* of 1660 confirmed that he was a master of contradictions and reversals), J. G. Herder (in *Über die neuere deutsche Literatur: Erste Sammlung von Fragmenten* of 1767 the word 'fragment' appeared as an organizing form of literature and study), and Nicolas Chamfort. Chamforts's popular *Maximes et pensées, caractères et anecdotes* of 1796 – a collection of aphorisms, maxims and sayings – influenced Schlegel greatly, and he often referred to the fragment as the 'Chamfortian form'. In Schlegel's opinion, 'Chamfort was what Rousseau liked to pretend to be: a genuine cynic, more of a philosopher in the classical sense than a whole legion of dried-up school philosophers' (1991: p. 45).

Rodolphe Gashé sees Schlegel's fragment responding directly to the Kantian 'Idea' (the concepts of reason) and the Copernican revolution. In light of Kant's complex philosophical systematization, the fragment served as a powerful form to critique systems of thought,

and it revealed, by its very fragmentariness, how 'from a theoretical
viewpoint, the concept of a whole cannot be experienced . . . The idea
achieves presentative value exclusively as fragment' (p. xxvii). In the
Critique of Judgment, for example, Kant analyses the aesthetic feelings
associated with the beautiful and the sublime, concluding that the
sublime, not the beautiful, creates a presentation of limitlessness. The
sublime was for Kant the 'Idea' of limitlessness, always the victor over
the imagination, yet for Schlegel, the fragment approaches such
limitlessness as a conceivable whole. The 'Idea' *is* the fragment; the
'Idea' – as schema, organon, system or the sublime – is beyond
experience, and yet, nevertheless, participates in it. 'Aren't all systems
individuals just as all individuals are systems at least in embryo and
tendency?' asks Schlegel. 'Aren't there individuals who contain within
themselves whole systems of individuals' (1991: p. 50). Thought of as
more than just the remnant of a once unified whole, the fragment for
Schlegel not only combined the complexities of genres like poetry and
philosophy, but also used incompleteness in a more critical fashion to
scrutinize the very concept of completion whatever its guise. His
theory of Romantic poetry, so important in the advancement of
nineteenth-century poetics, relies on this sense of incompleteness, or
as he put it, 'becoming', to express the expansiveness of poetry. The
fragment's self-containment ultimately freed it from being con-
strained by conceptions of wholeness:

> Romantic poetry is progressive, universal poetry. Its aim isn't merely to
> reunite all the separate species of poetry and put poetry in touch with
> philosophy and rhetoric. It tries to and should mix and fuse poetry
> and prose, inspiration and criticism, the poetry of art and the poetry
> of nature; and make poetry lively and sociable, and life and society
> poetical . . . Other kinds of poetry are finished and are now capable of
> being fully analyzed. The Romantic kind of poetry is still in the state of
> becoming; that in fact, is its real essence: that it should forever be
> becoming and never be perfected. It can be exhausted by no theory.
> (1991: p. 32)

There is undeniably a similarity between Schlegel's poetic 'becoming' and the *PrCs*. Schlegel invited his reader to reconsider the
part/whole relationship prevalent in Western metaphysics: the fragment does indeed presuppose a totality, and yet, while it points beyond
itself, it still maintains its self-referentiality and its meaning as a
fragment. 'If the fragment is indeed a fraction', Lacoue-Labarthe and
Nancy propose, 'it emphasizes neither first nor foremost the fracture

that produces it. At the very least, it designates the borders of the fracture as an autonomous form as much as the formlessness of deformity of the tearing' (p. 42). This conflictive movement and containment (the border produced in the 'tearing' from the whole) structures the *PrCs* in how the poetry combines oppositional ideas that not only reveal the part/whole relationship between the poetic and the philosophical, the idea and the system, and the individual poem and the larger *oeuvre*, but also challenge the reader to participate in the conceptual play that results from all of it. Poem lxxv (*NC*) provides us with a good example of how these oppositional ideas unfold. In this poem Machado refers to the folkloric 'ingenio gitano' to present his reader with a paradox:

> Conversación de gitanos:
> – Para rodear,
> toma la calle de en medio;
> nunca llegarás.[11]

If one wished to take the most circuitous route to any location, travelling the straight line of the 'calle de en medio' would never accomplish this end; however, travelling the straight line is certainly a circuitous route if one intends to 'rodear'. The verb 'rodear' is polysemic, and in its figurative sense also means 'usar de rodeos al hablar', an equivalent to the English idiom 'beat about the bush'. Given the poem's conversational context, Machado exploits the polysemy of 'rodear' to create a duality of meanings: location and movement; and to speak, literally, in a roundabout way. In this poem Machado illustrates how language signifies through conceptual differences. The verb 'rodear', in the roundabout directness/circuitousness opposition it suggests, will endlessly defer any stable meaning or closure, and for this reason it complements the irony and infinitude alluded to in the final verse: 'nunca llegarás'. The poetic-conceptual 'tearing' comes by way of the poem's self-referentiality on the one hand (the gypsies' roundabout conversation about travelling from A to B), and its resistance to closure on the other hand (signified by an unreachable destination). The poem at once conjures up, sustains and destabilizes, in the most limited of spaces, the part/whole relationship in a conceptual play of opposites. Poem lxvi (*NC*) is structured in a very similar fashion. The polysemic term 'dar vueltas' below can mean to circle a given location, and also to ponder:

> Conversación de gitanos:
> – ¿Cómo vamos, compadrito?
> – Dando vueltas al atajo.

Machado again establishes a directness/circuitousness opposition in 'dar vueltas' and the 'atajo' to imagine an implied – yet unreachable – destination. This part/whole rapport, as in poem lxxv, also refers to the act of thinking in circles (a circularity of thought with the potential to lead to negation and aporia). Poem lxxxvi's (*NC*) playful contradiction hides a clever wordplay in a presence/absence antithesis: the speaker's friends are present in his solitude when he is far from them, yet when he is among them, they vanish with his solitude:

> Tengo a mis amigos
> en mi soledad;
> cuando estoy con ellos
> ¡qué lejos están!

A similar affirmation/negation circularity informs poem xciv (*NC*) concerning the dispensation of advice:

> Doy consejo, a fuer de viejo:
> nunca sigas mi consejo.

What Machado suggests is that the *PrCs*, quite simply, resist any conceptual completion. Although it can be argued that almost any poetry resists completion in some way, the *PrCs*, particularly given the oppositional tensions that arise from the part/whole dynamic, disclose poetry's problematic relationship with language and meaning. After all, the gypsies' 'ingenio' in poem lxxv, although lighthearted on the surface (the gypsy 'gracia'), reveals deeper constructions that endlessly refer beyond themselves and make any gesture toward wholeness difficult, if not impossible. Similarly, the speaker's friends in poem lxxxvi can never be present when they *are* present, and following the advice offered in poem xciv implies a self-negating contradiction. These types of constructions allude to how language is erected upon an endless chain of signifieds, and like Schlegel's poetic 'becoming', the poetry remains in a state of progression for there is no transcendental signified that can be grasped in its wholeness.

What is perhaps more revealing – and Romantic, we could say – about these questions of oppositions and incompletion is how they bring to the fore the poet's creative freedom. In both opposing and uniting several concepts, Machado immerses himself in the complex territory of the finite and the infinite, the singular and the universal.

As with Schlegel, who considered these types of part/whole tensions as 'perfect' examples of poetic irony because they established 'a constant alteration of self-creation and self-annihilation', Machado is aware of the difficultiy in effectively communicating with the world (1991: p. 24). While Schlegel spoke of the 'impossibility and necessity of complete communication' in his famous fragment 108 (1991: p. 13), Machado adopts the 'rodeo' and 'atajo' of poem lxvi as metaphors for this same impossibility and necessity of poetic communication:

> Lo natural suele ser en poesía lo bien dicho, y en general, la solución más elegante del problema de la expresión. *Quod elixum est ne assato,* dice un proverbio pitagórico . . . Sabed que la poesía – sobre todo en poesía – no hay giro o rodeo que no sea una afanosa búsqueda del atajo, de una expresión directa; que los tropos, cuando superfluos, ni aclaran ni decoran, sino complican y enturbian; y que las más certeras a lo humano se hicieron siempre en el lenguaje de todos. (1971a: p. 263–4)

The Pythagorean proverb *Quod elixum est ne assato,* which appears in poem xxii (*NC*), has to do with measuring poetry against Pythagoras' truism that there should be nothing superfluous in the poetic word, nothing 'extra' that can obscure meanings that are already indeterminate and entangled in contradictions:

> Sólo quede un símbolo:
> *quod elixum est ne assato.*
> No aséis lo que está cocido.

Nowhere is this plea for directness of meaning clearer than in Machado's critiques of baroque poetry. He believed ingenuity for ingenuity's sake generated difficulties in meaning where there should be none. Juan de Mairena was more direct about his dislike for baroque poetry. In seven theses he criticized its lack of intuition, its artifice, its indirectness, its obliqueness, its lack of sincerity and its aristocratic pretensions, particularly when it came to Góngora's *culteranismo.* In poems lxxx and lxxxviii (*NC*), Machado believes that the baroque *concepto* inspires an ornate and 'empty' thinking:

> Concepto mondo y lirondo
> suele ser cáscara hueca;
> puede ser caldera al rojo.
>
> El pensamiento barroco
> pinta virutas de fuego,
> hincha y complica el decoro.

Yet if we approach the following poem lxxxix (*NC*) as a summation of
this critique (a poem that appears after lxxxviii and begins with the
connective 'sin embargo'), it is plain to see that baroque theatre is
saved from this criticism. This change in tone is understandable
considering that Machado admired Lope de Vega, a major inspiration
during his formative years:

> Sin embargo. . .
> –Oh, sin embargo,
> hay siempre un ascua de veras
> en su incendio de teatro.

It is this question of poetic communication that brings Bécquer into
the discussion. Even though the Schlegel brothers' influence – particularly Friedrich's – on Spanish writers was partial at times throughout the nineteenth century, it is possible to discern how it affected
Bécquer's poetry and his thinking on poetic language. By now it is well
established that the Hispanist and bibliophile Juan Nicolás Böhl de
Faber popularized the Schlegel brothers' Romantic theories in Spain
in the early nineteenth century. His famous disagreements with the
journalist, poet and writer Joaquín de Mora that were published in
Cádiz and Madrid between 1814 and 1820 concerned German
Romanticism's underlying literary and symbolic tenets, and these
publications back and forth between Böhl de Faber and Mora provided the former with a welcome outlet to clearly lay out the Schlegel
brothers' Romantic theories, especially those of August.[12] In his
Vienna lectures between 1808 and 1811, August discussed many of the
foundational ideas that had stimulated early German Romanticism,
and in lecture XXIX specifically he praised Calderón's theatre because
it was steeped in the time-honoured values of religion, heroism, nation
and chivalric honour. In August's opinion, 'honour is always an ideal
principle; for it rests . . . on that higher morality which consecrates
principles without regard to consequences . . . I know no apter symbol
of tender sensibility of honour as portrayed by Calderón' (p. 421). As a
Catholic sympathizer of Fernandine absolutism who was wary of
imported neoclassical models of art (especially those from France),
Böhl de Faber used August's ideas to champion a return to nationalist
traditions, the monarchy, Christian ideals, and a distinctly Spanish (or
'native') aesthetic sensibility. With time, 'Böhl was able proudly to
reiterate a new theory of literary evolution', Flitter points out, one that
displaced neoclassical aesthetics and ideology and looked to Spain's
medieval past for traditional values (p. 7–8). Thanks to figures like

Böhl de Faber, Romantic historicism in Spain was Schlegelian and, to a lesser extent, Herderian in character, at least until 1833 when Ferdinand VII died and Spanish Romanticism became a much more complex phenomenon as exiled intellectuals began returning to Spain from abroad with new ideas about literature and art.

Although critics of Spanish Romanticism like Navas-Ruiz, Silver, Carnero, Juretschke and Sebold may disagree on the exact periodization of the movement and the fundamental sociopolitical character it exuded (whether it was more inherently liberal or conservative at the highest intellectual levels), they agree with Flitter in underlining how significantly the Schlegel brothers' ideas influenced how Romantic ideals were interpreted, institutionalized and opposed in Spain. Eustaquio Tomé was one of the first critics to provide a broad understanding of how this German influence had affected Bécquer's work in particular. As he explains it: 'Desde 1839 corrían por España traducidos ... los cuentos de Hoffmann centellantes y fantásticos, varios cuentos de los hermanos Grimm y algunas baladas alemanes ... Bécquer sintióse atraído por esos relatos idealistas que entretenían "el lado nocturno de nuestro espíritu" como dicen los alemanes' (Turk, p. 2). Bécquer's contact with German Romanticism began in early childhood, a time when he studied various German authors in his godmother's library. Later, he read journals like *Correo de la Moda* and *La América* that published translations of German poetry, yet he also became very interested in flamenco and the Spanish *cantar*. Thus, 'lo alemán y lo andaluz, la balada y el cantar, el lied y la soleá son las dos ricas vertientes que se aúnan en el hondo caudal becqueriano' (Pedro Díaz, p. 211). Bécquer learned of Friedrich Schlegel through the work of the Catalan poet Pablo Piferrer, who was well-acquainted with Böhl de Faber's Schlegelian theories of German Romanticism; so much so in fact, that Piferrer was considered 'el schlegeliano español más puro' (Pedro Díaz, p. 73). H. C. Turk also examines Schlegel's influence on Bécquer, and shows how he adopted Schlegel's ideas to develop some of the thematic aspects of his short stories:

> In his essay *La pereza*, Bécquer shares the sentiments expressed in Friedrich Schlegel's chapter 'Idylle ueber den Muesziggang' from his well-known and 'scandalous' *Lucinde* [...] Bécquer, exactly like Schlegel, whom he is apparently quoting, begins by saying: 'La pereza dicen que es don de los immortales' (a most radical point of view, for Schlegel, whose race has the saying 'Arbeit macht das Leben suesz').

Here Bécquer displayed his humorous side (seldom found in his other writings), on a subject seriously treated by his German predecessor. (pp. 48–9)

In more recent criticism, Irene Mizrahi has argued that Friedrich Schlegel's theories on the fragment influenced Bécquer's work in several key ways. Firstly, Bécquer's short poems of the *Rimas* can be conceived in terms of Schlegel's idea of poetic autonomy: that is, the poems can be considered autonomous yet interrelated texts that resist establishing a totalizing and grand *obra*. As Bécquer often lamented, he was incapable of adequately expressing the 'grandura' of his inner world. How can the infinite and opaque universe of feeling, he often asked, be expressed in words? As Bécquer understood it, the poet had to struggle with translating the untranslatable, of imposing form on what was, in essence, formless. In his famed 'Rima I' he provided a partial answer to this quandary: he imagined an altogether new language in which words functioned as words, but they also carried that ineffable quality of 'risas y suspiros, colores y notas'. But even this new language, he admits, was inadequate: 'Pero en vano es luchar, que no hay cifra / capaz de encerrarle'. Bécquer opts instead for poetic openness, contradiction and infinitude when attempting to articulate the inner world. 'El fragmento', Mizrahi clarifies, 'es el recurso que permite que la poesía escrita se integre en el constante fluir del tiempo. Un texto lógicamente organizado y acabado paraliza su objeto haciéndolo prisionero de las categorías del discurso' (1994: p. 49). The concise *Rimas* acquire more movement (intertextuality) and meaning when read as open-ended and incomplete pieces. That is, the reader never gains any sense of absolute knowledge or finality in the *Rimas*, but is left with a collection of fragments that point – as Bécquer intended – to the infinite expanses of the inner world. 'Es cuestión de evitar que la "historia" del espíritu humano tenga un fin o último capítulo', Mizrahi explains (1994: p. 54). Bécquer's poetry, both in its brevity and content (the alterations in metre; the subtleties of assonance versus perfect rhyme; the ambiguous language; the themes of imagination and infinity; the symbolism), resists the idea of closure. The reader has to involve himself in the poetry's 'symphonic music'. In Mizrahi's words:

El entendimiento del fragmento, que se resuelve en un sistema de interacciones con el resto de los textos, obliga a seguir un movimiento de ida y vuelta constante porque siempre tenemos que pasar de la obra becqueriana a las referencias internas y externas [. . . La] aparente desorganización [de las *Rimas*] abre la puerta a una indeterminada manera de asociarlas, no sólo con ellas mismas, sino con todos los demás textos que integran el sistema de correspondencias intertextuales de su obra. Aunque ésta es auto-referencial y omni-interpretativa, como los textos bíblicos, su totalidad refleja la unidad orgánica del Cosmos infinito. (1998: p. 12)

Eugene del Vecchio has also demonstrated Friedrich Schlegel's influence on Bécquer in the concept of Romantic irony, a concept closely related in the German literary tradition to the fragment. For del Vecchio, Bécquer poetizes the infinite world of 'sentimiento' while at the same time acknowledging the limits of language in expressing this world (pp. 220–2). In Bécquer's *oeuvre*, irony stood as 'an intermediate position between enthusiasm and skepticism . . . the attainable and the ineffable . . . meaning through words and suggestion through music in words' (p. 226). His use of irony was one way of drawing attention to the limits of language in expressing what was inexplicable or infinite, and in the ironic gesture itself all types of oppositions manifested themselves, as the knowable versus the unknowable, or the impossibility of absolute understanding versus the necessity of poetic communication. It is apparent what Bécquer found so appealing in Schlegelian irony: irony, Schlegel tells us, is a paradoxical 'permanent parabasis' (the *parabásis* represents the critical moment in ancient Greek drama when an actor speaks to the audience and breaks the dramatic illusion) that opens a critical space between self and object of inquiry in which to explore the world through a type of authentic and creative *poïesis* (1968: pp. 123–5).[13]

In his 'Prólogo' to Augusto Ferrán y Forniés' *La soledad*, Bécquer considered the *cantar* – and folkloric poetry more generally – as a perfect medium to express his ideal of poetic communication. In his mind, a folk poetic form like the *cantar* or *copla* was 'una forma libre' that required both 'sentimiento' and 'pensamiento'. Thus, 'la poesía popular es la síntesis de la poesía' (and his word 'síntesis' referred to that type of 'poesía natural, breve, seca') (pp. 187–8). Although I will speak more of Ferrán in the following section, for now it is sufficient to note that his influence on Bécquer was considerable. In Robert Pageard's opinion, Ferrán's knowledge of Heine's poetry, and his knowledge of folk forms like the *soleá*, which brought to mind what German Romantics such as Goethe, Schiller and Uhland were doing with shorter poetic forms, directly affected Bécquer's *Rimas* (pp. 270–1).

It goes without saying that the *Rimas* influenced Machado greatly. He was well aware that Bécquer was, as he explained it in 1904, the first innovator of modern Spanish poetry.[14] From Bécquer he learned to be sceptical of language's capacity to convey meaning, and how to use the oppositional dialectic between 'sentimiento' and 'pensamiento' with the absolute minimum of poetic materials. It is perhaps for this reason that he believed the *Rimas* could not be adequately interpreted without appreciating their Romantic dialogicism, and he refers to Bécquer's poem 'Volverán las oscuras golondrinas' to make his point:

> La poesía de Bécquer . . . tan clara y transparente, donde todo parece escrito para ser entendido, tiene su encanto, sin embargo, al margen de la lógica. Es palabra en el tiempo, el tiempo psíquico irreversible, en el cual nada se infiere ni se deduce. En su discurso rige un principio de contradicción propiamente dicho: '*sí, pero no; volverán, pero no volverán*'. (1971a: p. 239)

While Schlegel and Bécquer provide us with crucial insights into the mechanics of Machado's fragmentary poetry, Nietzsche's idea on the fragment also influenced his work. Machado admired the iconoclastic Nietzsche for his ability to distil philosophy into fragments and aphorisms. In Nietzsche, the fragment became more discursive, transgressive, and metapoetic, and his 'Prelude in German Rhymes' in *The Gay Science*, or his 'Apothegms and Interludes' in *Beyond Good and Evil*, or the various aphorisms in *Human, All Too Human*, to name a few examples, function not only to recast the major themes we find in the more extensive works, but also provide the reader with several of his core arguments in distilled forms. The fragment provides Nietzsche with a certain freedom in establishing a rapport and intimacy with his reader while at the same time criticizing philosophy, society and religion. His writings were 'free-spirit' works in this sense, and the success of his truth perspectivism owes a great deal to his style of presentation. 'The Maxim of the Brute', for instance, reveals – and in a sense makes explicit – such foundational themes as master morality, the godless world and the superman in a new way that is both proverbial and poetic:

> Never ask! Why cry and shake?
> Please, I ask you, simply take.
> (1974: p. 47)

Blanchot identified a new order of philosophizing in Nietzsche because he spoke 'according to a different language: no longer for the whole but of the fragment, of plurality, of separation' (p. 152). For Blanchot, Nietzsche's fragment abjures the idea of unity as somehow attainable – or even desirable – in philosophical thought. Sarah Kofman echoes Blanchot noting that the 'brevity and density' of Nietzsche's aphorism 'is an invitation to dance . . . The aphorism, by its discontinuous character, disseminates meaning and appeals to pluralism of interpretations and their renewal' (pp. 115–16). For Machado, Nietzsche's philosophy was an 'open' infrastructure, yet it was also figurative in that it brought together concept and language effortlessly, and for this reason he considered Nietzsche *almost* a poet. Mairena explains it as follows:

> Su lectura es mucho menos divertida que la de Schopenhauer, aunque éste es todavía un filósofo sistemático, y Nietzsche, casi un poeta, señaló para siempre ese *resentimiento* que tanto envejece y degrada al hombre. Yo os aconsejo su lectura, porque fue también un maestro del aforismo y del epigrama.

> Ejemplo:

> > *Guárdate de la mano grácil:*
> > *cuanto en ella cae*
> > *se deshace.* (1971a: p. 256)

Through Mairena, Machado lauds Nietzsche with two references to *Human, All Too Human*. The first one derives from aphorism 333 in 'Man and society', and the second from aphorism 580 in 'Man alone with himself':

> Sobre el sonido de nuestra propia voz . . . quiero recordar esta fina observación de Federico Nietzsche: *A veces, en la conversación, el sonido de nuestra propia voz nos causa una cierta inquietud y nos lleva a afirmar cosas muy contrarias a nuestras opiniones.* El hecho, cuya causa no indaga Nietzsche, es cierto. (1971a: p. 34)

> Decía Federico Nietzsche que la ventaja de una mala memoria consiste en poder gozar varias veces de una misma cosa por primera vez. La frase . . . es ingeniosa y, *sin embargo*, no es ninguna tontería. (1971a: p. 37)

In the end, Machado took from Nietzsche the idea that the fragment straddled the realms of both philosophy and poetry. Sobejano has suggested that Nietzsche and Machado coincide in their near obsession with epigrammatic fragments, and how these fragments enrich the presentation and form of poetic expression: 'En resumen, Antonio Machado coincide con Nietzsche formalmente como poeta epigramático, y creemos es influido por él como pensador aforístico y fragmentario y en algunos puntos de vista psicológicos y estéticos' (p. 430). Yet Machado was also guarded in his admiration for Nietzsche in areas of his work, and he criticized his will to power and his idea of a noble ruling class, preferring in the end what he called 'el buen Nietzsche', the diagnostician of common-sense values that used aphorisms '[para] acercar de nuevo el pensar filosófico a las *mesmas* [*sic*] *vivas aguas de la vida*' (1986: p. 95).

To read the *PrCs* by way of Schlegel, Bécquer or Nietzsche is to subject Machado's poetry to a comparative analysis, which is not my intention. Although Machado knew Bécquer's poetry well, it is doubtful he was well-acquainted with Friedrich Schlegel's full work, or had read much of Nietzsche when his first *PrCs* appeared in 1909 (in his 'Carta abierta a don Miguel de Unamuno', dated 14 August 1903, he mentioned Nietzsche's writings for the first time). Indeed, there are several formulations of the fragment in the nineteenth century. There are Baudelaire's fragments in *Mon cœur mis à nu*, for instance, where the spontaneity of writing created an assortment of finished and unfinished pieces. Kierkegaard used the fragment to escape the 'enchantments of the manifold', or the grand systems of metaphysical thought – particularly Hegel's – that were unreliable because of their contradictions. Wordsworth and Coleridge left behind fragments, but as Marjorie Levinson demonstrates, the type of fragment normally associated with them 'acquires its formal distinctiveness *ex post facto*, or after it enters the marketplace or tradition and is found to resemble a host of poems' (p. 11). I have spent some time on Schlegel, Bécquer and Nietzsche because they coincide in Machado's *PrCs* and represent different ways of conceiving the fragment. In sum, I want to show to what extent Machado inherits a mostly Romantic tradition of 'fragment thinking' and makes it his own through the use of polysemy, irony, indeterminacy, *mise en abîme*, contradiction, and, perhaps most importantly, a critical inquiry into the limits of reason.

The 'proverbio' and 'cantar': A Brief Genealogy

The fragment's self-reflexivity, scepticism and infinity dwell at the heart of the *proverbio* and *cantar*. Yet, what is it about the *proverbio* and *cantar* that makes self-reflexivity, scepticism and infinity conceptually possible or even desirable? How do the *proverbio* and *cantar* function as open forms that facilitate Machado's concept of otherness? To answer these questions, we must begin by defining the *proverbio* and *cantar*.

A proverb is a short and popular saying that communicates a general truth. Although the origins of proverbs are unclear and date back to at least 2500 BC, it is in ancient Greece where the proverb takes hold etymologically in the *paroemia* and evolves into its present-day understanding. 'The word παροιμία, paroemia', according to Karagiorgos, 'is known from Aeschylus' play Agamemnon (lines 264–5), written in 458 BC' (10). Karagiorgos also refers to Hesychios of Alexandria, a fifth-century Greek lexicographer, who defined the proverb as 'a statement useful to life which is said along the road, i.e. a by-the-way saying; for oimos means road' (pp. 10–11). As Hesychios suggests, the suffix *oimos* (road) forms the word *paroemia*, or 'proverb' in Greek and from where the word paroemiology derives. The proverb, then, represented a certain type of knowledge that guided travellers passing along a road:

> Another theory about the etymology of the word paroemia is that it is made up of the preposition παρά (near, by) and the word οιμός (oimos), which in ancient Greek meant way, road (cf. προοίμιον, preamble). In antiquity there was a custom to engrave short, succinct slogans on the marble under the statuettes of the god Hermes, protector of pedestrians. These statuettes were posted in central spots, crossroads and other central places of cities to guide strangers. Such slogans, and brief, wise statements, gradually became popular and passed from mouth to mouth as proverbs. (p. 10)

Proverbs guided strangers and travellers on their journey. Statues of Hermes, god of travellers, among other things, were erected in specific transit spaces and inscribed with proverbs, thus invoking both literally and symbolically the *oimos*. The name Hermes derives from *herma*, or pile of marker stones along a road, and Hermes statuettes, known as *herms*, and usually constructed as rectangular pillars with the god's head adorning the top and his genitals adorning the bottom, were also implemented as road and boundary markers throughout Greece. As a god capable of not only demarcating boundaries, but also transgressing them, Hermes was a trickster, a guide of souls to the underworld, and a messenger of the gods. The proverbs, along with the statues they were inscribed on, signal a limit or place, but a limit or place that points to a *plus ultra* (a destination).

By the Middle Ages, the proverb – known in Latin as *proverbium* or *adagia* – evolved into a complex form of knowledge transmission and circulation. The proverb was used with didactic ends in preaching (most notably from the Book of Proverbs in the Bible), as explanatory references in the margins of religious texts, as moral guides and precepts, as stylistic and rhetorical tools, and as mnemonic devices, among other things. Erasmus's popular *Adagia*, published in 1500 and consisting of some eight hundred proverbs, is one the best examples of how folk wisdom and general moral teachings collected over the ages were disseminated throughout Europe. In Spain the most direct transmission included Francisco de Espinosa's *Refranero* begun in 1527 and Mal Lara's *Philosophia vulgar* of 1568. Spain had a long tradition of proverbial wisdom by this time, and other scholars like Sebastián de Horozco (*Refranes golsados*, 1550) and Hernán Núñez (*Refranes o proverbios en romance*, 1555) were also collecting and publishing *refranes* during this period. One of the most renowned compilers of proverbs was the humanist and grammarian Gonzalo Correas, who amassed over twenty-five thousand proverbs and proverbial phrases in his vast *Vocabulario de refranes y frases proverbiales* of 1627.

The Greek *paroemia* and the Latin *proverbium/adagia* have much in common. They both share the same sense of movement in how they 'guide' one to a destination or some form of revelation. The *paroemia*'s road, bringing to mind the traveller, and the *proverbium*'s/*adagia*'s didacticism, are fitting for Machado, since his poetry is rife with all types of symbolic *caminos* that guide, instruct, reinterpret, comment on, or simply clarify some idea or concept for the willing reader.

Juan Ramón Jiménez understood the *proverbio*'s epistemological significance in Machado's poetry. He compared Machado to the rabbi, philosopher and proverbialist Sem Tob de Carrión (1290?–1369) when he praised the 1912 edition of *CC* shortly after its publication: 'tal vez sean los *Proverbios y cantares* lo que más me gusta de tu admirable libro último. Dom Sem Tob revive en ti, como si en todo el tiempo que ha estado muerto hubiese robado a lo eterno tesoros májicos e inefables' (2001b: p. 328). Sem Tob's *Proverbios morales*, as Juan Ramón had realized, presented moral teachings in a proverbial fashion much like the *PrCs*, and Machado was indeed familiar with Sem Tob, who appears in poem lxi of *NC* ('Como don San Tob / se tiñe las canas, / y con más razón'). Like Machado, Sem Tob poetized the distinction between reality and illusion, the evils of greed, pride and false modesty, as well as the beauty of wisdom. Segundo Serrano Poncela also notes the similarities in theme and proverbial tone between Sem Tob's *Proverbios* and the *PrCs*:

Razona don Sen Tob con lenguaje de refranero, característica ésta muy hispánica [. . .] algunas de estas sentencias y otras análogas quedaron bien grabadas en la memoria del poeta [Machado] y se hilvanaron, más tarde, en sus Proverbios y Cantares [. . . existen] ciertos paralelos temáticos que se dan entre los Proverbios de Sen Tob y los Proverbios y Cantares, de Machado. La tendencia al sermonarismo, la contracción lírica dentro del poema gnómico. (pp. 180–3)

Unamuno also understood the importance of the *proverbio* in Machado's poetry. The *PrCs*, he believed, had surpassed the longstanding Platonic quarrel between philosophy and poetry by establishing a discursive space in which Machado condensed the very best of his poetic thinking: 'Y en estos proverbios y cantares de Antonio Machado se condensa y concreta su amarga sabiduría poética' (1968: p. 95). More concretely, Unamuno liked how Machado used of the *pueblo*'s folklore to add lyrical and philosophical depth to his own work:

Otros poemas en que el poeta penetra en las reconditeces del alma humana contiene este libro de *CC*, y hacia el fin ya hay una serie de pequeñas composiciones – las más de sólo cuatro versos – bajo el título de Proverbios y cantares, en la vena de aquel judío de Carrión, don Sem Tob, nuestro clásico poeta gnómico. Este género de la sentencia rimada, al que, en rigor, pertenecen los refranes y no pocos cantares didácticos, tiene en España largo y glorioso abolengo y encierra lo más y mejor de nuestra sabiduría popular. (1968: p. 97)[15]

The *cantar,* as a folk genre of poetry and song, is much like the *copla.* It consists mostly of four verses, eight syllables per line, and it is typically composed in consonant rhyme. Although Machado does use *cantar* to refer to a folk genre of poetry and song, he also uses it as a broader term to denote the many folk forms he adopts in the *PrCs* (like the *soleá, solearilla, saeta, seguiriyas gitanas* and *serranas,* among others). The *cantar,* however, as a verb, also imbues the poetry with a poetic presence (the poet or singer, as in flamenco). Yet what is perhaps most significant for Machado is the *cantar*'s oral tradition, and how the anonymous *cantar* is passed from person to person and brings to mind the *pueblo.*

The years between 1850 and 1895 witnessed a resurgence of the *cantar* in Spain. Antonio Trueba, better known as 'Antón de los Cantares', popularized the *cantar* in his famous *Libro de los cantares* of 1851, but it was Augusto Ferrán's 1861 collection *La soledad: colección de cantares por Augusto Ferrán y Forniés* that inspired a generation of younger poets to discover the lyrical potential of folk poetry. Ferrán's close friend Bécquer, who was also exploring Spanish folklore during this period (including flamenco and the *cante jondo*) in what would become his legendary *Rimas* and *Leyendas*, praised Ferrán's *cantar* as a liberating form of expression in a review in *El Contemporáneo* shortly after the publication of *La soledad*. Bécquer believed Spain was left wanting for more poets like Ferrán, poets who could revitalize poetry at the highest lyrical and intellectual levels. Others like Rosalía de Castro (*Cantares gallegos*, 1863), García Ladevese (*Baladas y cantares*, 1867), Ruiz Aguilera (*El libro de la patria: Nuevos ecos nacionales, baladas y cantares*, 1869), Caballero y Martínez (*Escenas populares: Cuadros de costumbres basados en los cantares del pueblo*, 1880), Manuel del Palacio (*Melodías íntimas: Sonetos, cantares y coplas*, 1884), and Enrique Paradas and Manuel Machado (*Tristes y alegres: Colección de poesías*, 1894), developed the *cantar* successfully in later years, but it was the poet, critic and politician Ramón de Campoamor who most openly championed the *cantar* and sought to elevate its standing among the literary establishment in late nineteenth-century Spain.

For Campoamor, the *cantar* was a timeless poetry that could translate reality into a simple and direct language, and yet it could express the most intricate of philosophical problems. In *Cantares* (1846), and later in *Dolorosas y cantares* (1882), he used the *cantar* to examine all types of philosophical questions. In his prose study *La metafísica y la poesía, polémica* (1891) – penned not only as a response to Valera's (in)famous claim that metaphysics was a useless science and poetry a useless art, but also as an instructive exposition on his own poetic praxis – he sought to demonstrate, once and for all, the intimate relationship between metaphysics and poetry.[16] In the prologue to Manuel de la Revilla's *Dudas y tristezas: poesías* (1875), Campoamor writes that poetry provides a lyrical voice to the 'pensamiento' and eternalizes thought: 'la poesía es la manifestación más íntima del pensamiento del hombre, pensamiento que, cuando está bien formulado, hace tan eterna como él mismo la palabra en que está expresado' (p. 34).

The old guard of Spanish poetry was sceptical about the sudden popularity of *cantares*. Núñez de Arce was convinced that the popularity of the *cantar* owed a great deal to translations of German poets like Heine that were in wide circulation at the time, and he believed it was too short to communicate much of anything lyrically speaking. In the prologue to the 1890 edition of *Humoradas; cantares y fábulas*, Campoamor criticized Núñez de Arce's lack of poetic vision, and he argued that the *cantar* was the most suitable form for lyrical poetry:

[M]e propongo rehabilitar con esta publicación, en lo que sea posible, esa poesía, ligera unas veces, intencional otras, pero siempre precisa, escultural y corta, que nuestro eminente poeta D. Gaspar Núñez de Arce ha estigmatizado con la expresión desdeñosa de 'Suspirillos líricos, de corte y sabor germánicos, exóticos y amanerados' . . . Esa poesía que algunos llaman *lapidaria*, es la más propia para que se graben los pensamientos, no sólo en las piedras, sino en las inteligencias. (p. 237)

Undeniably, there was some truth to Núñez de Arce's claim. Heine's poetry was very fashionable at the time thanks in large part to Ferrán, who had studied in Munich in his youth and had discovered Heine's poetry as well as the lieder of Mendelssohn, Schubert and Schumann. What attracted Ferrán to Heine's poetry was its simplicity and deep lyricism and its use of common language to convey the most intimate emotions. Upon his return to Spain in 1859, he founded the short-lived journal *El Sábado* dedicated in large part to publishing translations of German poetry and short stories. In 1861, the same year *La Soledad* appeared, he published *Traducciones e imitaciones del poeta alemán Enrique Heine*, as well as several translations of Heine's poetry in the journal *El Museo Universal*. Subsequent translations appeared over the years in *El Eco del País* (1865) and *La Ilustración Española y Americana* (1873). In *El Contemporáneo* (1877), he also published Heine's intro-duction to the German edition of *Don Quijote*. Another Spanish Heine follower included the poet, author and diplomat Eulogio Florentino Sanz, who during a diplomatic mission to Berlin between 1854 and 1856 had read much of Heine's poetry and had translated fifteen of his lieder in *El Museo Universal* in 1857. Thanks to Ferrán's and Sanz's efforts, Heine was read, discussed and imitated (through the *cantar* mostly) in Spanish literary circles, even though the translations of his work were often not very accurate and focused on his early *Poems* (1821) and *Book of Songs* (1827).

The *proverbio* and *cantar* experienced a resurgence in *fin de siglo* Spain thanks in part to new concepts of Romantic nationalism and the Romantic movement's discovery of the traditions and poetry of a rural *Volk*. As Stuart Joseph Woolf explains, 'the rapid spread of nationalism owed much to the language of romanticism . . . Political romanticism signified the cult of a folkloric (and hence distant and authentic) past, language as the Herderian expression of a *Volk*'s soul' (p. 11). It was King Charles III's measures in the 1770s and 80s to consolidate a national unity that gave new vigour to the Spanish regionalist revival. A century later, this revival had effectively united folklore with, and in some cases, as with Rosalía de Castro's poetry, politically fused it to, a nationalist sentiment.[17] Regions like Cataluña, Galicia and País Vasco, which historically had evolved with a distinct culture and language (arguably as a result of poor communication networks and weak State centralization), began to establish the proto-nationalist discourses of a *patria chica*. Folklore and folkloric movements in the final decades of the nineteenth century, like those pioneered by Machado's father, provided much needed legitimacy to these national sentiments.

That said, could Machado's *proverbio* and *cantar* be expressions of this popularist movement in Spain? Could he not have wanted simply to pen folkloric poems of Andalusia or Castile in the *PrCs*? After all, Campoamor, Valera, Unamuno, Pereda, Maetzu and Ganivet were exploring Spain's past, its customs and *casticismo*, and looking at folklore for a more authentic sense of Spanishness. Even Menéndez Pidal documented in 1900 how the oral *Romancero* – an excerpt of *Muerte del príncipe don Juan* dated to 1497 – could still be heard in El Burgo de Osma, a remote village in Soria. Although the *PrCs* do appear at the cusp of the folklorist wave extending from 1860 to 1939 and explore folk poetic forms and the idea of Spanishness, their poetic and philosophical concepts move beyond the *tipismo*, the stereotypes, the imagery, and even the Romantic sense of *patria chica* that we often find in the folklore of this period. Machado's brother Manuel, for instance, was considered one of the finest folk poets of the early twentieth century, and he was praised with the epithet 'el poeta de los cantares'. From his first poems that appeared in the early 1890s, he explored the full range of folk poetic forms, and in early works like *Tristes y alegres* we find sections like 'Cantares' and 'Más coplas' devoted entirely to *seguidillas* and *soleares*. Yet many of Manuel's poems were overly effusive in their descriptions of Andalusia and bordered on the stereotypical: the proliferation of *¡ayes!*, the flamenco guitar, the colourful *juergas*, the seductive women, the love trysts, etc. In *Alma* (1900), he defines the *cantar* by conjuring up this type of romanticized image of Andalusia:

> Vino, sentimiento, guitarra y poesía
> hacen los cantares de la patria mía. . .
> Cantares. . .
> Quien dice cantares, dice Andalucía.
>
> A la sombra fresca de la vieja parra,
> un mozo moreno rasguea la guitarra. . .

Cantares. . .
Algo que acaricia y algo que desgarra.

La prima que canta y el bordón que llora. . .
y el tiempo callado se va hora tras hora.
Cantares. . .
Son dejos fatales de la raza mora.[18]

In *Fiesta nacional* (1906) and *Alma, Museo y Los Cantares* (1907) we find poems that exhibit more of Manuel's social awareness, and in *Cante hondo* (1912) in the poem 'Cantares' he recognizes the *cantar*'s anonymity, but the general themes of 'dolor' and 'amor' still prevail, and the *cantar* is vaguely personified as a love interest in the themes of intimacy and loss. The final imagistic play of the *cantar* taking flight like a lark and grazing the lips of strangers, as if in a kiss, once again evokes folk poetry's more colourful vein:

Cuando la gente ignore
que ha estado en el papel,
y el que lo cante llore,
como si fuera de él:
copla de mis amores,
cantar de mis amores,
entonces tú serás
la copla verdadera,
la alondra mañanera
que lejos volarás. . .
Y en labios de cualquiera
de mi te olvidarás.[19]

These themes and images are mostly absent from the *PrCs*. There are no dark-skinned men or women to speak of, no wine or plaintive songs of pain and unrequited love, and a national sentiment cannot be gleaned from these poems without a familiarity with Machado's poetic 'metafísica' and his concept of otherness. What binds the *proverbio* and *cantar* for Machado is the dialogue between poet (self and inwardness) and world (Other and objective social reality). In the *proverbio* and *cantar*, and even more so in their complementarity, the entire drama of human existence plays itself out, and as we shall see, the self–Other relation is at the heart of this problematic. Moreover, folklore, as Machado learned from his father Demófilo and his folklorist uncle Agustín Durán, had to do with bridging the *pueblo*'s present with its mythic-historical past in the timeless *Romancero*. As Machado understood it in poem lxxix (*CC*):

Del romance castellano
no busques la sal castiza;
mejor que romance viejo,
poeta, cantar de niñas.
Déjale lo que no puedes
quitarle: su melodía
de cantar que canta y cuenta
un ayer que es todavía.

This link to the past is critical for Machado in that he discovers the Spanish land and its people, and it sets the stage for what he called 'lo elemental humano', an earlier form of the 'comunión humana' that he referred to in his *Proyecto de un discurso*. Without a doubt, 'lo elemental humano' is one of the most important themes in his *PrCs*, and it acknowledges the Other in the world as an integral part of any good lyrical poetry. In the often cited prologue to the 1917 edition of *CC* Machado writes:

> Me pareció el romance la suprema expresión de la poesía y quise escribir un nuevo Romancero ... pero mis romances no emanan de las heroicas gestas, sino del pueblo que las compuso y de la tierra donde se cantaron; mis romances miran a lo elemental humano, al campo de Castilla y al libro primero de Moisés, llamado Génesis. (2001a: p. 79)

Although terms like 'humano' and 'hombre' connect with the social ideals of Francisco Giner de los Ríos and the philosophy of Friedrich Krause that Machado learned during his early formative years in the Institución Libre de Enseñanza, it was his father Demófilo who taught him to ask: '¿Queréis conocer la historia de un pueblo? Ved sus romances. ¿Aspiráis a saber de lo que es capaz? Estudiad sus cantares' (1884b: p. 6). We shall explore these topics in the following chapter.

Chapter 2

Towards Conceiving the Other: The Formative Years

Para mí hoy el pueblo como la humanidad no existen; existen hombres.

Antonio Machado y Álvarez 'Demófilo', *Cantes flamencos*.

Machado had very fond memories of his early childhood. He was born in the enchanting Palacio de las Dueñas in Seville, where he spent the first years of his life before relocating with his family to Madrid. In the capital, he was enrolled in La Institución Libre de Enseñanza, one of the most progressive schools in Spain at the time, where he was introduced to the Krausist philosophy that would stay with him for the rest of his life. His family of distinguished folklorists, particularly his father Antonio Machado y Álvarez 'Demófilo', the founder of Spain's modern folklore studies, supplied him with an incomparable source of intellectual stimulus. Even during his bohemian years in Madrid in the 1890s, Machado sought out the same liberal circles of folklorists, poets and politicians that surrounded him in his childhood, and it is no wonder that his formative years offer revealing insights into how the *PrCs* came about. These years demonstrate that the ideas and themes in these poems played an important role in his maturation as a poet and thinker, and without a doubt the *proverbio* and *cantar* ran deep within him and shaped his concept of otherness from the very beginning.

The Machado Family

Before becoming one of Spain's pre-eminent folklorists, Machado's father had studied philosophy and law at the University of Seville. He had entered the legal profession as a young man, but soon chose to teach metaphysics for brief periods at his alma mater and dedicate himself exclusively to the study of folklore. Throughout the years he published seminal works like *Cantes flamencos* (1881), the series *Biblioteca de las tradiciones populares españolas* (1883–6), as well as *Estudios sobre literatura popular* (1884), which included dozens of essays on everything from Andalusian phonology to poetic riddles. Over the years he also collaborated with other European scholars in the field such as Dutch Arabist Reinhart Dozy, the Austrian linguist Hugo Schuchardt, and the English anthropologist Edward Tylor, whose *Primitive Culture* of 1871 – a work he had reviewed and translated – had a considerable influence on his work.[1] The Machado household in Madrid was also a popular gathering place for scholars and politicians, and it was not uncommon for Joaquín Costa or Giner de los Ríos to participate in the family *tertulias*. Demófilo's influence on Machado, directly and indirectly, was instrumental in fostering in him what his brother José called his 'amor al saber popular':

> La influencia familiar en el desarrollo del espíritu de Antonio, la ejerció al comienzo nuestro padre, que era un ilustre y original escritor que, como es sabido, fue el fundador del Folklore en España . . . En su condición de fundador del folklore español ha dejado varios libros . . . La influencia de todos estos libros – tan relacionados con el pueblo – es indudable que dejó en Antonio una huella imborrable . . . Este amor al saber popular es algo que palpitaría siempre a lo largo de toda su obra. (pp. 8–13)

To collect and publish proverbs, songs, *coplas* and other folk poems was not a mere pastime for Demófilo. As a committed Krausist in the 1860s and 70s under the tutelage of Federico de Castro (a well-respected professor of metaphysics at the University of Seville and one of the most able interpreters of Sanz del Río's Krausist philosophy), he collected and analysed folk pieces to demonstrate the relevance of folklore in understanding the Spanish *pueblo* within a broader sociohistorical context. Reminiscent of Herder's 'patriotic spirit', Demófilo conceived the *pueblo* during these years within the Romantic tradition as an ennobled rural community that upheld the time-honoured values of togetherness and mutual respect, and he recognized folk poetry as a living expression of a people's true identity:

> No es sólo un deber lo que a estudiar las obras artísticas del pueblo nos impulsa; no es tampoco puro entusiasmo por las cosas propias lo que a ello nos mueve, es también nuestra íntima convicción de que la belleza no se encuentra vinculada en la clase determinada y cierta, antes a todo pertenece . . . ¿Por qué desdeñar las *bellezas de nuestra propia casa,* que en forma de cantares, romances, leyendas y tradiciones por todas partes se nos ofrecen, revelando nuestra índole propia y peculiar[?].
> (Pineda Novo, p. 42)

In fact, folklore constituted the *pueblo*'s 'alma', and it was capable of fomenting a national regeneration movement at the root of Spanish culture. The folklorist was thus obliged to study, interpret and disseminate folklore for the betterment of society.

After 1879 Demófilo, like many Krausists, had been seduced by positivism and his methodologies changed drastically. He now defined folklore as a new science of the popular spirit ('el sentir popular') based upon observation and scientific analysis.[2] In the prologue to Manuel Balmaceda y González's study *Cancionero de coplas flamencas,* Demófilo formulates a type of *Völkerpsychologie* to study the *pueblo*'s character as a whole and, perhaps most significantly, prognosticate its future development as a society bound to observable biological and evolutionary laws. There was a larger enterprise at hand, then, in introducing folklore studies in disciplines like linguistics, anthropology, sociology and even political theory in that it could establish a much broader 'conocimiento de la naturaleza y evolución del espíritu humano y de las leyes biológicas a que está sometido' (Pineda Novo, p. 88). Demófilo believed that the *pueblo*'s folklore should never be critically interpreted, but observed and studied with methodical rigour to determine correlations, patterns, associations and the like, which could reveal the universal principles of man's social evolution:

> No basta decir existe una literatura popular y sus formas son tales o cuales; es necesario estudiar esas formas y señalar su naturaleza y eslabonamiento con las anteriores y siguientes . . . Las coplas no han de estudiarse por bonitas . . . han de estudiarse como materia científica. (Pineda Novo, p. 53)[3]

Demófilo's folklorism can thus be classified in two distinct periods; the first one can be considered his Krausist period – the interpretative approach to folklore – of the 1860s and 70s that was influenced predominantly by Federico de Castro, and the second can be considered his positivist period – the observation and evolutionary approach – that appears roughly after 1879 and was influenced by Darwin, Spencer, Tylor and Huxley.[4] These two periods moulded his intellectual identity, and during his positivist years he lamented having ever committed the blunder of subjecting folklore to literary analysis during his early Krausist period. 'Esta tendencia [Krausista],' he explained, 'transcendental sin duda, pero exclusiva para mí entonces, me hizo incurrir en el error de vestir con forma literaria los cuentos populares, pecado imperdonable' (1884b: pp. xiii-xiv). Yet, the Krausist and positivist Demófilo were almost indistinguishable in the belief that folklore expressed a people's world view through long-held traditions and values. By revealing how this world view came into existence ('tradición'), and by establishing what forces exerted influence upon it ('progreso'), it was possible to trace the historical trajectory of the entire nation:

> La historia, verdadera maestra de la vida, enseña hasta qué punto carecen de razón los que pretenden prescindir de cualquier de los dos términos aludidos: la tradición o el progreso. Bajo este amplio sentido creo firmemente no sólo que el estudio del F*olk*-L*ore* [*sic*] deben dedicarse los representantes de todas las escuelas filosóficas, sino que es de absoluta necesidad que en esta obra, en España de verdadera transcendencia nacional, tomen parte tanto los literatos y artistas, como los dedicados a ciencias naturales o sociológicas. (1884a: p. xxii)

Machado and his generation took Demófilo's lessons to heart. Favouring his father's Krausist viewpoints in writings like 'Sobre pedagogía', Machado outlined his pedagogical theories for Spain's regeneration, which included sending 'investigadores del alma campesina' into the farthest reaches of the country to analyse the people's customs and way of life: 'Es preciso enviar los mejores maestros a las últimas escuelas . . . es preciso enviar también investigadores del alma campesina, hombres que vayan no sólo a enseñar, sino a aprender' (2001b: p. 322). Unamuno's doctoral thesis *Crítica del problema sobre el origen y prehistoria de la raza vasca* of 1884 is also significant in this respect. This early work reveals how receptive the young Unamuno was to the concept *pueblo* after the promulgation of the 'Ley abolitoria de fueros' of 1876 that threatened the Basque Country's language and customs. In the essays in *En torno al casticismo* (1895) he expressed his concern regarding the future of the Spanish *pueblo* and its folklore: '¡Ojalá una verdadera juventud, animosa y libre, rompiendo la malla que nos ahoga y la monotonía uniforme en que estamos alineados, se vuelva con amor a estudiar el pueblo!' (p. 168). Azorín también studied the *pueblo* as he travelled the country as a chronicler for various newspapers in the early years of the twentieth century, and he reported that the *pueblo* was as socio-economically downtrodden in 1904 as it had been in 1578 (pp. 29–32).

Demófilo taught Machado how to appreciate folklore and reflect upon its importance in understanding Spain's sociohistorical reality. Several of Demófilo's lessons bring to mind Mairena's pedagogic philosophy of the imaginary Escuela Popular de Sabiduría Superior, a secondary school whose curriculum was based on folk wisdom. Take for example the following excerpt from Demófilo's prologue to *Cantes flamencos* that, much like Mairena advocated decades later, considered folk poetry superior to learned poetry because it spoke the voice of the people: 'la copla popular o anónima es superior, casi siempre, a la hecha por el erudito' (1947: p. 13). Carvalho-Neto has demonstrated that Demófilo's ideas and themes are indeed present in Machado's work (they used a similar poetic language at times) (pp. 83–93), while Vázquez and Costa Medel propose that father and son were so analogous in their views on folklore that there is barely an appreciable difference between them in this respect (pp. 151–60). Dámaso Chicharro and Cruz Giráldez also identify what they believe is Demófilo's influence on the Machado brothers' theatre, and they have argued that their works *La Lola se va a los puertos*, *Desdichas de la fortuna* and *La duquesa de Benamejí* reveal '[una] imitación consciente' of Demófilo's work (their argument rests on the fact that a handful of the *coplas* in these plays can be found, with some minor variations, in Demófilo's *Cantes flamencos*).[5]

Demófilo's teachings are clearly present in Machado's poems and prose works, and it is indeed plausible that he took a few of the popular *coplas* that his father had published in his books and included them in his own work. Yet Demófilo's influence on Machado is most identifiable in how he conceived the relationship between folk poetry and intersubjectivity (the *yo* and *tú*). More specifically, Demófilo left him specific lessons on this topic in his extensive field studies collected in *Cantes flamencos*. The first lesson had to do with the *copla*'s dialogical structure: in its brevity, lyricism and ease of social exchange, the *copla* revealed as much about the poet as it did the objective world he poetized. In the *copla*, the lyrical *yo* spoke directly with the objective *tú*, both as an individual Other and as a collective group, and it served as a

communal poetic site that validated and circulated (mostly anonymously) all types of social values, feelings and popular wisdom. In the
Cantes flamencos, Demófilo explained it in philosophical terms as a
multiplicity within oneness, and in literary terms, as an anonymous
lyrical voice within the collective symphony:

> [E]ste Juan del Pueblo no es en definitiva más que una serie de Juanes,
> Juanitos y Juanillos que nacen y mueren continuamente para dar lugar a
> otros Juanillos, Juanitos y Juanes, que así perecen y retoñan como los
> brotes de los árboles, dentro de aquel gran Juan a quien yo, como mi
> querido amigo, tanto amo . . . la poesía épica del pueblo, como todo se
> distingue y *Juanifica*, por decirlo así, engendrando lo que los filósofos
> llaman lo vario dentro de lo uno, lo que literariamente pudiéramos
> llamar lo lírico dentro de lo épico . . . La copla romanceada octosílaba
> por su brevedad y especial estructura, responde, en mi sentir, a esta
> condición: el hombre del pueblo no refleja en la copla más que su propio
> sentimiento; la copla es, dentro siempre de límites convencionales, una
> poesía lírica dentro de lo épico; lo menos lírico, si se quiere, dentro de lo
> lírico; lo menos épico, si se quiere, dentro de lo épico. (1947: pp. 291–2)

The idea of multiplicity within oneness appears throughout
Machado's work, and it constitutes one of the cornerstones of his
concept of otherness. Martín's philosophy begins with a multiplicity–
oneness binarism founded upon Leibniz's monadic theory. Leibniz
postulated that the universe consisted of an infinite number of sub-
stances called monads (from the Greek *monas*, for unit or atom), and
each was unique, indivisible, constantly in flux and internally determined with its own field of perception. The individual monad, in its
relationship with other monads and its role in the expression of the
infinite God, mirrored the unity of the universe, and in so doing
constituted a microcosm of it. For Martín, the monad represents an
expansive consciousness of the many within the one, or '*el gran ojo que
todo lo ve al verse a sí mismo* . . . una autoconciencia integral del universo
entero' (1953: p. 11). From this multiplicity–oneness binarism,
Machado's later criticisms of solipsistic thinking come into sharper
focus, and he develops the binarism in much of his work following his
father's precept of locating some semblance of the self in the collective. Poem 1 (*NC*), for instance, expresses these two distinct yet corresponding levels of understanding in the folkloric song:

> Con el tú de mi canción
> no te aludo, compañero;
> ese tú soy yo.

Machado's *solearilla* speaks of the intersubjective *canción*, and it acknowledges the anonymous 'tú', the 'compañero', in the 'yo'. In this simple poem Machado touches upon one of the most significant principles of subjectivity in Western philosophy: the I as a subject (the observer) is also a you as an object (the observed) from the perspective of another I as a subject. Although subjectivity proclaims its independence from the Other, it actually depends on the Other for recognition. In *Phenomenology of Spirit*, Hegel had developed this idea in very concrete terms explaining how self-consciousness may indeed exist prior to any concept of Other, but it is through contact with the Other in the world that the self develops. 'Self-consciousness', he declares, 'exists in and for itself when, and by the fact that, it so exists for another; that is, it exists only in being acknowledged' (p. 92).

Demófilo's second lesson was an extension of the first and had to do with the language and lyrical immediacy of folk poetry. In folk forms, the poet transmitted his most intimate of sentiments to the world in a very direct and immediate way that was easily comprehensible: 'La poesía de los hombres del pueblo expresa siempre una relación más directa entre el objeto sentido y el sujeto que siente, que la poesía reflexiva' (1947: p. 300). In poem lxxvi (*NC*), it is language that binds poet and the concrete world:

> El tono lo da la lengua,
> ni más alto ni más bajo;
> sólo acompáñate de ella.

Machado refers to the flamenco *cante* in the above *soleá*. The folkloric image it suggests, particularly in terms of the relationship between language and music (the polysemic verb 'acompañar') is that of a flamenco performance. Yet why does Machado insist on the tone and volume of language? The *soleá* has a specific tone and delivery that is vital to a *cantaor* when 'liberating' the *duende* in flamenco song, and the sounds and tonalities of words add to the hermeneutical experience of their meanings. In so doing, poetry – particularly the *soleá* that can effortlessly merge poetry, music and dance – reveals how a language's volume and tone is also a voice. This poem lends itself to a metapoetic reading in that the *soleá* poetizes the *soleá*; the poem makes known, through its own reflection on language and music, its very nature as *soleá*.

While shorter folk forms collapsed the distance between self and world, they also contained a degree of indeterminacy that resisted poetic closure in the traditional sense. This was Demófilo's third

lesson: 'la indeterminación de las coplas populares . . . lejos de ser un
defecto de tales producciones, es una condición que las abrillanta'
(1947: p. 21). Poem xcic (*NC*) echoes this sentiment. How do we
define Art, Machado asks? Art is an infinite play of meanings:

> –¿Mas el arte? . . .
> –Es puro juego,
> que es igual a pura vida,
> que es igual a puro fuego.
> Veréis el ascua encendida.

The fourth lesson proposed that good poetry was brief: 'la mejor
poesía es la que dice más en menos palabras' (1947: p. 13). Poem viii
(*NC*), consisting of only four words, demonstrates Machado's fondness
for sententiousness: 'Hoy es siempre todavía'. In this poem, he seems
to refer to time in the present with the initial 'hoy', yet the present slips
into infinity with the final words 'siempre' and 'todavía'. The poem's
temporality provides a glimpse of how important time was for
Machado in grappling the very essence of Being. As Mairena put it: 'es
el concepto de la eternidad que tiene el sentido común, concepto, en
el fondo, mucho más trágico que metafísico' (1971a: p. 81).

Finally, tradition did not ossify folklore; on the contrary it kept
various poetic forms in circulation, and so-called scholarly poets –
those who favoured sonnets, alexandrines and other forms of 'poesía
erudita' – would do well to know them: 'los poetas eruditos en mi
opinión, no perderían el tiempo en estudiar [las coplas populares]
como gérmenes de poesías más complejas' (1947: p. 21). In poems xli
and lxv (*NC*), Machado tells us that the 'palabras viejas' are always
relevant in poetry. Once again, folklore's orality (its volume and tone)
comes to the fore with the verbs 'oír' and 'sonar':

> –Ya se oyen palabras viejas.
> –Pues aguzad orejas.
>
> Bueno es recordar
> las palabras viejas
> que han de volver a sonar.

Demófilo's *Cantes flamencos* outline *in nuce* the essential character-
istics of the poetic fragment in the *PrCs*: sententiousness, movement,
immediacy, indeterminacy, lyricism, infinity, openness (resistance to
closure), the mixing of genres and the multiplicity of voices
(self/Other). Through his father, then, Machado appreciated what
made folklore so poetically and philosophically expansive, and he was

provided with a thorough education in the field, learning of the various popular forms, their traditions, performativity and structural nuances from one of Spain's foremost folklorists. Like Demófilo, he recognized the significance of folklore in questions of intersubjectivity, yet he did so as a poet who lived and witnessed first hand Spain's rural life and customs. In forging his own folk-inspired poetry, he responded not only to more contemporary and transnational cultural influences (Becquerian romanticism and German philosophy, for instance), but also his own developing sense of ethics, which his rural surroundings and his occupation as a rural French teacher sharply affected after 1907. In 'Poema de un día – Meditaciones rurales', a type of interior monologue, he demonstrates to what extent rural life in Baeza had influenced his poetry. By describing the solitude of rural life one cold winter evening the speaker ponders his existence through the themes of time ('En estos pueblos se lucha / sin tregua con el reló / con esa monotonía / que mide un tiempo vacío') and death (¡Oh, tú, que vas gota a gota, / fuente a fuente y río a río, / como este tiempo de hastío / corriendo a la mar remota'). He then turns to the philosophy of Unamuno and Bergson to understand better the meaning of life but comes away with no clear answers (¿Todo es / soledad de soledades, / vanidad de vanidades / que dijo el Eclesiastés?'). Folklore, then, also emanated from a personal experience for Machado, and for this reason it lacked Demófilo's scholarly detachment. The intimacy of Machado's folklore engendered on the one hand the strong lyrical 'sentimentalidad' of his poetry, and on the other hand its deep contemplative quality.

Other family members influenced the young Antonio who I will mention as a conclusion to this section. His uncle Agustín Durán, director of the Biblioteca Nacional and Royal Academy member, was a respected folklorist in his own right. In the 1917 prologue to *CC*, Machado cites Durán's *Romancero* as the book he first used to learn how to read: 'Cierto que yo aprendí a leer en el Romancero general que compiló mi buen tío don Agustín Durán' (2001a: p. 79). Antonio Machado y Núñez, Machado's grandfather, was also an important figure in his life. As a professor of Natural Sciences at the University of Seville (later the Central University in Madrid), and as a progressive liberal in the revolutionary *junta* during the 1868 revolution, he loomed large in the family. Thanks to Machado y Núñez's efforts, Darwin's evolutionary theories flourished at the University of Seville, and in 1871 he founded Seville's Anthropological Society. Even a figure as distant as José Álvarez Guerra, Machado's great-grandfather,

could also have been somewhat influential. As a lesser-known philosopher and author of a four volume series spanning from 1837 to
1855 titled *Unidad simbólica y destino del hombre en la tierra o filosofía de la
razón, por un amigo del hombre*, he may have inspired Machado to give
life to his alter-egos Martín and Mairena as Valverde has suggested.[6]
Ian Gibson points to similarities between Álvarez Guerra's treatise and
Machado's concept of Other:

> Hay momentos en el tratado de Álvarez Guerra – y en el *Complemento*
> publicado en Sevilla en 1838 – en que es imposible no pensar en el
> poeta Antonio Machado. Por ejemplo, cuando 'Un amigo del
> Hombre' habla del prójimo, del otro, y dice que, una vez vuelto el
> hombre a su Creador, "la felicidad misma inherente a este bien
> imposibilitaría reincidir en el mal por el amor mismo que nos
> inundaría hacia nuestro semejante, hacia ese *tú* segundo *yo* que todos
> querríamos sin que pudiese haber fuerzas humanas que nos
> arrancasen este deseo, este amor"'. (pp. 27–8)

Finally, Machado's grandmother Cipriana Álvarez Durán was a published folklorist and a recognized landscape artist who habitually read
Durán's *Romancero* and Bécquer's *Leyendas* to the young Antonio and
Manuel, and as both brothers admitted later on, these readings were
influential in their early education.[7]

The Institución Libre de Enseñanza and the Krausist 'hombre'

The Institución Libre de Enseñanza (ILE), a progressive secondary
school in Madrid whose curriculum was largely modelled on the
principles of philosopher Friedrich Krause's (1781–1832) harmonic
system, had a profound impact on Machado's sense of otherness.
Machado himself spoke of his intellectual debt to the ILE on several
occasions, and the years he spent there with Giner de los Ríos – its
much-admired founder and rector – and other Krausist teachers, were
some of the happiest of his life. The ILE's liberal pedagogy instilled in
him his love for nature and the outdoors, and it awakened in him those
famous 'gotas de sangre jacobina' that influenced his sociopolitical
beliefs later on in life: 'Estudié en la Institución Libre de Enseñanza y
tuve por maestros a Giner de los Ríos, Cossío y Salmerón ... mi
formación había de ser liberal y republicana, que por otra parte había
de coincidir con la historia política de mis antepasados, ya que mi

padre y mi abuelo eran republicanos fervorosos' (Pineda Novo, p. 20). In a letter to Ortega y Gasset he added further: 'en mí no hay otro bagaje cultural que el adquirido en mis años infantiles de los 9 a los 19 en que viví con esos santos varones de la Institución Libre de Enseñanza' (2001b: p. 304). Although much can be surmised from these childhood and early adolescent years at the ILE, I will limit myself to demonstrating how its Krausist pedagogical theories cultivated a sociophilosophical concept of Other in Machado, one that further complemented Demófilo's teachings.

The ILE provided Machado with a liberal education, and under Giner's guidance, everything from personal hygiene to ethics and folklore appeared on the curriculum in some fashion. In every discipline students learned aspects of Krause's philosophy as it was translated and interpreted during the 1850s and 60s by Julián Sanz del Río, the university professor chosen by the Spanish government in 1843 to develop German philosophy in Spain. The Krausist world view is founded on the belief in a panentheistic God: unlike pantheism, panentheism proposes that while God is the universe, He nevertheless transcends it in an infinite and timeless perfection. God and universe are therefore distinct but also one, so that 'all things are part of God, yet he has unity and identity of his own which is not simply that of his finite parts. God is not identical with the cosmos, but neither is he separated from it. Rather, he lives his own life in and through it: The world is God's body. And we ourselves are parts of God' (Hasker, p. 111). Within this panentheistic cosmology, man was formed in God's image and conceived as a finite, essentially moral and perfectible being who progressed toward an ideal potentiality through a social process of self-creation. Through Giner's example, Machado learned of Krause's ideal of humanity ('ideal de la humanidad'), as invoked by the German philosopher, in which reason bonded men in mutual obligation and a common ethical purpose:

> Porque este reconocimiento de lo común y constante de nuestra naturaleza y el de las exigencias positivas que de ello resultan nos enseña a guardar medida en nuestra conducta individual y social, a estar siempre en el justo *medio* de nuestras relaciones propias o ajenas, cercanas o lejanas, con individuos o con pueblos. (p. 7)

Krause's ideal recognized the Other in oneself; that is to say, the very concept of Other, of being Other, was inextricably intertwined with subjectivity. At every turn, the Other's existence involved the self ethically, and it forced the self to strive toward the perfection of reason. The Other was thus ontologically necessary.

At the heart of Giner's Krausist pedagogy there dwelled the belief that education not only opened the mind to reason, but it was also part of the larger national (and spiritual) project of 'making men' ('el hacer hombres'). In López-Morillas words, 'hacer hombres equivale a educarlos, a cuidar que del brote del párvulo y la flor del niño se desarrolle y sazone el fruto del adulto. En tamaña potenciación humana radica para Giner la única esperanza de salvación' (1971: p. 53). The Krausist *hombre* Giner imagined – a term imbued with as much Romantic idealism as philosophical import – had the potential to morally elevate all *hombres*, and indeed, Krause's ideal of humanity depended on this reciprocatory self–Other relation:

> ¿Qué resta, pues, al hombre de sano sentido, al que ama todavía su naturaleza, al que sabe que esta naturaleza quiere ser reconocida y realizada, sino levantar la vista a la idea fundamental de la humanidad, en la que todos como hombres y pueblos nos reunimos, la que a todos nos liga con lazo indisoluble para el cumplimiento de una misma ley común y de un definitivo destino? (p. 15)

For Giner, the *hombre* was conceived both as an ideal *hombre* (the rational man universalized through reason and his socio-ethical commitment to the Other) and as an individual *hombre* (the person who is different from the Other, free to make decisions and listen only to himself). 'Todos somos al par *el* hombre y *este* hombre', Giner believed (1899: p. 25). Only by living up to the ideal *hombre* could the individual *hombre* be perfected, and understanding this ideal *hombre* meant becoming conscious of how the universal bond of reason united the self and Other in the world. Yet this intersubjectivity progressed somewhat organically as reason itself was cultivated in the individual's life, from his friends and family to his education and the spheres of politics and government that involved him. Moreover, the *hombre*'s duality, as Giner conceived it through Krause's philosophy, depended on the ideal *hombre* always transcending the individual *hombre*'s egotism for the collective good: 'Ningún hombre, por lleno que esté de sí mismo y de su interés egoísta, deja de hallar en su conciencia una perenne aspiración a que el bien se produzca, no sólo en su vida personal, mas en la de todos los seres, sin excepción ni restricción alguna' (1969: p. 27). According to Giner, the very possibility of our being able to continually perfect ourselves and transcend our own egotism for the Other reflected an immanent reason (a type of divine *logos*), and in the end the individual *hombre* always aspired to become the ideal *hombre*. This process of continual approximation to the ideal, of striving toward perfection, produced a superior harmonic 'social being' that not only acquired its own unique national character, but also projected some form of collective teleology.

There is little doubt that Krause's philosophy influenced Machado's concept of Other. Krause's principle of social harmony in the ethical 'camino obligado', with the self–Other relation as its primary foundation, appears in one of Machado's earliest letters to Unamuno in 1904:

> Nos miramos por dentro y, al ver nuestros defectos, no tenemos el heroico valor de confesarlo, sino que se lo arrojamos en forma de catilinaria a nuestro vecino. Apenas si surge un adjetivo que no se lo tiren a la cabeza todos a todos, con el santo deseo de descalabrarse. En realidad es que a todos nos duele. Pero en el fondo de esta gran miseria hay algo que nos llevará a todos a unificar nuestros esfuerzos hacia un ideal que está más alto que nuestra vanidad. No cabe duda. (2001b: p. 199)

Machado's idea of Other, however, slowly evolved beyond Krausism, as we shall see, although it always retained its underlying idealism. The 'mala gente' he speaks of in poem II of *SGOP*, for example, or the fratricidal tragedy of 'Recuerdo infantil', demonstrated how far he had come in positing the *hombre* in far less abstract terms between 1903 and 1907. The same can be said of many poems in *CC* like 'Por tierras de España', 'Un loco', 'La tierra de Alvargonzález', and 'Un criminal' (this last poem inspired by the brutal murders committed in the small village of Carrascosa de Abajo in 1908). Machado grew sceptical of Giner's faith in the collective goodwill of his fellow man, partly because his years in Soria and Baeza revealed to him the irrational 'hombre malo del campo y de la aldea / capaz de insanos vicios y crímenes bestiales' who he poetized in 'Por tierras de España'. In his writings, Giner often condemned Restoration Spain's sociopolitical predicament, and he was by no means naïve about the failures of reason during this period, but he believed that a methodical rationality practised in all spheres of society and governance was the one and true path to national renewal. To understand the *hombre*, Machado believed that it was perhaps of little use to propose 'rational' ideals of any kind if one had not first confronted the individual *hombre*'s socio-economic reality, which required an active learning about the Other, particularly as this Other lived and suffered from day to day. As he explained to

Ortega y Gasset in 1912: 'Cuando los intelectuales, los sabios, los doctores se dignen ser algo folkloristas y desciendan a estudiar la vida campesina, el llamado problema de nuestra regeneración comenzará a plantearse en términos precisos' (2001b: p. 306). To learn about the Other, as I will demonstrate in chapter 5, required, ironically, a continual practice of self-edification on the subject of ignorance, the main obstacle preventing the individual *hombre* from becoming the ideal *hombre*. Spain was a rural country with an appallingly low level of literacy during this period, as Machado knew first hand, and any pedagogical programme, no matter how rational it purported to be, had first to tackle the realities of what became known as 'el problema de cultura'.

Although significant differences are discernable between Machado's and Giner's concepts on otherness, the ILE's Krausist education allowed the young Antonio to formulate the idea of Other through panentheism, social harmony, the individual/ideal *hombre* and the simple dictum of honouring others. After Giner's death in 1915, Machado celebrated 'don Francisco' in a short article in *Idea Nueva* that revealed just how much the ILE had influenced his poetry and thinking. Mairena, for instance, could well have been fashioned in Giner's image, given the following description:

> Su modo de enseñar era el socrático, el diálogo sencillo y persuasivo . . . Desdeñaba don Francisco Giner todo lo aparatoso, lo decorativo, lo solemne, lo ritual, el inerte y pintado caparazón que acompaña a las cosas del espíritu y que acaba por ahogarlas . . . Era don Francisco Giner un hombre incapaz de mentir e incapaz de callar la verdad . . . Carecía de vanidades, pero no de orgullo; convencido de ser, desdeñaba el aparentar. (2001b: pp. 387–8)

Machado also offers kind words for Giner's principle of self-betterment. Giner believed that one had to be true to oneself and act in accordance with the highest ethical good, and this kind of 'self-truth' was the only feasible way to build up the nation: 'Lo que importa es aprender a pensar, a utilizar nuestros propios sesos . . . y a calcar fielmente la línea sinuosa y siempre original de nuestro propio sentir, a ser nosotros mismos, para poner mañana el sello de nuestra alma en nuestra obra' (2001b: p. 387).[8] In the poem 'A don Francisco Giner de los Ríos', Machado reflects upon Giner's death recreating his life and works as those of a saint, and the final verses of the poem perhaps best express his debt to Giner: 'Sed buenos y no más, sed lo que he sido / entre vosotros: alma'.

The ILE also served Machado as a sociopolitical lens through which the sorry state of Spain's Restoration government came into sharper focus. The ILE's very existence spoke to the failure of the liberal 1868 Revolution and the short-lived First Republic of 1873–4. The liberal decree of 21 October 1868, granting university professors freedom of curriculum, doctrine and method was hotly disputed, and it soon unraveled into a power-play between liberals and conservatives known as 'la cuestión universitaria' in which Spain's pedagogical philosophy and the role of Krausism in university education were at stake. The *Decreto de Orovio* promulgated on 26 February 1875, replete with concessions made to the Church by Prime Minister Cánovas del Castillo's new government, finally forced out the liberal and Krausist faculty – Salmerón, Giner de los Ríos, Azcárate, Castelar, Montero Ríos, Moret and others – from universities across Spain, and replaced them with conservatives like José Manuel Ortí y Lara and Menéndez y Pelayo. According to regenerationists like Joaquín Costa, these conservatives would work to disseminate 'ese convencionalismo criminal que ha postrado a la nación y la tiene en trance de expirar' (1998: p. 188). And thus Giner's pedagogical programme, initially devised for university implementation, was relegated to a single privately-funded secondary school, the ILE. Thereafter, the Krausist regenerationists, many of them teachers at the new school, were even more convinced that Spain's future depended as much on political reform as it did on a national education programme based on Krausist collectivism.

There is one last childhood experience that affected how Machado conceived the Other. This experience came about just as he finished his schooling at the ILE at the age of fourteen, and it effectively marks a transition point for him into a type of social awareness that would develop during his bohemian years in Madrid. In 1889, he attends a political rally in Madrid led by Pablo Iglesias, the founder of the Spanish Socialist Workers' Party (PSOE, 1879) and the Spanish General Workers' Union (UGT, 1888). Through passionate Marxist rhetoric, Iglesias reveals the realities of Spain's divided and unjust society for Machado, and the socialist leader's 'humanidad auténtica' aroused in him what he remembers as '[mi] primera meditación infantil', or a social awareness of the deep socio-economic divide that distanced him from 'existencias más pobres':

> Lo cierto es que las palabras de Iglesias . . . implicaban una revelación muy profunda para el alma de un niño. De todo el discurso . . . sacaba yo esta ingenua conclusión infantil: 'El mundo en que vivo está mucho

peor de lo que yo creía . . . ¡Cuantas existencias más pobres que la mía hay en el mundo, que ni siquiera pueden aspirar, como yo aspiro, a entreabrir algún día, por la propia mano, las puertas de la cultura, de la gloria, de la riqueza misma!' (1953: p. 154)

The Madrid Years: Folk Poetry in the Age of Romantic Exhaustion

Machado's first publications in the weekly journal *La Caricatura* dating from 1892 to 1893, and his friendship in the mid to late 1890s with poets and intellectuals like Enrique Paradas, Salvador Rueda and Eduardo Benot, also provide clues to his nascent sense of otherness. By 1892, Machado had completed his studies in the ILE and the Instituto de San Isidro and was enjoying a casual, bohemian lifestyle with his brother Manuel in Madrid. The brothers idled away their days reading Lope and Góngora in the Biblioteca Nacional, hopping from café to café with their friends, and attending the socialite Victoria Minelli's lively *tertulias*, where the discussion of recent plays fuelled their interest in theatre. More importantly, they were regulars at the flamenco *tablaos*, where they would spend countless hours soaking up the *coplas* that some of Spain's best performers had to offer:

> Allí van *en serio*, enamorados del cante y del baile, que merecen honores de gran arte popular. Mas su café preferido es el de La Marina, en la calle de la Reina. No se cansan de ensalzar su *cuadro flamenco*, que actúa y que está formado por la célebre Matilde Prada, *bailaora* de lo fino; el *cantaor* Revuelta, las Coquineras, Medina, *la Camisona, la Macarrona*. (Ferrero, p. 39)

During this period Machado took his first steps as a writer in *La Caricatura*. From his very first contributions, his discontent with Madrid's literary scene was apparent. He believed that Romantic and Parnassian forms of poetry had played themselves out in poets like Núñez de Arce, Emilio Ferrari and Manuel Reina who did little except recycle the same antiquated formulas and affected sensibility ad nauseum. Under the pen name 'Cabellera', Machado harshly criticized Spain's late Romanticism in the article 'Dios los cría y ellos se juntan' by describing what exactly transpires in Madrid's literary salons:

> Don Estanislao Parnaso, que goza entre sus amigos fama de gran poeta, ha dado en la manía de celebrar reuniones literarias, y todos los sábados por la noche, recibe en sus salones una multitud de vetas, provisto de sonetos, quintillas, décimas y demás municiones literarias

... Este caballercito es recibido con visibles muestras de disgusto, porque, no en balde, la literatura marcha por otros derroteros, y la sociedad moderna prefiere una poesía más ligera, feliz y ocurrente . . . Aquel inconsciente, que acapara la noche para sí, acaba por aburrir y desesperar a la tertulia. (2001b: p. 122)

With a wit reminiscent of M. J. Larra's 'Castellano viejo', the character poignantly named don Estanislao Matacán del Parnaso bores his guests with dozens of cantos. The guests believe that don Estanislao's poetry is outdated and they fancy something fresh, something different and new, 'una poesía más ligera, feliz y ocurrente'. Machado questions the public's poetic sense, since the remainder of the evening is dedicated not to poetry, but to a dull discussion on Cervantes's maimed arm and Homer's myopia. In 'Los Bohemios', he continues this line of criticism by expressing his bewilderment at how many sham poets he sees crowding the cafes and literary salons in Madrid: 'La clase de bohemios o perdidos, la de aquellos que tienen esta vocación, que viven a expensas de la humanidad escudados en un romanticismo ficticio que les impide doblegarse al trabajo, aún muy numerosa y cuenta multitud de individuos en todas las grandes poblaciones' (2001b: p. 116). In 'Moscardón literario', it is clear that he believes these 'bohemios' did poetry a great disservice: they understood lyrical poetry as a question of quantity (number of rhymed verses) rather than quality (pure sentiment):

Conozco un caballero de esta índole, que ha logrado con la práctica una tal facilidad de hacer versos (claro está que los hace muy malos), que llegó a apostar en un café con un amigo suyo, a que antes de terminar éste la media tostada que tenía entre manos, habría compuesto un romance heroico a la toma de Granada por los Reyes Católicos, cuatro sonetos, conceptuosos los cuatro, y un himno a las cerillas de Cascante. (2001b: p. 125)

Machado's articles, brimming with satire and all types of bohemian poets, reveal not only the poetic impasse reached in Spanish literary circles at the time, but the larger *mal du siècle* and the crisis of values of the age. *Modernismo* and the so-called Generation of 98's still emergent 'existential' sensibility provided Machado, like most up-and-coming artists of the day, with a renewed social awareness. A crucial facet of this awareness was what Machado explained as 'el santo deseo de despertar al prójimo', or his desire for new forms of poetic expression capable of speaking directly to the day-to-day realities of Spain's hardworking people that were nowhere to be found in Madrid's cafés and *tertulias.*

He explained it to Ortega y Gasset as a type of sociopolitical coming-of-age for a whole group of intellectuals:

> Amargura, desengaño, descontento, rencor, en un caso pasional vivíamos; fue aquello el despertar bilioso de una gran pesadilla. Se gritaba, unos iracundos, otros compungidos, y en algunas voces, no las menos sinceras, difícilmente se distinguía el disgusto de haber despertado el santo deseo de despertar al prójimo. Hubo entonces una gran virtud: la sinceridad, llevada hasta el absurdo, hasta el suicidio. (2001b: p. 305)

It is during this time of disillusionment that Machado turns his attention to *cantares* for a sense of what he called 'poesía moderna', and he soon discovers the work of Enrique Paradas. In his article 'Enrique Paradas' of 1897, he states: 'Es Enrique Paradas el poeta popular por excelencia, entre nuestros poetas modernos' (2001b: p. 149). At the time, Paradas was known for a collection of *cantares* titled *Agonías* (1891), and as managing editor and founder of *La Caricatura,* he had published various first-rate *cantares* and folk poems in his periodical.[9] José María de Cossío considered him a pivotal figure in popularizing the *cantar* in Spain at the turn of the century:

> Si quisiéramos dar con el poeta al que puede asignársele el papel de enlace y el oficio de puente entre el cantar del siglo XIX que vengo considerando, el cantar de intención culta o de intención popular y la estilización popular que en pleno modernismo ha de culminar con el nombre de Manuel Machado, creo que este nombre sería el del poeta y autor teatral madrileño Enrique Paradas. (p. 495)

Doubtless Machado was impressed with Paradas's frugal *cantares* because they were able to condense an entire tragedy or epic drama into a three-verse *soleá.* Moreover, Paradas was a poet in touch with the *pueblo,* whose poems, far from relying on stereotypical imagery of Andalusia and hollow *¡ayes!,* spoke directly to the common man's reality: 'El espíritu de Enrique Paradas sufre en sus coplas admirables la más completa metamorfosis. Tan pronto le vemos identificado con la desgracia del mendigo, que gime y padece implorando la caridad del prójimo' (2001b: p. 150). Manuel Machado was also inspired by Paradas, whom he considered Spain's finest poet of *cantares*. Paradas went on to publish *Undulaciones* (1893) (with an epilogue written by Manuel), and then *Tristes y alegres* (1894) and *& (Versos)* (1895) in collaboration with Manuel, yet he never forgot Antonio, often referring to their friendship in epigraphs like 'A mi amigo de verdad, Antonio Machado', or 'Al gran poeta, mi excelente amigo Antonio

Machado'. And Machado, it seems, never forgot Paradas either, since he reappears years later in a brief note in 'Cancionero apócrifo, Doce poetas que pudieron existir' in *Los complementarios*:

> ENRIQUE PARADAS
> Autor de: *Agonías, Undulaciones, Tristes y Alegres, Impresiones y Cantares.*
> Tiene algunas coplas bellas ej.:
>> Dijo a la lengua el suspiro:
>> échate a buscar palabras
>> que digan lo que yo digo.
>
>> Se le fue al pastor la honda
>> y vino a caer la piedra
>> en una ovejita coja. (1971b: pp. 147–8)

Paradas also appears in Mairena's *Sentencias* accompanied by some of Machado's most significant writings on folk poetry. The words associated with the *copla* in the following excerpt are revealing ('sincero', 'ingenuidad', 'experiencia', 'modestia', 'canción') and complement what Machado wrote almost four decades earlier on the candour and modernity of Paradas's *cantar* during the *fin de siglo* period:

> El hombre, para ser hombre,
>> necesita haber vivido,
>> haber dormido en la calle
>> y, a veces, no haber comido.

> Así canta Enrique Paradas, poeta que florece – si esto es florecer – en nuestros días finiseculares. (Habla Mairena hacia el año 1895). Yo no sé si esto es poesía, ni me importa saberlo en este caso. La copla – un documento sincero de alma española – me encanta por su ingenuidad. En ella se define la hombría por la experiencia de la vida, la cual, a su vez, se revela por una indigencia que implica el riesgo a perderla. Y éste *a veces*, tan desvergonzadamente prosaico, me parece la perla de la copla. Por él injerta el poeta – ¡con cuánta modestia! – su experiencia individual en la canción, lo que algún día llamaremos – horripilantemente – la vivencia del hambre, sin la cual la copla no se hubiera escrito. (1971b: p. 195)

Machado came to appreciate how the *cantar* could distil (the 'depuración') the singular, lyric voice of the poet and the *pueblo*'s collective voice into the most sententious of forms. Much as Demófilo had proposed, he recognizes that folk forms like the *cantar*, especially in the hands of a talented *rimador* like Paradas, said as much of the poet, lyrically speaking, as it did about the objective world that inspired him. When Cossío examined Paradas's collection of poems *Tristes y alegres*, he noted this candour and lyricism of his poetry stating: 'Su carácter popular tiene una autenticidad verdadera . . . porque no son imitaciones o transcripciones que pretendan una identidad con las coplas del pueblo en carácter, en tono o en lenguaje, sino una depuración de los rasgos más selectos y significativos de tales cantares' (pp. 495–6). Paradas's *cantar* was lyric poetry at its finest, Machado believed, and it had nothing to do with the empty and prosaic verses of the second-rate poets who littered Madrid's cafés and literary salons. In Machado's opinion, 'Enrique Paradas exprime su espíritu en todas sus composiciones, y por eso siente una invencible repugnancia y un desprecio sin límites hacia esos poetas, que merced a una labor mecánica y grosera producen obras desprovistas de todo sentimiento' (2001b: p. 151). This distinction between lyrical and 'soulless' poetry would resurface years later in Machado when he criticized the avant-garde.

If we take a closer look at Paradas's *cantares* in *Tristes y alegres* we find that they reveal striking similarities with Machado's *PrCs*. These similarities suggest that Machado may have incorporated some of his poetic themes and stylistic touches into his own poetry, particularly as they pertained to the use of symbolic language. Isabel de Castro has gone so far as to suggest that several of the major themes of the *PrCs* of *CC* and *NC* echo Paradas's later poetry of *Impresiones. Cantares* (1913). Part of Castro's argument rests on the fact that Paradas's poetry, much like Machado's, does indeed become more concise and conceptual over the years: 'En 1913 publica Paradas *Impresiones. Cantares* . . . Antonio Machado ha publicado ya *Campos de Castilla*. En estos cantares de Paradas se observa una marcadísima inclinación hacia lo gnómico . . . Sorprende la estrecha relación temática y formal de estas composiciones con los proverbios y cantares machadianos de *Nuevas Canciones*' (x). In the following *cantar*, Paradas likens solitude – and social incommunicability in general – to the anonymity of a coin:

> Te pasas la vida
> como la moneda
> sin querer a nadie, de una mano en otra,
> rueda que te rueda.[10]

The coin for Machado is a symbol of intersubjectivity and it represents the social 'currency' of truth and feeling in communicating the inner life to the Other. Like a coin that passes from hand to hand, the poet's

ethos – his lyrical 'oro' – is given to the Other in the *copla*, a recognizable 'coin' stamped and circulated by the poet and honoured by the
collective. For Mairena, 'lo poético, en el poeta mismo, no es la sal,
sino el oro' (1971a: p. 103). In poem lxxii (*NC*) we read:

> Mas no te importe si rueda
> y pasa de mano en mano:
> del oro se hace moneda.

Paradas often pondered how dreams projected all types of personal
ideals, yet the ideals he imagined in the oneiric realm – mostly those
associated with a Becquerian love and intimacy – are never fully
realized because they are continually thwarted or ruined by the reality
that comes with awakening:

> Me han dicho que la otra noche
> soñé que tú me querías
> y que si no me despiertan
> me muero de la alegría.

> 'En esta vida. . . '
> Soñé que era tu dueño
> ¡que triste despertar, qué dulce sueño!

Machado believed dreams had definite symbolic potential in revealing
the self's innermost desires. Over the years, the dream in his poetry
transformed from evoking a fragile sphere of essences, colours,
nymphs and childhood remembrances in the manner of *modernista*
verse (perceptible in 'La fuente' or 'Preludio – IV' of *Soledades*, poems
that express a nostalgia for days past), to later recreate an elaborate
sphere of failed ideals that guided the speaker toward a sociopolitical
'awakening'. In poems xxi (*CC*) and liii (*NC*), Machado tells us:

> Ayer soñé que veía
> a Dios y que a Dios hablaba;
> y soñé que Dios me oía . . .
> Después soñé que soñaba.

> Tras el vivir y el soñar,
> está lo que más importa:
> despertar.

There is little doubt that Paradas exerted great influence on the
young Antonio during these bohemian years in Madrid, particularly
when it came to revealing the lyrical depth of the *cantar*, and from the
little that is known of Machado's relationship with Paradas we know

that he had read his poetry and considered him a great poet. After Demófilo and his Krausist teachers at the ILE, Machado admits that Paradas was instrumental in instilling in him his core humanistic values, which is high praise indeed considering how he revered his father and the 'santos varones' of the ILE when it came to his concept of 'lo humano': 'Para mi hermano y para mí fue Enrique Paradas – bien lo recuerdo – un hombre providencial . . . cuya mano ruda y cariñosa nos ayuda a pasar las fronteras un pocos artificiales de la infancia. Es el hombre que, acaso, después de nuestros padres y maestros, deja más honda huella en esta experiencia humana'.[11]

The Influence of Eduardo Benot

Eduardo Benot's *tertulias* are also relevant during this time for Machado. As a former minister of the First Republic and a renowned linguist and grammarian associated with the ILE, Benot's *tertulias* attracted all types of poets and politicians. It was through these *tertulias* that Machado met Valle-Inclán, Federico Balart and the Andalusian poet Salvador Rueda, at the time known for his *cantares* in *Cuadros de Andalucía* (1883) and *Aires españoles* (1890). Antonio and Manuel very much admired Rueda, since he too felt stifled by Madrid's literary scene. 'Está cansado nuestro público', Rueda declared, 'de los endeca-sílabos de tono *quintanesco*; de los versos resonantes como sacudido saco de nueces . . . de la grandiosidad escultórica vacía de jugo y de belleza y de tanto trompetazo rimado. Parece que se encastilló entre nosotros la vacía retórica' (González-Blanco, p. 294). Rueda's *cantares* were a welcome breath of fresh air for Antonio and Manuel, and during the Benot *tertulias* they expressed their liking of Rueda's folk poetry: 'Casi siempre que se toca el tema poético en la reunión es en honor de algún poeta visitante. Los mayores guardan grandes consid-eraciones a Balart, mientras que los dos mozos [Antonio y Manuel] otorgan su predilección a Salvador Rueda' (Ferrero, pp. 41–2). And Rueda was also quite fond of the Machado brothers, particularly Manuel, and he even penned a brief 'Contera' to Manuel's and Paradas's *Tristes y alegres* of 1894 in which he praised their *coplas*: '¿No le parecen al lector estos cantares de [Manuel y Paradas] lo mejor que en España se ha producido en su clase? ¿Y no es cierto que esto vale infinitamente más que los millares de odas huecas y versos *arqui-tectónicos* y limados, de que tanto se ha abusado [?]'.[12] According to Pérez Ferrero, however, most of Benot's *tertulias* were not really about poetry and literature, but tended to revolve around Spain's political difficulties in revolutionary Cuba (p. 50). Yet, if we examine the Benot–Machado relationship a little more closely, we find that there are several literary and philosophical points of contact worth mentioning.

To begin with, Machado was involved in helping Benot finalize *Diccionario de ideas afines* (1897), a study dedicated to Spanish grammar and lexicography. Though he was a well-known statesman in late nineteenth-century Spain, Benot is remembered mostly as a grammarian and linguist, and his *Arquitecturas de las lenguas* (1889), and the posthumous *El arte de hablar – Gramática filosófica de la lengua castellana* (1910), are considered foundational in the field. In the Introduction to a 2001 edition of Benot's *Breves apuntes sobre los casos y las oraciones* (originally published in 1881), Juan Lope Blanch notes that before Benot, 'nunca . . . se había intentado hacer una clasificación amplia y sistemática de las oraciones dependientes de otra, por subordinación o por coordinación. Ni siquiera los conceptos mismos de hipotaxis y de parataxis habían sido establecidos con claridad' (v). While Machado assisted Benot in preparing the *Diccionario* for publication, it is safe to assume he had become familiar with Benot's scholarship (if he had not done so already, since works like *Breves apuntes* were critically acclaimed at the time and had run through several reprints by 1900). Benot had also penned several works on French grammar such as *Gramática francesa y método para aprenderla* (1858), *Programa del primer curso de francés* (1887), *Programa del segundo curso de francés* (1888), and *Versiones francesas recopiladas de los mejores hablistas* (1889), and they may have inspired Machado's plans to pen his own historical grammar of the French language. Shortly after his arrival in Paris in January 1911 to study in the Collège de France, he wrote a brief letter to the Junta para Ampliación de Estudios stating: 'He empleado los primeros días de mi residencia en París en recordar mis estudios de gramática histórica y filología medieval' (2001b: p. 246). In March, he wrote to the Junta once again on this same matter: 'Desde mi llegada a París . . . estoy trabajando para reunir materiales con que emprender una Gramática histórica de la lengua francesa, algo más lógico y ordenado que lo que tenemos en España' (2001b: p. 255).

Benot's approach to language is generally considered to fall within what is known as philosophical grammar.[13] After tracing the roots of philosophical grammar to Antoine Arnauld's and Claude Lancelot's 1660 publication *La grammaire de Port-Royal*, Noam Chomsky points out that its evolution is still little understood today. What philosophical

grammarians had in common was that they sought a psycho-
philosophical explanation of language:

> Philosophical grammarians had little interest in the accumulation of
> data, except insofar as such data could be used as evidence bearing on
> deeper processes of great generality. The contrast then . . . is between
> grammar as 'natural history' and grammar as a kind of 'natural
> philosophy' . . . The clear intent of philosophical grammar was to
> develop a psychological theory, not a technique of textual explanation.
> (pp. 13–16)

It is perhaps this natural philosophy of language and its inseparability
of meaning, production and thought that is most clearly discernible in
Benot's method of exposition; a method replete with both linguistic
and philosophical examples, a number of which refer to ancient Greek
philosophy. In his *Breves apuntes*, for example, he lays out one of the
core principles of his linguistic philosophy: to learn a language
requires more than internalizing a grammar or linguistic rules, but
comprises a more complex system of interpersonal communication
(an idea he developed more thoroughly in *Arquitecturas de las lenguas*
where he posited the existence of universal structures shared by all
languages that made it feasible to conjecture a universal grammar). Of
interest is not Benot's theory of language per se – although his belief
in interpersonal communication and universal understanding is con-
genial to Machado's thought – but one of the many examples he uses
to further his argument:

> Decía Cicerón que, con ser los ojos los que todo lo ven, no se ven, sin
> embargo, a sí mismos. Y en verdad, que ni aun les es dado verse bien
> por medios indirectos. Cuando miran en los espejos, juzgan a la
> izquierda lo que se encuentra realmente a la derecha, y suponen a la
> derecha lo situado a la izquierda. (pp. 5–6)

Benot refers to Book I 'On the Contempt of Death', chapter XVIII of
Cicero's *Tusculan Disputations*, where the Roman orator speaks about
the soul's immortality and the idea that death should be regarded as a
blessing. For Cicero, the soul is much like an eye: while it can see
everything in the world, it is incapable of seeing itself. Yet, more
significantly, it acquires its being, as it were, from the world outside
itself:

> The soul has not sufficient capacity to comprehend itself; yet, the soul,
> like the eye, though it has no distinct view of itself, sees other things: it
> does not see (which is of least consequence) its own shape; perhaps

not, though it possibly may; but we will pass that by: but it certainly sees
that it has vigor, sagacity, memory, motion, and velocity; these are all
great, divine, eternal properties. What its appearance is, or where it
dwells, it is not necessary to inquire. (p. 313)

Such a theory of the soul brings to mind poems i and xl (*NC*) of the
PrCs that seem to echo Cicero's eye metaphor in a similar manner.[14]
An eye is an eye, Machado proposes, not because we believe it is, or
even because it is seen by others, but because it *sees* beyond itself to the
tú. The *tú* impresses itself upon the self through the gaze and gives it
meaning:

> El ojo que ves no es
> ojo porque tú lo veas;
> es ojo porque te ve.
>
> Los ojos por que suspiras,
> sábelo bien,
> los ojos en que te miras
> son ojos porque te ven.[15]

We cannot say for certain if Machado discovered Cicero through
Benot, or even if he had Cicero in mind when he wrote these poems,
yet Benot clearly encouraged him to broaden his literary and philosophical horizons during this formative period of intense readings in
Madrid. Often overlooked is that Benot was also a philosopher of sorts.
His study *En el umbral de la ciencia* (1889) outlines to what extent
idealism, atomism and extension – all relevant subjects in Machado's
metaphysics – were still important in contemporary European
thought, and his book marshals all the major philosophical principles
since Descartes to tackle the problem of subjectivity in the late
nineteenth-century context. After summarizing Enlightenment idealism in Berkeley and Hume in a chapter titled '¿La vida es sueño?',
Benot asks: 'Siendo las sensaciones fenómenos de nuestro ser interior,
¿cómo probar que al conjunto de ellas corresponda un conjunto de
realidades, toda vez que no hay más que fenómenos internos, subje-
tivos, y, en saliendo de la experiencia subjetiva, no exista ya ciencia
posible? Consecuencia: El mundo es, pues, pura objetivización del YO'
(1889: p. 336). Benot is interested in exploring the limitations of
idealist philosophy to prove the existence of some form of subjectivity
that is not solipsistic. Covering the gamut from Heraclitus to Dalton,
his writings are devoted to critiquing idealism through the age-old
questions of the unity, divisibility and multiplicity of matter.

Contemporary science and philosophy, he concludes, do not provide any clearer solutions to the questions of subjectivity and objectivity than did the ancients, and while the reader is often left with more questions than answers in *En el umbral de la ciencia*, Benot's analytical spirit, even his philosophical language and familiarity with the subject, are reminiscent of Martín's monadological concept of alterity. In fact, many of Benot's conclusions on the unity of matter reappear to some degree in Martín's monadic philosophy. As Benot put it:

> Existe la materia; La materia es una; Está constituida por moléculas o átomos simplicísimos; Esta moléculas pueden agruparse diferentemente; Son susceptibles de diferentes movimientos; No percibimos la materia universal; Pero sentimos la acción de su diversidad de agrupaciones y de movimientos; Y creemos, por ilusión, que esa diversidad de distribuciones y de DINAMISMOS es multiplicidad de sustancias diferentes. (1889: p. 339)

Benot was also recognized in his time as a poet. A few of his more notable publications included *Patria* (1890) and *España. Poesías* (1905). His *Estudio acerca de Cervantes y el Quijote* (1905), a short study that had originally been written as an introduction to Ramón León Máinez's popular *Cervantes y su época* (1901), later appeared as a separate book. He also published short articles and poems in *modernista* publications like *Alma Española*, *Vida Nueva* and *Electra* – all publications in which Machado's poetry had appeared –, and he was even lauded by the young Antonio in an epigraph to 'Fantasía de una noche de abril' in *Soledades* ('Al venerable maestro D. Eduardo Benot'). Benot's theory of art, with its admission that thought ('el pensamiento') was the foundation of artistic form, is also noteworthy in terms of Machado's search for new forms of poetic expression. In Benot's words: 'El pensamiento es la esencia de las artes, y la obra será lo que el pensamiento fuere; porque si la forma es consustancial con la idea, la idea es el verbo que se encarna. Las formas son sólo condición constituyente, no esencial' (1901: p. xxi).

Benot's Shakespeare scholarship could also have influenced Machado. It was only in the late nineteenth century that Shakespeare's *oeuvre* was systematically translated into Spanish, prompting a general interest in his plays in Spain. Benot not only wrote the critical foreword to William Macpherson's *Obras dramáticas de Guillermo Shakespeare* of 1885 (one of the most popular translations of Shakespeare at the time), but also to one of the volumes of José A. Márquez's and Menéndez y Pelayo's translation *Dramas de Guillermo Shakespeare*, a four volume set that was first published in 1881. Benot's forewords are considered the first modern criticism of Shakespeare in Spain, and they could well have left their mark on Machado who was reading Lope's and Calderon's theatre in the 1890s. Although there is a significant reference to Hamlet in poem xlviii (*CC*) of the *PrCs* (in the *Unicaja* workbooks, we know to what extent Machado was captivated by Hamlet's 'to be or not to be', since it appears repeatedly in several pages), in 1904 he mentions Shakespeare for the first time in a review of Jacinto Benavente's *Teatro*. Shakespeare, he says, '[es] aquel sublime creador' (2001b: p. 188).[16]

Early Poetic Symbolism: The *Soledades*

By 1903, the year *Soledades* appeared, Machado's had published his first poems in the journal *Electra*, and he had travelled to Paris on two separate occasions with his brother Manuel, in 1899 and 1902. These trips to Paris inspired Machado to explore Symbolism and *modernismo* more fully (he met Jean Moréas, Oscar Wilde, Paul Fort and Rubén Darío, among others), and it also inspired him to write the poems that would appear in *Soledades*. By analysing some of the poems in *Soledades*, we can gain a more complete picture of Machado's poetic thinking at the turn of the century. During the 1902 visit, for instance, Darío noted Machado's tendency, especially during their late-night get-togethers when they read poetry and drank wine, to recite philosophical *paradojas* and song-like *saetas*:

> Antonio Machado es silencioso, meditabundo, lleno de honda y suave filosofía. . . Yo le conocí antaño, en noches jóvenes, de cerveza y lirismo. El silencioso se tornaba conversador y conversador gentil y chispeante. Tenía fáciles la saeta y la paradoja, y su ideología encantaba el ánimo. Su aspecto de joven lord descuidado parecía blindado de resignación y su paradoja y su saeta siempre iban suavizadas de indulgencia. (2001b: p. 321)

Although the first *PrCs* appeared in 1909, Machado himself acknowledged that many of his poems were written considerably prior to publication.[17] According to Juan Ramón Jiménez, 'Antonio Machado escribió un libro de cantares, anterior a *Soledades*, y Manuel, a sus diecisiete años (de hecho tenía veinte), publicó otro. . . Ellos procuraron destruir todos los ejemplares y nunca más quisieron acordarse de tales libros' (1958: p. 57). Why Machado destroyed his

first book of *cantares,* and how much of this initial poetic material
found its way into his later work, is unknown, but what is certain is that
various references, symbols and themes in *Soledades* and *SGOP* augur
the *PrCs.* An introductory comparison beginning with poem I in
Soledades will clarify further:

> Daba el reloj las doce . . . y eran doce
> golpes de azada en tierra . . .
> . . . ¡Mi hora! —grité— . . . . El silencio
> me respondió: —No temas;
> tú no verás caer la última gota
> que en la clepsidra tiembla.
> Dormirás muchas horas todavía
> sobre la orilla vieja
> y encontrarás una mañana pura
> amarrada tu barca a otra ribera.

Poem I begins with a clock striking midnight, the witching hour of
metamorphoses and enchanting transformations. Time and death are
one in the clepsydra, and the steady drip of its water from one vessel to
another signals the speaker's passage from the earthly to the spiritual
realm. Although a daunting experience, Silence appears and tells the
speaker not to fear death because death is nothing more than a restful
sleep followed by the purest of mornings. Given the references to the
death-journey by boat ('amarrada tu barca a otra ribera'), this sleep
evokes the cosmological waters of *Oceanos,* the river surrounding the
earth beyond which lies the kingdom of Heaven. This preoccupation
with death is prevalent throughout Machado's work. In the poem 'El
poeta' of *SGOP,* for instance, it returns precisely in the water-drop
metaphor:

> Maldiciendo su destino,
> como Glauco, el dios marino,
> mira, turbia la pupila
> de llanto, el mar, que le debe su blanca virgen Scyla.
> El sabe que un Dios más fuerte
> con la sustancia inmortal está jugando a la muerte,
> cual niño bárbaro. Él piensa
> que ha de caer como rama que sobre las aguas flota,
> antes de perderse, gota
> de mar, en la mar inmensa.

Although this poem is dedicated to the poet's discovery of pain and
melancholia, its initial verses speak of death in the tragic myth of

Glaucus and Scylla. Much like Glaucus who never won the love of the beautiful water-nymph Scylla, the speaker yearns for what is unrealizable knowing that God is playing with his destiny with the same disregard as a mischievous child. Faced with the omnipotent God, the speaker imagines himself subject to the whims of destiny in a tragic progression towards death in the images of a branch floating on the surface of the water, and then a drop of water lost in the sea. This progression towards death brings to mind how after ingesting magic herbs, Glaucus too was welcomed to the sea wholly transformed, and all that was mortal in him was cleansed forever. In poem xlv (*CC*) of the *PrCs*, Machado uses this water-drop metaphor to ponder the inevitability of death, yet he is in a much more existential frame of mind. Can death be simply nothingness, he asks, much like a drop of water whose distinctiveness and oneness is lost forever in the sea?:

> Morir. . . ¿Caer como gota
> de mar en el mar inmenso?
> ¿O ser lo que nunca he sido:
> uno, sin sombra y sin sueño,
> un solitario que avanza
> sin camino y sin espejo.

Or perhaps death is a transformation from the physical realm to the realm of solitary and ethereal essences, where being one – the *only* one (a type of spiritual dispersal into the infinite cosmos, free from matter, hopes, dreams and self-consciousness) – is the destiny that awaits the dead? In 'Poema de un día' of *CC*, Machado once again compares time and death with the sea, but he uses a symbolism reminiscent of Jorge Manrique's *Coplas* to make his point: '¡Oh, tú, que vas gota a gota, / fuente a fuente y río a río, / como este tiempo de hastío / corriendo a la mar remota'.

In *Soledades*, Machado also uses the image of the crystalline glass ('vaso') to refer to the soul in poem V:

> Crear fiestas de amores
> en nuestro amor pensamos,
> quemar nuevos aromas
> en montes no pisados,
> y guardar el secreto
> de nuestros rostros pálidos,
> porque en las bacanales de la vida
> vacías nuestras copas conservamos,

mientras con eco de cristal y espuma
ríen los zumos de la vid dorados.

‒‒‒‒‒‒‒‒‒‒‒‒‒‒‒‒

Un pájaro escondido entre las ramas
del parque solitario,
silba burlón . . .
     Nosotros exprimimos
la penumbra de un sueño en nuestro vaso . . .
Y algo, que es tierra en nuestra carne, siente
la humedad del jardín como un halago.

The speaker ponders the illusory nature of longing itself. The 'fiestas de amores' are many times only the mind's wishful fantasies ('crear'), and in the bacchanalias of life (the echo of clinking glasses so evocative of *modernista* poetry), one seldom discovers the meaning of life one had hoped for. The poem concludes in a symbolic garden, the inner life's repose: the most one can aspire to, especially in matters of love (I return to the opening verses and the contrast they establish with the speaker's mortality in the final verses: 'tierra en nuestra carne'), is extracting ('exprimir') some semblance of meaning and comfort from one's hopes and dreams ('sueño'). The glass in this poem perhaps derives from Darío, particularly his poem 'Nocturno' ('Como en un vaso vierto en ellos mis dolores / de lejanos recuerdos y desgracias funestas'), but Bécquer's 'Rima V' also comes through clearly: 'Yo, en fin, soy ese espíritu, / desconocida esencia, / perfume misterioso / de que es vaso el poeta'. In the poem 'Luz', published in *Alma Española* in 1904, Machado uses the symbolic glass to tackle questions of love, longing and the soul:

Pero en tu alma de verdad, poeta,
sean puro cristal, risas y lágrimas;
sea tu corazón arca de amores,
vaso florido, sombra perfumada.

The same is true in poems XL and LXX of *SGOP*:

De tu morena gracia,
de tu soñar gitano
de tu mirar de sombra
quiero llenar mi vaso.
Me embriagaré una noche
de cielo negro y bajo
[. . .]

‒‒‒‒‒‒‒‒‒‒‒‒‒‒‒‒

Y nada importa ya que el vino de oro
rebose de tu copa cristalina,
o el agrio zumo enturbie el puro vaso. . .
Tú sabes las secretas galerías
del alma [. . .]

In *CC*, Machado distinguishes between the glass's use for drinking and thirst itself. As his poetry became more socially aware, the glass assumed a more critical meaning. In the *PrCs*, the glass is considered through the properties of the vessel itself as a symbolic object of unity, reconciliation and brotherly love, as in poem xxxviii (*CC*):

¿Dices que nada se crea?
No te importe, con el barro
de la tierra, haz una copa
para que beba tu hermano.

In quenching the brother's thirst, we can better appreciate the significance of thirst in poem xli (*CC*):

Bueno es saber que los vasos
nos sirven para beber;
lo malo es que no sabemos
para qué sirve la sed.[18]

As we shall see in chapter 3, these poems refer to the book of Genesis to explain the symbolic significance of satiating the brother's thirst and granting him new life. Fraternal union promises a new order of ethical responsibility between the *yo* and *tú* that will surface in the *PrCs* in the Cain and Abel tragedy.

There is a definite continuity between Machado's short 'Consejos' and 'Glosa' on Manrique in *SGOP* with the later *PrCs*. Consider, for example, the verse in poem I of 'Consejos' '¡Ayer es Nunca jamás!', and its antithesis in poem viii of the *PrCs* in *NC*: 'Hoy es siempre todavía' (in poem VII of 'De mi cartera' in *NC* we also find these variant verses: 'del Hoy que será mañana, / del Ayer que es Todavía'). Similarly, the 'moneda' of poem II in 'Consejos' reappears throughout much of Machado's poetry, even in Mairena's writings of the 1930s. The poem 'El poeta' in *SGOP* that I used to discuss briefly the water-drop metaphor also provides clear evidence of Machado's progression towards the *PrCs*. There are a few verses of the poem that refer to the first chapter of the book of Ecclesiastes attributed to Solomon (and we know that Machado admired Solomon for his wisdom poetry: 'Reparad en que Salomón – único sabio verdaderamente popular –

fue, aunque amargo y negativo, un poeta que hizo, ante todo, obra de vivo sentimiento') (2001b: p. 206). Machado's famous phrase 'vanidad de vanidades' appears in these verses for the first time:

> Con el sabio amargo dijo: Vanidad de vanidades,
> todo es negra vanidad;
> y oyó otra voz que clamaba, alma de sus soledades:
> sólo eres tú, luz que fulges en el corazón, verdad.

Ecclesiastes is a book of cynical wisdom full of proverbs and practical advice, and it is also the book of vanity of vanities (a Hebrew idiom meaning 'utter vanity') that questions the purpose of human existence, as in chapter 1:14 that reads: 'I saw all the deeds that are done under the sun; and see, all is vanity and a chasing after wind'.[19] Everything under God is vanity of vanities, meaningless, and only He can illuminate the path to truth, love and salvation. Yet in chapter 3:11, the path to God is a mystery to humans, since God 'has put a sense of past and future into their minds, yet they cannot find out what God has done from the beginning to the end'.[20] God gave man the ability to conceive the notion of eternity and other-worldliness, but He did not provide him with the means to grasp it fully. Thus, ultimate meaning exists but man can never attain it, and so the speaker in 'El poeta' listens instead to the inner voice that urges him to seek some form of truth on earth. Poem xxvii (*CC*) develops the distinction between truth and vanity, a distinction that establishes a leitmotif throughout Machado's work. The speaker equates truth to the vanity of vanities; that is, to establishing a truth within the self:

> ¿Dónde está la utilidad
> de nuestras utilidades?
> Volvamos a la verdad:
> vanidad de vanidades.[21]

From his early formative years, Machado inherited a keen sense of folk poetry and learned the expressive and conceptual range of its pithy forms, especially the *cantar*. Nearly every member of the Machado family, from Agustín Durán to Cipriana Álvarez, had a significant connection to folklore. Demófilo's folkloric studies alone stretching from the 1860s to the 1890s, not to mention his sociopolitical ideology that sought to situate folklore at the heart of questions on national identity and philosophy, provided the young Antonio with a foundation from which to develop his own unique poetic ideas. Yet perhaps most significant of all was his father's theory of the pithy *copla*.

Sententiousness did not mean a diminution of poetic quality or
lyricism for Demófilo: on the contrary, it was the very essence of rich,
suggestive poetry. Shorter forms like the *copla*, especially considered
within the oral poetic tradition, allowed the poet to contextualize the
lyrical juncture between the self and Other within a larger framework
of social relations. Under Giner's guidance, the Institución Libre de
Enseñanza's instruction on Krausist reason and God only strengthened Demófilo's lessons by conceiving the concept of Other as a
significant part of an individual's perfectibility. In fact, the few times
Giner discussed folk poetry (for instance, in his 1863 article 'Poesía
erudita y poesía vulgar'), he alluded to the strong relationship
between the poet and the *pueblo*:

> la poesía *popular*, riquísima elaboración del sentimiento de un pueblo
> en lo que tiene de más personal y característico, eco armonioso de su
> vida interior . . . es, en efecto, la más alta manifestación que hacen de
> sí las naciones . . . en ella, el poeta es la patria, que derrama su corazón
> y fantasía en formas encantadoras, y reúne en santa comunidad del
> sentimiento a todos sus hijos, vivificando sus tradiciones, perpetuando
> su pasado. (1876: pp. 96–7)

From Machado's writings in *La Caricatura*, we also know that he was
not only sensitive to the *fin de siglo* crisis of culture and values in
Restoration Spain, but that he sought new forms of poetic expression.
He yearned to renew poetry beyond clichéd Romantic models, and he
was drawn to Enrique Paradas and Salvador Rueda, both celebrated
poets of *cantares* who he considered 'poetas modernos' during these
years of *modernismo* and Symbolism. Paradas and Rueda revitalized
poetry during this period of lyrical exhaustion, and Machado learned
of the *cantar* first hand from their work. Moreover, when he began
writing the *Soledades* in Paris, many of the themes and symbols of the
PrCs, although still embryonic, are present from the very beginning in
his work.

With the lessons Machado learned from his family and his bohemian years in Madrid leading up to 1903, he developed his own ideas
of what constituted the *proverbio* and *cantar*. Yet it was a lengthy process
that took on a new sense of urgency after 1903 when he came into
contact with the scholar, novelist and philosopher Miguel de
Unamuno, and began to distance himself from *modernismo* and
Symbolism to define a new poetics of otherness.

Chapter 3

From Art to Life: Critical Inquiries and a New Poetry

Yo nunca os aconsejaré que escribáis nada, porque lo importante es hablar y decir a nuestro vecino lo que sentimos y pensamos.

Antonio Machado, *Juan de Mairena*

How could poetry, Machado pondered in 1903, delve fully into the poet's inner life without ignoring the world of social engagement? How could it strike that delicate balance between a lyrical ideal (a poetics of self-interrogation) and a social ideal (a poetics of collective experience)? These difficult questions were important in the development of Machado's poetry and thought in the decade from 1903 to 1913, particularly when they are considered in light of the problem of subjectivity presented in chapter 1.[1] In this chapter it will become clear that the *PrCs* were a crucial part of Machado's shift away from the preciosity in style and sentiment of his early poetry to a more objectivist world view. Indeed, the contribution of the *PrCs* has never been adequately appraised in this light. As I hope to demonstrate, they played a significant role for Machado in opening up a unique discursive space in his work in which to examine the poetic-philosophical links between concepts of self and Other in the Cain and Abel tragedy, among other ways. To properly contextualize this discursive space, we must first carefully examine Machado's correspondence with Miguel de Unamuno between 1903 and 1905. Although the Machado–Unamuno correspondence offers revealing insights into various aspects of Machado's work, I will limit my analysis to his beliefs concerning the relationship between 'arte' (Art; how the poet can express his inner self with honesty and truth) and 'vida' (Life; the objective and social world of day-to-day existence). In his letters to

Unamuno, Machado speaks candidly of what he believes constitutes Art and Life and how they influence his concept of Other (as he admitted to Unamuno, 'en las cartas se dice lo que se siente'), and as such they are valuable in establishing a clearer picture of Machado's thoughts on poetry and philosophy at the time (2001b: p. 425).

The Machado-Unamuno Correspondence 1903–1905

In February 1903, Machado began an epistolary relationship with Unamuno when he received a brief note of congratulations from him for the recently published *Soledades*.[2] In a short reply a few weeks later, Machado expressed his gratitude to the rector of the University of Salamanca for his gracious words, and he took the opportunity to share with him what he was working on during the months following the publication of his first book. What most immediately occupied him during this time was the relationship between Art and Life: 'Empiezo a creer, aun a riesgo de caer en paradojas, que no son de mi agrado que el artista debe amar la vida y odiar el arte. Lo contrario de lo que he pensado hasta aquí' (2001b: p. 165). Unamuno was impressed with Machado's insights, and considered his distinction between Art and Life so convincing that he wrote a short reply to its basic premises in the August edition of *Helios* titled 'Vida y Arte'. In this reply, Unamuno cautioned Machado to ignore the solipsistic trends popular in contemporary poetry, for they were capable of leading a poet down a self-obsessed and narcissistic path and away from any true lyrical expression (not to mention the fact that they almost always resulted in second-rate poetry according to Unamuno). He suggested that a poet, if he were true to himself, should find his own voice by creating Art from the stuff of life experience: 'Huya, sobre todo, del "arte de arte", del arte de los artistas, hecho para ellos solos . . . Bueno es que busque su arte en la vida, y en la vida sin arte reflexivo; pero mejor será que afirme su propia estética y acepte la batalla en su terreno' (1971: pp. 879–90). When these words appeared in *Helios*, Machado's views on the subject had sharpened considerably, and in his review of Antonio de Zaya's *Joyeles bizantinos* that appeared that same month of August in *El País* he stated: 'Malos son estos tiempos para que alcancen estimación las obras donde sólo se manifiesta una pura intención de arte' (2001b: p. 175). Soon afterwards, he entered into a more open discussion with Unamuno on how to create a poetry 'torn' directly from Life. In his 'Carta abierta' he says to Unamuno: 'Aborrezco esto que usted llama *arte de arte* ... y aunque tal no fuera del todo despreciable, habríamos de convenir en que es algo muy inferior a la obra del verdadero artista; la cual se arranca directamente de la vida' (2001b: p. 177).[3]

As presented in the previous chapter, this desire for poetic directness and authenticity had appeared in Machado's writings during his formative years when he was in close contact with his father and folk poets such as Paradas and Rueda. Yet during this period between 1903 and 1913, Machado is looking for ways to poetize a larger social experience without having to sacrifice the lyricism of his poetry, and he slowly begins defining what he called his 'misión'. This 'misión' consisted in revealing the social reality of 'lo elemental humano', that is, the social reality that united individuals within a community (as Juan de Mairena would later clarify: '[e]ntre españoles, lo esencial humano se encuentra con la mayor pureza y el más acusado relieve en el alma popular') (1953: p. 111). Coming to terms with this reality involved not only distancing himself from the hermeticism of symbolist and *modernista* poetry, but also becoming more socially conscious of the Other as Other. There was no naivety on Machado's part when he formulated the poet's 'misión', but quite to the contrary, this 'misión' illuminated how pivotal otherness had become in his poetry during the 1903–13 period. As he saw it, he had to engage his fellow *hombre* in a larger communal context, and clearly, the very idea of 'lo elemental humano' (the bonds of feeling and understanding between the *yo* and *tú*) offered him a new way of conceiving how to do it. In time, it would change the direction of his poetry entirely and coincide with his *PrCs* in 1909 and his vision of Castile in 1912.

The concern for poetic directness and authenticity revealed that Machado was struggling with what Unamuno had discussed in 1900 in an article titled 'Turrieburnismo' (a neologism that refers to Sainte-Beuve's well-known phrase *la tour d'ivoire*). Unamuno defined the excessively hermetic art that was popular in contemporary cultural circles in Europe as *turrieburnismo*, or 'ese encastillarse con armiñesco egoísmo en la torre ebúrnea, debilidad de los literatos sobre todo, que les lleva al literatismo y a la vacuidad al cabo' (1971: p. 178). From his younger years as a committed socialist, Unamuno had always believed in Art's pedagogical function: 'La verdadera función del arte es una función educadora' (1971: p. 698). In fact, Art was a form of intuitive knowledge about the self and its place in the world. In response to what he believed were the shortcomings of the Naturalist novel (Zola's positivist works in particular), he proposed in 1898 that 'el arte es un saber intuitivo, gráfico podría decir, que nos presenta realidades que la ciencia . . . no consigue determinar' (1971: p. 771). Even in later years, when this pedagogical function was perhaps less explicit in his work, it was identifiable in the thought-provoking and more agonic/dramatic narratives that begin with _Amor y pedagogía_ in 1902. In _Niebla_ (1914), for instance, Victor Goti – often considered a mouthpiece for Unamuno – tells us that 'lo más liberador del arte es que le hace a uno dudar de que exista' (p. 257).

In light of Art's relationship with social experience, Parnassian impassibility, followed by the symbolists's claim that Art should express the most concealed aspects of the inner life, seemed a somewhat superficial – if not altogether irrelevant – proposition for Unamuno. How could Art represent any kind of pedagogical or revelatory function in Life if it strove to do away with emotion from the work of art in the Parnassian manner? How could Art render the world beyond the self if it represented, as the symbolists proposed, only the inner life, and even then, mostly through what Mallarmé coined as _suggérer_? _Turrieburnismo_, which reappears in the Machado–Unamuno letters, expressed this deep scepticism about the _l'art pour l'art_ stance and its Parnassian and symbolist roots, and it was even broad enough to include _modernismo_, which at the turn of the century was perhaps more influential in Spain than any ideas that were imported directly from France. Unamuno's dislike for _modernismo_ (its excessive ornamentation mostly) was apparent in his 1912 article 'Arte y cosmopolitismo', where he declared: '[E]ternismo y no modernismo es lo que quiero; no modernismo, que será anticuado y grotesco de aquí a diez años, cuando la moda pase' (1951: p. 1189).

Unamuno's role in developing Machado's ideas on Art and Life is often unclear. Obviously, there were many forces acting upon Machado during this period, and as Richard Cardwell has demonstrated, these forces often complemented one another to influence his thinking in significant ways.[4] What is perfectly clear, however, is that through his epistolary dialogue with Unamuno he articulates many of his core concepts on Art and Life, and perhaps most importantly he questions the direction of his poetry. Unamuno challenges Machado to think about such things as lyrical expression, language usage and poetic meaning, yet he also urges him to look into the world and poetize a larger social experience. And certainly Machado's recently published _Soledades_, with their enchanted gardens and murmuring fountains, reveal the unmistakable influence _modernismo_ and French

Symbolism had on his poetry (the type of hermeticism Unamuno was referring to with *turrieburnismo*).[5]

Under Unamuno's guidance, Machado also better interprets the sociohistorical and spiritual crisis prevalent in Restoration Spain, and in his letters we can see how he develops a more critical perspective of the country's sociopolitical state of affairs. In a letter to Juan Ramón Jiménez in January 1904, for instance, he believed that dealing with the country's sociopolitical problems required a bold collective protest: 'Pero pienso, queridísimo amigo, que es necesario afrontar una gran lucha contra la ignoble [*sic*] chusma nutrida de la bazofia ambiente. Pero hay que luchar sabiendo que los fuertes somos nosotros' (2001b: p. 184). He reiterated this idea to Unamuno a few months later stating: 'Pero hoy después de haber meditado mucho, he llegado a una afirmación: todos nuestros esfuerzos deben tender . . . hacia la conciencia' (2001b: p. 198). He also begins thinking about how this social awareness might influence his poetic praxis: 'Yo no puedo aceptar que el poeta sea un hombre estéril que huya de la vida para forjarse quiméricamente una vida mejor en la que gozar de la contemplación de sí mismo' (2001b: p. 190). In his review of Antonio de Zayas's *Noches blancas* published in April 1905, his position had all but crystallized in this respect: 'Muchos son los caminos de la poesía moderna, hasta vemos que cada poeta tiende a seguir el suyo; mas, para encontrar fortuna en todos ellos, la directa contemplación de la vida es condición principal' (2001b: p. 202).

In Machado's emerging social awareness, we can begin to see how he was gradually distancing himself from Symbolism and *modernismo* and advancing toward a more critical and 'communal' poetry concerned with what he termed 'los otros'. In this respect, Unamuno served as a mentor – Machado often imagined himself as his 'discípulo' – whose publications and encouragement influenced him to shun *turrieburnismo* and discover what was authentic in social experience as the source of meaningful poetry. Machado reached many of the same conclusions as Unamuno on poetry's social significance: a poetry that privileged only the inner, private life ignored what he now understood as the 'vida activa' (a socially committed existence), what he also called the 'vida militante' (an expression that speaks clearly to his developing sociopolitical awareness during this period). Similarly, a poetry that favoured descriptive, non-personal themes and attempted to eliminate emotion from the work of art also committed the same blunder.[6] In adopting this stance, Machado, like Unamuno had done before him, is perhaps oversimplifying turn of the century aesthetics without fully considering the larger socio-economic factors influencing its development (that is, how decadent art, with all of its ornamentation and solipsistic excesses, could serve as a window into the perceived social 'degeneration' of bourgeois values that Max Nordau and others criticized during the *fin de siècle* period).[7] Nevertheless, he concluded that the 'vida activa', and the social truth it revealed, should most immediately occupy the poet: 'La mejor intención de un artista [es] arrancar un poco de verdad de la vida, a esta pobre vida que tanto tiene ya de suyo, de vacío simulacro' (2001b: p. 187). Yet the question still remained: how could the poet incorporate the 'verdad de la vida' into his work without ignoring the inner life? In his 'Carta abierta' to Unamuno, he took his first steps at answering this question:

> Pero ahora que nos encontramos enfrente de la vida para hacer arte de ella, detengámonos un momento a meditar . . . Con el mote de *arte de arte*, rechazamos toda la producción de pretensiones artísticas que no tenga una honda raíz en la vida. Mas ¿cuál ha de ser esa vida en que el arte arraigue? Yo creo que no ha de buscarla el artista fuera de sí mismo . . . porque resultaría de nuestros esfuerzos que, por la vana pretensión de ser artistas, dejaríamos de sentirnos vivir, considerando la vida como una cosa externa. (2001b: p. 177)

Machado realized that the poet could not ignore the inner life and had to approach Life – or what he was beginning to recognize as a more profound communal being-in-the-world – as an integral part of the poetry itself and not as something that existed 'outside' it. Art demanded from the poet a clearer concept of how the individual lived in the concrete world, a proposition that implied, particularly considering Machado's Krausist and folkloric background, a deeper ethical sense of otherness (to which we will return later). By 1912, he believed Art, to be socially relevant, had no choice but to accommodate the poet's deep experiential concept of Life: 'Tengamos en cuenta que sólo se puede llamar alegre en arte aquello que nos reconcilia con la humanidad' (2001b: p. 313). Through his letters, we know that he seeks this balance between Art and Life in his own poetry. As he now understood it, poetry should never obviate the inner life or a lyrical and self-revelatory mode of expression, but inwardness required a certain objectivity to safeguard the poet from falling into solipsistic thinking or a realm of abstractions: 'Con todo lo cual no hago sino dar en este fondo de mi pobre pensar: la mayor de todas las vanidades es la

de enamorarnos de cuanto bulle en nuestros sesos . . . Además, siempre he aborrecido el pensamiento abstracto, por haber sospechado
desde muy niño que era éste trivial o inútil pasatiempo del espíritu'
(2001b: p. 176). If poetry could strike this balance, if it could locate
this middle ground between self and world, then the most intimate
and lyrical poetry could also be the most universal: 'Creo, sin
embargo, que una poesía que aspire a conmover a todos, ha de ser
muy íntima. Lo más hondo es lo más universal. Pero mientras nuestra
alma no se despierte para elevarse, será en vano que ahondemos en
nosotros mismos' (2001b: p. 191).[8]

To better illustrate this balance between self and world, Machado
speaks of dreaming awake. Although seemingly antithetical, each pole
of the dream/awake binarism allows him to explore this poetic middle
ground. To dream awake – not to be confused with the escapism of
daydreaming as Machado was quick to clarify – is to recognize the
importance of the larger 'vida activa' through lyrical poetry. In the
poetic space between self and world, a meaningful, direct and lyrical
connection with the Other was possible, but a connection that allowed
the poet to 'tear' the most intimate of experiences from a communal
experience of which he formed part. He explained it to Unamuno in
1904 as follows: 'Y hoy digo: Es verdad, hay que soñar despierto. No
debemos crearnos un mundo aparte en que gozar fantásticamente y
egoístamente de la contemplación de nosotros mismos; no debemos
huir de la vida para forjarnos una vida mejor, que sea estéril para los
demás' (2001b: p. 198). What is crucial for Machado is that to dream
awake required not only a re-evaluation of one's sense of self (the
pitfalls of egocentrism), but it demanded a conscious acknowledgement of the Other in the world: 'Hombre es el más alto poeta, y
nada suyo debe ser vedado a los humanos. Ahondemos, pues, en
nuestra propia alma, no con la vana pretensión de encontrar en ella
algo en que fundar privilegio alguno; sino deseosos de arrojar luz
sobre el alma de los otros revelando la nuestra' (2001b: p. 178).

This entering into the self to discover the Other and conceiving Art
as inseparable from Life (defined through the lens of 'la vida activa')
greatly influenced Machado's poetic 'misión' in the *PrCs*. Although he
is still far from Martín's idea of otherness, these years laid the groundwork to his concept of Other and point revealingly to his later interest
in philosophers like Kant, Socrates, Bergson and Heidegger. In April
1904, he had already begun speaking of writing a *new* poetry to express
his ideas of Art and Life: 'No estoy muy satisfecho de las cosas que hago
últimamente. Estoy en un período de evolución y todavía no he

encontrado la forma de expresión de mi nueva poesía' (2001b: p. 194). In the following years, this period of 'evolution' places the Other increasingly at the centre of his work, and he returns to the store of folkloric forms he had discovered in his youth to better consolidate the rapport between self and Other. The 1907 publication of *SGOP* is revealing in this respect. Although this collection of poetry includes poems from the 1903 edition of *Soledades*, it demonstrates to what extent Machado had not only renewed his poetic voice through a more direct and simple language, but also how he felt he had to edit many of his earlier Symbolist and *modernista* poems. In fact, thirteen poems from *Soledades* were deleted entirely in the new edition, and almost every remaining poem was edited in some fashion.[9]

This process of paring down the poetry, of letting it speak in the most open and unfettered way possible, most clearly resulted in the *PrCs*. It allowed Machado to articulate that balance between interiority/exteriority, subjectivity/objectivity and self/Other that he was seeking, and this explains why the first twenty *PrCs* published in *La Lectura: Revista de ciencias y de artes* in February and May 1909 effectively mark a point of departure of a new type of poetry. Machado locates the 'forma de expresión' that he pursued in questions of otherness in the *PrCs*, which will remain from that point onwards an open site for this topic all the way up to Mairena's *Sentencias*. These poems represent his most succinct and 'simple' poetry at the time, and their structure, tone and direct form of address (a form of address that is increasingly ontological in character) depart from the rest of his work and both introduce and develop several of the core themes of much of his poetry thereafter (envy, vanity, narcissism, wisdom, truth, time, nothingness, fratricide and Jesus).

One of the most significant publications that illustrates the paring down of the poetry in the *PrCs* is a parable titled 'Las nueces y la ingratitud humana' that appeared in *Renacimiento* in March 1907. This often overlooked parable is significant for several reasons: firstly, it reveals to what extent Machado had returned to his folkloric roots for poetic inspiration; secondly, it shows how he was branching off into philosophy and ethics as he explored the concept of Other; thirdly, it demonstrates how his idea of Other appears in the first *PrCs*; and lastly, it reveals to what extent his idea of Other, even within a few short years, had evolved into something more substantive and complex beyond what he had outlined in his letters to Unamuno.

'Las nueces y la ingratitud humana' relies upon a binary *uno/otro* structure: a kind man ('uno bondadoso y discreto') helps his egocentric fellow man ('otro egoísta e insensato'). As the two men amble through a forest, the egotist, try as he might, is unable to break open the nuts he carries in a bag. This activity is kept secret because, true to his nature, the egotist only thinks of himself and does not want to share his food with the kind man. But after the kind man questions his odd behaviour, the egotist asks for his help:

–¿Y quieres decirme porque te retrasas en el camino para comértelas a espaldas mías?

El insensato respondió:

–Te hablaré con franqueza. Me gustan tanto las nueces, que quisiera comérmelas todas . . . He tratado de comerme las nueces, como tú sabes; pero tienen la cáscara muy dura y mis dientes son débiles. . . Si quisieras probarme tu amistad harías una cosa.

–¿Cuál?

– Tú partirías la nueces una a una y yo las iría comiendo. (2001b: p. 218)

The kind man agrees to help the egotist knowing full well that his efforts will go unrewarded, yet he asks the egotist only for a sincere display of recognition (through gratitude), to which he replies: 'Si tú me partes las nueces para que yo me las coma, no dudes de mi agradecimiento' (2001b: p. 218). The kind man breaks open nut after nut, but each is empty, and the egotist is furious, and far from expressing any gratitude, the egotist accuses the kind man of theft and of depriving him of his meal. The parable ends with the egotist collecting the empty shells in his bag and walking off.

Like all parables, 'Las nueces y la ingratitud humana' has different levels of meaning. The most obvious level is that good deeds often go unrewarded, yet another reading suggests itself if we draw a sharper contrast between the kind man's selflessness and the egotist's ingratitude and how it plays out in the symbolic *uno/otro* structure. In selflessly agreeing to help the egotist and labouring for his welfare, the kind man asked only for recognition. This recognition from the Other, through gratitude, is the parable's underlying message, yet rather than originating from any universal ethical basis in gratitude's implied social reciprocity or logic of mutual appreciation, Machado makes recognition contingent on self-gain. It follows that while the empty nuts show that the egotist comes away with no material profit, they similarly point to the kind man's sacrifice. In other words, the egotist fails to see that he was, in fact, rewarded with the kind man's selflessness, and he was given all that he asked for (breaking open the nuts). This revelation, although lost on the egotist, explains why the kind man's final words read: 'Yo he hecho – se decía – un gran favor a este desventurado, porque ahora aprenderá a elegir nueces' (2001b: p. 219). The parable makes clear the deep ethical basis Machado began to recognize in questions of otherness, as well as the pedagogical effort involved in meaningful intersubjectivity. This effort is alluded to in the lesson of recognition itself, as well as the egotist's refusal to look beyond his own self-interest. Understandably, then, the parable's final image is that of the egotist returning to the broken shells, the symbols of his 'empty' and alienating self-love.

It is significant that Machado presents this lesson on egotism and otherness in parable form (all the more so if we consider that 'Las nueces y la ingratitud humana' was published anonymously in one of the most important *modernista* publications in Spain at the time). There is no affectation in this text, no elaborate language, only direct and plain meanings. Like his poetry during this period, the parable is pared down, and Machado distils its underlying ethical message into two poems in the *PrCs*: the first one, poem II (iii in *CC*), is a variation on a *serventesio* (it includes hemistiches and a paired rhyme scheme) published in February 1909; the second one, poem VIII (xix in *CC*), is a *redondilla* published in May 1909:

> A quien nos justifica nuestra desconfianza
> llamamos enemigo, ladrón de una esperanza.
> Jamás perdona el necio si ve la nuez vacía
> que dio a cascar al diente de la sabiduría.
>
> El casca-nueces-vacías,
> Colón de cien vanidades,
> vive de supercherías
> que vende como verdades.

Although the empty nut ('nuez vacía') remains a symbolic anchor to the original theme of recognition and alludes to the larger parabolic context, the poems' proverbial message opens the self-Other relation to such things as forgiveness, wisdom and vanity. The poetry enriches the parable with a new symbolic language ('desconfianza', 'necio', 'sabiduría', 'vanidades', 'verdades', etc.), particularly if we consider how this language reappears in other *PrCs* published in 1909 (such as poem I – xiv in *CC* – on virtue, or poem IX – xvii in *CC* – on hypocrisy). These poems rely on a more complex dialogic context not only within Machado's *PrCs*, but also within his larger *oeuvre*. From his letters to Unamuno, it has been apparent that he reveals a deeply personal aspect of the self-Other relation in these poems (the need to acknowledge the Other in some direct fashion), yet their folklorism also speaks to the collective, which points to the broader social sphere where he intended to lead this emerging ethical discussion of the 'nuez vacía' with his poetry.

Modernismo

For many readers, Machado's poetic shift between 1903 and 1913 demonstrates his almost complete distancing from his early influences, particularly *modernismo*. This claim, however, requires further examination if we are to appreciate the factors that motivated him to explore a more social poetry, and it would be inaccurate to propose that his evolving views on poetry were not indebted to *modernismo* in significant ways. The next few pages make no pretence of tackling the difficult task of explaining Machado's many ties to *modernismo*, but rather they attempt to reveal how *modernismo* played a part in his progression from his early period to the concept of Other in the *PrCs* of 1909.

Around 1903, Machado ponders how to write a poetry 'torn' directly from Life, which clears a path to his new poetry in the *PrCs* in 1909. According to Machado, his desire to create a new poetry appeared much earlier than 1909 as a response to *modernismo*, as the often-cited passage makes clear:

> Las composiciones de este primer libro, publicado en enero de 1903, fueron escritas entre 1899 y 1902. Por aquellos años, Rubén Darío, combatido hasta el escarnio por la crítica al uso, era el ídolo de una selecta minoría. Yo también admiraba . . . el maestro incomparable de la forma y la sensación . . . Pero yo pretendí – y reparad que no me jacto de éxitos, sino de propósitos, seguir camino bien distinto. (2001a: p. 78)

The early 1904 poem 'Al maestro Rubén Darío' reveals that Machado admired Rubén Darío, who he had met during his Paris visit in 1902, and he referred to Darío over the years as his 'admirado maestro', just as he did with Unamuno. And Darío also admiraba

Machado, and he had written the laudatory poem 'Oración por Antonio Machado' in 1905. Perhaps more than Symbolism, Machado's *modernismo* has been a source of considerable debate. Ricardo Gullón and Aurora de Albornoz have proposed that *modernismo* influenced the better part of Machado's poetry all the way up to *NC*, while critics such as Manuel Alvar have suggested that it influenced only his early poetry from 1900 to 1907.[10] In truth, the issue is not so clear, since there is no denying that *modernismo* influenced Machado's poetry after 1907, but not as significantly as it had prior to 1907. Although it is true that his attention to rhythm, language and form in *Soledades* is perhaps his most obvious debt to *modernismo*, there are other sensibilities that allied him with the movement. To begin with, Machado explored throughout much of his work the *modernista* idea – adopted directly from the Romantics – that the soul exists in emotive (dis)harmony with the universe. Also present in his work, although perhaps more tangentially, is the movement's belief in the spiritual bareness of modern existence. We also find that fragile sense of mystery and inner revelation in Machado's work that is discernible in *modernista* poetry when it comes to the strong experiences associated with love and loss. While he wrote poems in the so-called *modernista* style as late as 1906 – including poem LXVIII in *SGOP* that recreates a garden full of rose and jasmine-scented petals, or poem LXXXII, with its numerous nymphs, stars and dreamy images – Machado was also penning his famous 'Retrato' in which he criticizes in a simpler and more direct language the empty voices of the 'nuevo gay-trinar'. In fact, the paring down of his poetry, and the folklorism that it gave rise to, signals Machado's aesthetic break with *modernismo* in the *PrCs*, yet not necessarily a spiritual break, as we shall see.

It is true that *modernismo*, thanks in large part to Darío's interest in philology, rediscovered various forms of Spanish poetry. According to Darío, his first poems in *Primeras notas* demonstrated that he was well acquainted with Spain's literary tradition, and in his famous 'Palabras liminares' to *Prosas profanas* he professed his admiration for a long list of Spanish authors: 'El abuelo español de barba blanca me señala una serie de retratos ilustres [. . .] yo le pregunto por Gracián, por Santa Teresa, por el bravo Góngora y el más fuerte de todos, don Francisco de Quevedo y Villegas' (p. 49).[11] His poetry is full of allusions to Fray Luis de León, Garcilaso de la Vega, Calderón and San Juan de la Cruz, among others, and as Ricardo Gullón has noted, 'Rubén Darío es posiblemente el primero en el modernismo que intenta llevar a su plenitud la presencia de lo legendario, en las "Cosas del Cid", cosas por el estilo, en la figura del campeador, sobre todo' (1994: p. 48). Yet, what did 'llevar a su plenitud' really mean for Darío when he poetized Spain's traditions? What was Darío actually doing with 'lo legendario' in his work? His famous 'Cosas del Cid', often considered his most representative poem of Spain, is not inspired by El Cid directly, but by Barbey D'Aurevilly's poem 'Le Cid' in *Poussières* (the poem's first verses are dedicated to praising D'Aurevilly). The landscape El Cid inhabits is not touched by the sociopolitical realities of the Christian conquest of the peninsula after 722, but like D'Aurevilly's depiction, it is sketched as an idyllic countryside of musical sounds and flower beds. Similarly, in 'Letanía de Nuestro Señor Don Quijote', Darío imagines Don Quijote through the epic *La Chanson de Roland* as '[el] divino Rolando del sueño', and in 'A Maestre Gonzalo de Berceo', he praises Berceo's alexandrine by referring to Victor Hugo's innovations of the line.

Although these are only limited examples and allude to the much discussed topic of *modernismo*'s cosmopolitanism, they illuminate *modernismo*'s peculiar method of rediscovering Spain's folklore and historical figures. The poetry's preciosity (more so in early *modernismo*) displaces any sense of 'lo legendario' in these poems from its historical-geographical origins, yet we must be clear that this preciosity was much more than an aesthetic fancy (the famed 'galicismo mental'), as critics from José Enrique Rodó onwards have argued. It was Spanish America's complex response to the broader sociopolitical and economic crises of *la modernidad*, which included such things as the failure of positivistic reasoning, the disenchantment of spiritual and religious life and, more generally, the overall shifting of social values that came about with fast-paced modernization. Considering its scale and breadth, it is no small wonder that *modernismo* had such a transformative – and very often distorting – effect on 'lo legendario'. As Cathy Jrade summarizes it:

> [T]he *modernistas* were the first writers to experience and appreciate the all-encompassing alteration in the fabric of life in Spanish America brought by modernity [. . .] the first to witness the tragic face of science as it robbed legitimacy from the religious, magical, and animistic worldviews [. . .] the first to define the poet as both a visionary and outcast, at odds with dominant social values [. . .] the first to struggle with the newly commercialized social arrangements that were taking hold [. . .] the first to live the perhaps irreconcilable tension between the search for spiritual community and a sense of national identity, on the one hand, and a longing to participate in the world arena, on the other. (p. 5)

Machado's *PrCs*, their very *raison d'être*, marked a sharp departure from *modernismo*. One of *modernismo*'s core themes was the idea that the individual can somehow discover some form of ultimate truth. Most often, this truth reads as the individual's spiritual progression towards some type of transcendental harmony or ultimate ideal beyond the bleakness and sterility of the world, and it is literature – the space of self-construction, of identity and of legitimacy – that provides an ulterior form of knowledge about the ebbs and flows of modern existence. For Susana Rotker, 'modernists believed that everything, somehow, had to move toward a final harmony' (p. 8). There was a teleological rapport, almost mystical in character, between the individual and this almost cosmic 'everything', and language was critical in how the individual constructed and articulated his place within the cosmic whole. 'But the very concept of everything', Rotker continues, 'entered into the whirlpool of criticism. Modernists suffered – or began to perceive – an epistemological rupture' (p. 8). This rupture, particularly considered within the nineteenth century's shifting socio-economic landscape and its crisis of values, left 'the "I" [. . .] as the only way to achieve authenticity' (Rotker, p. 9). In many respects, this 'I' became the centre of ultimate truth, yet for Machado the 'I', quite simply, could not hope to achieve any type of truth without the Other. Much in a Krausist sense, truth depended on some form of recognition of otherness and the higher social good, and from here originates Machado's anti-solipsistic dictum in poem lxvi (*NC*):

> Poned atención:
> un corazón solitario
> no es un corazón.

'Fragment thinking' also illustrates Machado's distancing from *modernismo*. The fragment in Machado's work, its open-endedness (the 'duda' inherent in the incompleteness itself), its indeterminacy (the inarticulable inner life), and its underlying scepticism toward Absolutes (self, Other, God, truth, etc.), undermined *modernismo*'s faith in the referential function of language and its capacity to reveal nature's ultimate enigmas. The long alexandrine line privileged by many *modernistas*, with its hemistiches, elevated tone, cadences, complex interior rhyme and stresses, 'obliga a cálculos sutiles [. . .] un juego riguroso de pausas, esquemas rítmicos de diseños melódicos' (Zavala, p. 62).[12] This formal complexity – expansive, and yet exuding a sense of aesthetic perfection – runs contrary to Machado's belief in paring down the poetry in the folkloric *proverbio* and *cantar* and avoiding the poetic edifices that, as Schlegel understood them, are 'finished' and appear to be whole (Schlegel is referring to the necessity of that infinite expression in which the poem 'should forever be becoming and never be perfected') (1991: p. 32). In each word, verse, stanza and poem, Darío and other *modernistas* on both sides of the Atlantic tried to imagine and construct some form of completion and harmony, a way to contain the poetic word within a teleological projection: 'como cada palabra tiene un alma, hay en cada verso, además de la armonía verbal, una melodía ideal' (Darío, p. 49).

Gwen Kirkpatrick has demonstrated how some *modernista* poets and writers such as Leopoldo Lugones and Julio Herrera y Reissig had in fact wrought 'violence' to the movement's devotion to such things as wholeness and harmony, 'a violence turned inward against the grain of language and outward toward the usual signs of fulfilment, plenitude and richness' (p. 8).[13] José Asunción Silva is another *modernista* who went against such things as unity and wholeness, particularly in his disjointed prose work *De sobremesa*.[14] In this sense, *modernismo* played its part in clearing a path to the discoveries of the historical avant-garde, yet let us make no mistake: *modernista* poetry helped Machado define what he wanted to do in the *PrCs*. The fact that *modernismo* not only freed language from the need to reflect social reality (what is now understood as one of the movement's greatest achievements), but also considered the self, for better or worse, as the locus of truth, shed much-needed light on the gulf that divided the self from the Other. To bridge this gulf, as Machado realized, a new 'forma de expresión' was required, and it was not a question of values per se, but of social engagement, since *modernismo*'s belief in 'la alta idea' was very much in tune with his own Krausist-inspired idea of universality.

We must not infer from all of this that *modernismo* was blind to this self–Other gulf. Darío realized shortly after the turn of the century that his poetry could not continue along the same path, and it had to engage a larger social experience. In *Cantos de vida y esperanza* of 1905, Darío displayed a much deeper level of social awareness in poems like 'Salutación al optimista' or 'A Roosevelt', and he admitted in its 'Prefacio' that 'yo no soy poeta de muchedumbres. Pero sé que indefectiblemente tengo que ir a ellas' (Bordoli, p. 105). In the prologue to *El canto errante* of 1907, he argued that his wish had always been to universalize his poetic voice in order to commune with the Other: 'He meditado ante el problema de la existencia y he procurado ir hacia la más alta idealidad. He expresado lo expresable de mi alma y he querido penetrar en el alma de los demás, y hundirme en la vasta alma universal' (Bordoli, p. 178). By the time Darío came to this realization (and I have used Darío as the representative of a *modernista* sensibility that was indeed complex and involved several artists), it was perhaps too late for *modernismo* as a movement. The reaction against its language and forms – even from within its own ranks – had already taken hold, and many poets who would soon connect with the historical avant-garde were seeking to poetize the world more directly, precisely through such notions as fragmentation. This is the crucial point when, as Peter Bürger explains, 'the work of art entered into a new relationship to reality. Not only does reality in its concrete variety penetrate the work of art, but the work no longer seals itself off from it' (p. 91). And by not sealing itself off from concrete reality, Art had no choice, as Machado realized, but to acknowledge that truth required the domain of experience, contingency and social engagement.

Cain, Abel and the Thirsting Brother

To better appreciate Machado's self–Other relation in the *PrCs*, we must revisit the ethical dimension of his concept of Other in the first published poems between 1909 and 1913, particularly poems xxxvii and xxxviii (*CC*) on the biblical Cain and Abel story. In the brothers' tragedy, Machado adopts a different approach to otherness than he had prior to 1909, and he reveals how he was delving deeper into ontological questions in his *PrCs*.

Machado had discussed with Unamuno the subject of ethics as early as 1903 when he stated that 'me molesta la inmoralidad en la obra de arte . . . bien cuando se disfraza de *contramoral* o moral más sólida que opone la vida al espíritu religioso' (2001b: p. 178). Critics like Simón Guadalajara, Francisco Such and Elisa Rosales Juega have studied Machado's ethics closely, focusing on various social criticisms in the poetry, or in Juega's case, interpreting the poetry as a type of realization of the poet's ethical thinking.[15] However, the *PrCs* have seldom been considered a significant part of this discussion because Machado's larger work – including Martín's and Mairena's writings – provides rich insights into this topic. As we shall see, the *PrCs* furnish a symbolic depth to Machado's ethics when it comes to his concept of Other, and this symbolic depth is no more apparent than in the theme of fraternal reconciliation that he explores in the Cain and Abel tragedy.

In the poem 'Recuerdo infantil' of *SGOP*, Machado depicts a dead and bloodied Abel on a schoolroom poster. Fratricide, as readers learn in the enjambment of verses five to eight, is the classroom lesson ('Es la clase. En un cartel / se representa a Caín / fugitivo, y muerto Abel, / junto a una mancha carmín'). In *CC*, Cain reappears as a grim shadow in 'Por tierras de España' roaming Castile's godless lands fraught with violence and fratricidal envy, and in the epic 'La tierra de Alvargonzález', the Cain and Abel cycle continues unabated. In poem vii (*CC*), Machado suggests that envy is often at the root of such things as virtue, justice and even kindness:

> De lo que llaman los hombres
> virtud, justicia y bondad
> una mitad es envidia,
> y la otra, no es caridad.

Poem IX (x in *CC*) published in *La Lectura* in May 1909, praises the criminal Cain as a type of demigod. The poem's irony (the verse '¡Gloria a Caín!') only reinforces Cain's depravity:

> La envidia de la virtud
> hizo a Caín criminal.
> ¡Gloria a Caín! Hoy el vicio
> es lo que se envidia más.

For Machado, fraternal love symbolized one of the sincerest forms of recognition of the Other. To explore this point, he turns to the Bible, and more concretely, the Book of Genesis in poems xxxvii and xxxviii (*CC*):

> ¿Dices que nada se crea?
> No te importe, con el barro
> de la tierra, haz una copa
> para que beba tu hermano.

> ¿Dices que nada se crea?
> Alfarero, a tus cacharros.
> Haz tu copa y no te importe
> si no puedes hacer barro.

Machado alludes to the Book of Genesis (2:7) in the first poem ('barro de la tierra') to refer to man's creation from the dust of the ground. This reference to the creation story speaks not only to the symbolic significance of the task at hand (aiding one's brother), but also the new ethical foundation Machado perhaps believed the task implied.

The anonymous 'tú' in the first poem is urged to mould a cup to satiate his brother's thirst. In the second poem, a potter is commanded ('haz') to mould such a cup. The cup is intended to offer life-giving sustenance to the brother, and it transforms into a symbol of both salvation and fraternal union, but a symbol that involves acknowledging the brother's thirst. What establishes the dialogic relationship between these poems is how their initial question '¿Dices que nada se crea?' hinges on two related unknowns: the thirsting brother, and the as yet unformed cup.

The cup as a symbol of salvation and fraternal union has its roots in the Bible. In chapter 10:37–9 of the Gospel of Mark, James and John implore Jesus to show them the path to His glory. Jesus uses a cup to symbolize their shared sacrifice: 'The cup that I drink you will drink, and with the baptism with which I am baptized, you will be baptized'.[16] In chapter 26:27–9 of the Gospel of Matthew, Jesus offers His disciples His body and blood in the form of bread and wine during the Last Supper (the Eucharist). The cup of His blood is drunk by all: 'Then he took a cup, and after giving thanks he gave it to them saying, "Drink from it, all or you, for this is my blood of the covenant, which is poured out for many for the forgiveness of sins. I tell you, I will never again drink of this fruit of the vine until that day when I drink it new with you in my Father's kingdom"'.[17] Psalm 116:13 references the cup of salvation in honour of God: 'I will lift my cup of salvation and call on the name of the Lord'.[18] The Holy Grail in Christian mythology represents a cup or vessel capable of healing (Joseph of Arimathea collected Jesus's blood in it after His crucifixion). In all instances, the cup symbolizes union or healing, and it follows that without the symbolic cup, the brother will suffer from thirst.

Poem xli (*CC*) establishes an interrogatory structure that extends the dialogic relationship of the earlier poems xxxvii and xxxviii. It also begins with a question, but one that is antithetical to that of the earlier poems: instead of the life-affirming verb 'crear', it begins with the more ominous 'perder':

> ¿Dices que nada se pierde?
> Si esta copa de cristal
> se me rompe, nunca en ella
> beberé, nunca jamás.

Unlike the previous poems that dealt with the cup's creation, in poem xli the cup is materialized ('esta copa'), yet the symbolic vessel is not a potter's clay cup, but a brittle glass cup. The fragility of the cup, as suggested in the verbs 'perder' in the first verse and 'romper' in the third, threatens the fraternal union that has become more pressing with a first-person interlocutor. That is, the brother is given a voice in this poem, which brings to mind his thirst once again. In poem xliii (*CC*), this same sense of poetic presence informs the brother's fateful words on destiny (perhaps his own fate), which again include the repetition of the verb 'perder':

> Dices que nada se pierde
> y acaso dices verdad,
> pero todo lo perdemos
> y todo nos perderá.

Given the biblical context and the symbols associated with fraternal union, quenching the brother's thirst is presented as a deep ethical responsibility. Machado's message is clear: recognizing the brother is vital to transcending Cain's envy and realizing a meaningful self–Other relation. In these poems, envy is presented as a perceived absence or lack within the self that is transformed into a hatred for the Other, for what the self has in essence idealized in the Other and cannot attain. To put it another way, envy demonstrates how the self manifests, or exteriorizes in so-called 'projective identification', its self-hatred in violently imposing its will upon the Other. And not surprisingly, envy has been theorized psychoanalytically as a direct manifestation of the death instinct:

[E]nvy is an oral-sadistic and anal-sadistic expression of destructive impulses . . . It could be said that the very envious person is insatiable, he can never be satisfied because his envy stems from within and therefore always finds an object to focus on . . . Some people deal with their incapacity (derived from excessive envy) to possess a good object by idealizing it. The first idealization is precarious, for the envy experienced towards the good object is bound to extend to its idealized aspect . . . This tends to break down and then one loved object may frequently have to be exchanged for another; for none can come fully up to expectations. The former idealized person is often felt as persecutor (which shows the origin of idealization as a counterpart to persecution), and into him is projected the subject's envious and critical attitude. (Klein, pp. 1–27)

Yet why does the brother thirst? This unanswered question illustrates the openness of the *PrCs*, which in terms of the poems on the brothers' fate, places much of the ethical burden on the reader (the implied 'One *ought* to'). As the poems suggest, why the brother thirsts is perhaps not the matter of real importance, at least not at this stage. What is most important is an understanding of the thirsting itself (the physical need of the Other), for it represents that moment of self-transcendence, of recognition, when one looks beyond the egotistical self and acknowledges the Other. This thirst, so dramatically represented in these poems, also has the effect of casting doubt on the brothers' plight. Poem xli (*CC*) reiterates a core idea that is hinted at in the poetic irresolution: the self is seemingly ignorant of the ethical implications of the Other's thirst. After all, the brother's thirst is never quenched, but left as an unrequited yearning in the poetry:

> Bueno es saber que los vasos
> nos sirven para beber;
> lo malo es que no sabemos
> para qué sirve la sed.[19]

What consolidates the theme of fraternal union and recognition is the idea of how exactly to acknowledge the Other. To properly explore this subject, Machado's ideal of moderation must be explained first, if only briefly. For Machado, moderation was more than simply harmonizing extremes, for it involved, as in ancient Greek ethics, adhering to the highest ethical good. Poem xiii (*CC*) restates the age-old axiom of moderation, and it introduces one of his most revealing poems concerning the brothers' fate:

> Es el mejor de los buenos
> quien sabe en esta vida
> todo es cuestión de medida:
> un poco más, algo menos. . .

In the *Charmides*, Plato describes moderation as *sophrosyne*, a type of self-restraint and soundness of mind that had to do with moral fortitude, understanding right from wrong and distinguishing such things as virtue from vice, justice from injustice and contentment from envy. The ideal of moderation was a continuous process of ethical edification and self-mastery that came with true self-knowledge. Aristotle's 'doctrine of the mean' in the *Nicomachean Ethics* presents a similar principle of moderation, yet the 'good' for Aristotle also implied achieving excellence of character (*arête*, or virtue) which was 'a purposive disposition, lying in a mean that is relative to us and determined by a rational principle . . . It is a mean between two kinds of vice, one of excess and the other of deficiency' (p. 42). In poem xiv (*CC*), this type of moderation manifests itself in the virtuous man who does not judge

the Other; that is, he accepts the Other as Other. Machado invokes
Cato the Elder (234–149 BC), the Roman orator and statesman
remembered mostly for his incorruptible integrity, to propose that on
the *camino* of Life, it is the virtuous man ('el bueno') who tends to his
brother's thirst, yet he does so without passing judgement and with the
'good' in mind: he offers water to the thirsty and wine to the drunkard
because what is truly important is acknowledging the brother:

> Virtud es la alegría que alivia el corazón
> más grave y desarruga el ceño de Catón.
> El bueno es el que guarda, cual venta del camino,
> para el sediento el agua, para el borracho el vino.

By recasting the Cain and Abel story in the *PrCs*, there is an
accumulation of symbols, intra- and extratextual allusions and an
overarching sense of open-endedness (the brothers' fate hangs in the
balance from poem to poem), that confront the reader with the
complex ethical question of what 'good' ('bueno') really means. This
symbolic and contextual framework, particularly in relying on the
Book of Genesis (the book that lays the groundwork for man's knowledge of good and evil), provides much of the foundation upon which
Machado will develop his concept of otherness. In exploring Cain's
envy, the poetry suggests that the overarching ethical question 'Why
does my brother thirst?' requires the self to recognize the Other in the
world, and this might explain why envy is presented in such a visceral
and embodied way in these poems. Over the years, Machado understood that the key ethical question of alterity had to take root in a
recognition of the Other, and in his fratricidal problematic, recognizing the Other became an ethical problem that influenced almost every
aspect of his work. In most instances, what is 'ethical' in his poetry and
prose is not a defined set of normative principles that inform the way
one should specifically act and make judgements (although these
principles are certainly present: 'haz una copa / para que beba tu
hermano'; 'El bueno es el que guarda, cual venta del camino', etc.),
but rather it is an acknowledgement of a more fundamental 'comunión humana' between self and Other. This was a recognition of the
Other's separateness (what I have suggested takes symbolic form in the
Other's thirst) that preceded any ethical reasoning, theory or claim,
and the thirsting brother, as these poems suggest, can only be 'saved'
through this type of recognition. In sum, seeing the Other *as* Other –
in essence, bridging the divide between the *yo* and *tú* without the

violence to the Other that is born from envy – was one way of approaching the problem and illuminating its ethical imperative for Machado.

Poetic Inspiration: The Honeybee

In the *PrCs* of *NC* there are two poems on poetic inspiration that I present as both a summary and a conclusion to this chapter. Although published several years after Machado's poetic shift during the 1903–13 period examined in this chapter, these poems summarize one of Machado's most important discoveries about Art and Life that resulted in the *PrCs*. The discovery is simply this: lyric poetry is not synonymous with self-contemplation ('el cantarse a sí mismo'), but rather it reaches out to the Other within a larger and more inclusive existential context that directly involves the self. Without the Other, poetry simply could not be lyrical (and hence universal) in the truest sense of the word. The following poem xvi evokes the classic trope of the industrious honeybee, and contains two simple commands that develop these ideas:

> Si vino la primavera,
> volad a las flores;
> no chupéis cera.

The trope of the honeybee referenced in this poem derives from Machado's 1914 prologue to Manuel Hilario Ayuso's *Helénicas*. In this prologue, he discusses the relationship between inspiration and poetry, and he proposes that the poet must broach a larger social experience if he hopes to transmit anything true about Life:

> Porque el poeta no sacará nunca la poesía de la poesía misma. Crear es sacar una cosa de otra, convertir una cosa en otra, y la material sobre la cual se opera, no puede ser la obra misma. Así, una abeja consagrada a la miel – y no a las flores – será más bien un zángano, y un hombre consagrado a la poesía y no a las mil realidades de su vida, será el más grave enemigo de las musas. (2001b: p. 364)

Poetry cannot serve as its own well of inspiration. In fact, Life ('las mil realidades de su vida') provides the poet with the inspiration for his craft, never Art itself. The poet, like a honeybee, must never lose sight of the task at hand (the experience of Life, or 'las flores') for the 'sweetness' of what he produces (the poetry itself, or the 'cera').

Machado's trope of the industrious honeybee conjures up the ideal of poetic inspiration that appears in Plato's *Ion* where Socrates speaks of 'good lyric poets':

> [A]ll good poets who make epic poems use no art at all, but they are inspired and possessed when they utter all these beautiful poems, and so are the good lyric poets . . . The poets, as you know, tell us that they get their honey-songs from the honey-founts of the Muses, and pluck from what they call Muses' gardens, and Muses' dells, and bring them to us, like honeybees, on the wing themselves like the bees; and what they say is true. For the poet is an airy thing, a winged and a holy thing. (1961: p. 18)

In the short articles published in 'Los trabajos y los días' that appeared in *El Sol* in 1920, Machado extends the honeybee trope by revisiting poem xvi under the subheading 'Naturaleza y arte' and suggests that decadent art is superficial and self-referential. For Machado, the poet's preoccupation with the 'sweetness' of his own labours leads him astray:

> Si vino la primavera,
> volad a las flores;
> no chupéis cera

> El artista no copia la naturaleza; pero liba en ella. Llamo naturaleza todo lo que no es arte, y en ella incluyo al corazón del hombre. El arte decadente no es subjetivo – como pensaba Goethe – ni objetivo tampoco; es un arte de segunda elaboración, que pretende endulzar la miel, o, como decía Shakespeare:
> Añadir un perfume a la violeta. (2001b: p. 453)[20]

Machado goes on to criticize what he calls 'cosmetic' poetry by referring to Darío as 'el gran poeta y corruptor'. Poetry must acknowledge the complexities of social life, and he proposes that 'necesitamos finos aires de sierra no perfumes narcóticos. Porque es preciso madrugar para el trabajo y la caza' (2001b: p. 453). In poem lxvii, he calls on poets (the 'cantores') to draw their inspiration directly from Life: 'Abejas, cantores, / no a la miel, sino a las flores'. Likewise, he asks the 'cantores' to remain socially alert, vigilant, and awake in poems xxviii and xxix (*NC*):

> Cantores, dejad
> palmas y jaleo
> para los demás.

> Despertad, cantores:
> acaben los ecos,
> empiecen las voces.

From these early poetic ideas concerning Art and Life, Machado will approach subjectivity and otherness from a more metaphysical point of entry. As will become clear in the following chapter, he will seek to conceive the self and the Other in God, yet his God involves a collective 'sentimiento' known through the self–Other relation. The transcendental God, Machado tells us, is absent from the world, and only one's commitment to his fellow man will realize some form of the divine.

Chapter 4

The God of Intersubjectivity

The dimension of the divine opens forth from the human face. A relation with the Transcendent free from all captivation by the Transcendent is a social relation. It is there that the Transcendent, infinitely other, solicits us and appeals to us.

Emmanuel Levinas, *Totality and Infinity*

Machado often praised God, just as he often lamented His apathy and distance from the world. This dualism has led readers to consider his relationship with God through an assortment of critical lenses, and he has been deemed everything from a true believer and a pantheist to an agnostic and a committed atheist.[1] In reality, Machado's idea of God was very personal and often not very clearly defined because what He represented changed during different periods of his life. In parts of his work, God is presented in a very abstract way (in *Cancionero apócrifo*, for example, Abel Martín equates Him to a type of primordial nothingness), and it is not exactly clear at first glance if there is any overarching concern to his theism. Yet, in the *PrCs*, Machado provides us with a glimpse into a significant facet of his idea of God – and more generally, his notion of spiritual transcendence – that is expressed through the self–Other relation in a type of Christian 'communism' (a term he himself used to refer specifically to the deep spiritual communion and brotherhood among men). Although perhaps not immediately perceptible in his *oeuvre*, this God experience in the self–Other relation was essential when it came to his concept of Other. On the one hand, it advanced his idea of Other and its ethical imperative a step further into the realm of social life, and on the other hand, it demonstrated how he was symbolically wielding the fragment's inherent indeterminacy and oppositions in the *PrCs* to question God as the Absolute. What arises from this gesturing toward the Absolute is a reaffirming scepticism about God, a type of sustained inquiry into His nature that, rather than negating Him, conceives Him as an infinite possibility in the concrete here and now. As we shall see, this scepticism leads Machado to Jesus as a crucial symbol of an 'earthly' spirituality.

Before we can examine Machado's God in the *PrCs*, we must first outline his historic-theological context, since without this larger context it may not be entirely clear how and why he conceived the self–Other relation as an expression of God. Machado's idea of the divine was both traditional and transgressive, and it responded to the various shifts in philosophical, political and theological thinking that came about in the nineteenth century with God's so-called 'absence' from the world.

Spain's Spiritual Crisis and Unamuno's Lessons on God

Much as in the rest of Europe, organized religion began to be doubted in Spain in the nineteenth century. In the country's day-to-day life, the individual was confronted with a zealous Catholicism that had been steadily losing its footing for almost a century due to the gradual rise of industrialization and the emergence of the modern democratic State. Churches across Europe reacted to this loss of social power and relevance by not only publishing Pope Pius IX's controversial *Syllabus of Errors* of 1864 condemning such things as separation of Church and State and anticlerical propaganda, but also by attacking 'modernism' with texts such as the *Lamentabili sane exitu* in 1907 (a text containing a condemnation of sixty-five modernist errors) and the encyclical *Pascendi Dominici Gregis* explaining the dangerous 'doctrines of the modernists', also in 1907. From 1834 to 1868, a series of liberal administrations in Spain weakened the Church by disentailing vast expanses of ecclesiastical lands, and a substantial increase in peasant migration to industrial centres and mass emigration from rural areas to America also meant that countless churches were left without congregations. With the rise of liberalism and anti-aristocratic sentiment during this period, there was a sharp increase in violent anticlericalism. The radical mob, as Stanley Payne has documented, became a regular fixture in Spain's larger cities throughout the nineteenth century, and it laid waste to several Carmelite, Franciscan and Dominican monasteries (p. 82). As early as 1844 President R. M. Narváez had begun reshaping the Spanish constitution of 1837 under a socially conservative paradigm known as *moderantismo* to curb liberal radicalism and left-oriented social movements. The resulting constitution of 1845, which remained mostly unchecked until 1869, proclaimed 'sovereignty to rest not with the people, but with the monarch and the *cortes*; [it also] increased the power of the throne; proclaimed Spain to be Catholic; declared civil liberties to be subject to "regulation"' (Esdaile, p. 86). The Church's increased vulnerability in Spain during this time led to the Concordat of Catholic Unity of 1851 whereby Catholicism was recognized as the country's one true religion and thus assured permanent State protection (and this Concordat would stay in effect until 1953 when a new one was negotiated under the Franco regime). It is estimated that between 1797 and 1860, the number of clergymen in Spain decreased from 200,000 to 56,000 (Vicens Vives, p. 566). The 1868 liberal revolution and the subsequent and short-lived First Republic from 1873–4 further weakened the Church by introducing, among many other liberal policies, the right to freedom of religion.

The Spanish Church was resilient and it recovered significantly under the Bourbon restoration masterminded by Cánovas del Castillo in 1875. Cánovas established a parliamentary system based on a peaceful power exchange between moderate left- and right-winged parties known as the *turno pacífico*, while effectively excluding radical liberalism and ultra-Catholicism from the political process. Under his guidance, the Church's role in the country's sociopolitical affairs had been restored with the 1876 constitution, and in some cases even strengthened (its financing, for instance, reverted to pre-1868 levels) (Callahan, p. 23). The Decreto de Orovio promulgated in February 1875 succeeded in wresting control of Spain's educational system by replacing Krausist faculties in major universities with conservatives. Figures such as the Dominican Ceferino González, remembered mostly for his efforts to revive Thomism in Spain (he had written a three-volume work *Estudio sobre la filosofía de Santo Tomás* in 1864), succeeded in bringing a new energy to Catholic doctrine and scholarship. These measures amounted to a 'Catholic revival' in the *fin de siglo*.[2]

Although Catholicism did recover lost ground in turn of the century Spain, God's role in the individual's life had become suspect, if not altogether problematic, especially for the intellectual class and the burgeoning proletariat. The advent of positivistic rationalism, as well as the steady secularization of the State, had dealt a significant blow to the Church, and it had revealed its unyielding orthodoxy in not only sociopolitical matters, but also in terms of the exploding sphere of science and scientific discovery. In a world revolutionized by invention, liberal-minded intellectuals considered the Church an anachronism, an institution bogged down in its own shortsightedness. As Helmstadter explains it, '[in] the last 25 years or so of the nineteenth century, men of science and men of religion began to drift into separate spheres. In the new narrative of [the twentieth century] religion is marginalized and science, medicine, and technology become the central themes' (pp. 13–14). Even a devout Catholic like the Spanish Premier Antonio Maura, whose four administrations between 1903 and 1919 defined much of Spanish politics during the early twentieth century, believed that the country's socio-economic stability depended on a separation of Church and State.

One of the most symbolic reflections of this spiritual crisis in Spain, and certainly for Machado and his generation, is Unamuno's crisis of faith in 1897. Cloistered in a Dominican convent in Salamanca for three days, he abandoned his pursuit of a rational explanation of God and meaning in life. In his *Diario íntimo* written during this moment of crisis he acknowledges that 'con la razón buscaba un Dios racional, que iba desvaneciéndose por ser pura idea' (p. 15). In time, a deep existentialism occupied Unamuno's inner spiritual void, and it would set him on a course to what he termed 'agonismo'. Apparent as early as *Vida de Don Quijote y Sancho* (1905), he had conceived of 'agonismo' through the individual's inability to reconcile reason and faith, a failure that evoked the ever-present finality of a profound nothingness (and in fact, this nothingness had appeared briefly in *Paz en la guerra* of 1898 as 'el terror loco a la nada'). In a paradoxical fashion, Unamuno believed that the individual confronted this nothingness (through reason) to transcend spiritual doubt (through faith) to affirm the possibility of God. Yet the individual's ultimate realization that this cycle was marred by contradictions – the fact that God's existence was, in the end, always in doubt – urged him to perfect the self, to find something meaningful in the world. 'Me dicen que he venido a realizar no sé que fin social', Unamuno explains in *Del sentimiento trágico de la vida*, 'pero yo siento que yo, lo mismo que cada uno de mis hermanos, he venido a realizarme, a vivir' (p. 17). Although there is disagreement about what Unamuno's God meant to him exactly, it is clear that he believed the individual had to engage the world and interact with the concrete here and now to lead a fulfilling spiritual existence. 'Lo único de veras real', he tells us, 'es lo que siente, sufre, compadece, ama y anhela, es la conciencia; lo único sustancial es la conciencia. Y necesitamos a Dios para salvar la conciencia; no para pensar la existencia, sino para vivirla' (1967: p. 120).

From the Machado–Unamuno correspondence examined in the previous chapter, we know that Machado was familiar with Unamuno's thinking on a range of topics. His 1905 article 'Divagaciones (En torno al último libro de Unamuno)' dedicated to Unamuno's recently published *Vida de Don Quijote y Sancho*, reveals that he was also familiar with Unamuno's theism. He writes: 'Lo que conscientemente admiro en Unamuno es su heroica y constante actividad espiritual' (2001b: p. 206). He praises Unamuno's quest to regenerate the country spiritually, and compares him not only to Saint Ignatius of Loyola, but to Spain's great mystic saints. For Machado, Unamuno seeks a path of complete spiritual transcendence that will guide his fellow man to some type of ultimate truth, yet he recognizes that Unamuno's internal struggles of reason and faith sometimes got in the way: 'Mucho me recuerda Unamuno, en sus escritos, a nuestros mejores místicos . . . por el deseo de envolver y dominar espiritualmente y por el mucho pelear interior que no le deja punto de reposo' (2001b: p. 207). Machado concludes his article by noting the significance of Unamuno's underlying argument: ultimate truth is not to be found in organized religion or even reason, but in Life: 'Y abriendo el libro al azar, me encuentro con esta frase que no vacilo en reputar portentosa: "La verdad no es lo que nos hace pensar, sino lo que nos hace vivir". Y acaso esto resume todo el pensamiento de Unamuno' (2001b: p. 209).

In his 1907 article 'Tímidas consideraciones sobre el miedo de vivir y caminos para libertar a Dios, que está esclavo, según afirmó don Miguel de Unamuno', Machado demonstrates how he himself was confronting his own theism during his early years. As he saw it, God had to be liberated from a historical thinking marred by oppressive fear, guilt and melancholia. For God to be known more fully by man, He required a new individual who could overcome his death fear. Machado believed the individual had become so obsessed with death to the point of repressing his own *élan vital*. For this reason he draws an analogy between Life and bullfighting in which the individual's symbolic confrontation with the bull allows the individual to rehearse a death ritual as a reaffirmation of Life: 'debemos matar al miedo . . . Por eso propongo el *sport* taurino como uno de los medios de crear la energía suficiente para sacar a Dios de su cautiverio' (2001b: p. 213). God, then, was very much an attitude toward Life for Machado, a rethinking of one's understanding of Being and death. To liberate God was not a matter for the Church or Catholic orthodoxy, but instead His liberation came about in how one sacrificed himself for the Other. After confronting the death fear, one of the most revealing expressions of the individual's transcendence of fear, guilt and melancholia – and thus, the beginning of God's liberation as Machado proposes – was a deep altruistic bond with the Other:

> Comprenderéis que nuestro espíritu ha de ser, ante todo, generosidad, desinterés; pero nunca ascetismo. Debemos laborar sin esperanzas de lucro, sembrar para que otros cosechen; el altruismo es la ley esencial de la vida y único camino para libertar a Dios; debemos anteponer el interés de todos al interés individual. (2001b: p. 212)

Unamuno exerted a considerable influence on Machado's thinking on God, and we can see that his point of departure in the 1907 article is in fact Unamuno's poem 'Libértate señor' from *Poesías* (1907) that speaks of God as both liberation (revelation) and enslavement (blind faith). Aurora de Albornoz has revealed similarities between how Unamuno and Machado approached God, and while she suggests, and rightly so, that Unamuno's influence on Machado was significant, she confines it mostly to the period 1912–13. One of the major Unamunian ideas Albornoz discerns in Machado's notion of God is the 'Dios creado' that appears in his poetry during this period: 'Quiero adelantar que el concepto – o mejor, sentimiento – del "Dios creado" unamuniano, más que lejana o vaga presencia, es clara influencia [en Machado...] Mas sólo durante unos pocos años, que podemos fácilmente situar alrededor de 1912 y 1913' (1968: p. 230). Yet it is clear from these early articles that Machado was quite knowledgeable of Unamuno's theism much earlier than 1912. Although Unamuno's theism clearly progressed from his early work, Machado identifies many of its core arguments by 1905, one of the most important being that the country's sociopolitical regeneration demanded a collective spiritual renewal. In a 1909 letter to Rubén Darío, he echoes Unamuno when he proposed that any ideological programme seeking to restore the country socially and politically had to take root in a deep faith in God: 'Pensad en Dios, sentidlo en vosotros mismos y borrad el vicio de vuestras almas. No hay otro modo de hacer patria' (2001b: p. 231). Later he explained it as follows:

> El patriotismo de Miguel de Unamuno tiene una firme base religiosa como él mismo lo declara ... No está concebido este patriotismo de Unamuno en ningún campo político, no guarda relación alguna con interés de grupo, ni se roza en él la idea de patria con el ocio sectario ni con la seguridad personal de unos cuantos santones. (2001b: p. 349)

Another argument Machado adopts from Unamuno during this early period is that the very idea of God rested upon an 'existential' sensibility that had to do with lived experience and the day-to-day 'pormenores' that defined it (questions of human freedom, social responsibility, how to live, how to understand the inevitability of death, etc.). Unamuno had revealed God to be an intensely personal expression of Life. In *Mi religión*, he remarked: 'es obra de suprema piedad religiosa buscar la verdad en todo [. . .] mi religión es luchar con Dios desde el romper del alba hasta el caer de la noche' (p. 15). The individual could no longer imagine God, or even think or speak to Him, without a sense of agony, yearning, faith, hope and doubt (always doubt) pervading all aspects of his existence. To overcome doubt about God was a 'tragic' struggle for the individual because it made him aware of his desire for immortality and the inevitability of death.

The 1905 and 1907 articles also reveal how Machado differed from Unamuno, and how he was beginning to define his own understanding of God. Unlike Unamuno, he reconciled faith and God, as we shall see, in the very idea of Other he was defining during these early years. Unamuno had certainly concretized spiritual meaning in Life (in *Del sentimiento trágico* he recognizes the 'Dios humano' in love, pity and compassion in chapters VI and IX where he refers to his 'semejantes'), but his concepts of God and Life were intertwined with a very personal yearning for the soul's immortality:

> Quedémonos ahora en esta vehemente sospecha de que el ansia de no morir, el hambre de la inmortalidad personal, el conato con que tendemos a persistir indefinidamente en nuestro ser propio . . . es la base afectiva de todo conocer y el íntimo punto de partida personal de toda filosofía humana . . . Y este punto de partida personal y afectivo de toda filosofía es el sentimiento trágico de la vida. (1967: p. 35)

Alison Sinclair discerns two symbolic conflicts in much of Unamuno's work related to this inwardness of the tragic sense of life: 'living *with* another being [. . . and] living *without* the other being, and hence in a state of radical solitude, that condition . . . that dominates Unamuno's sense of self' (p. 126). Although Unamuno is aware of the Other in the world, it was the individual's relationship with God and his 'state of radical solitude' (the personal doubt and agony that came with the discovery of mortality) that was elevated to a universal – and many times abstract – condition for all men (and in this respect, it is often unclear how self and Other should share their ideas of 'un Dios colectivo').[3] This inwardness is perhaps best represented in

Unamuno's *San Manuel Bueno, mártir*. As a priest who secretly does not believe in God, San Manuel suffers his own internal struggles with his disbelief while publically upholding the Catholic faith and its message of hope for the collective good.

The Janus-faced God: Presence and Absence

From roughly 1907 onwards, Machado sought to 'liberate' God, but He became a more elusive idea the more he scrutinized Him. Although there is no question that he believed in Him (except a few profound moments, as we shall see, when he convinces himself that there can be no God), His relationship with the speaker in his poetry is often difficult and enigmatic. In poem LXXVII of *SGOP*, Machado admitted that he was a solitary and 'pobre hombre . . . buscando a Dios entre la niebla'. The fact is that he struggled with the idea of God, particularly following Leonor's death in 1912. Poem CXIX expresses his deep resentment towards Him for Leonor's death, since He had 'torn' her from his side against his wishes:

> Señor, ya me arrancaste lo que yo más quería.
> Oye otra vez, Dios mío, mi corazón clamar.
> Tu voluntad se hizo, Señor, contra la mía.
> Señor, ya estamos solos mi corazón y el mar.

The poem's biblical resonances (the speaker's exhortation to God in each verse; its overall tone of lamentation; its psalmic form and style) intensify the emotive power of the speaker's words to God. After the death of the loved one, the speaker is left alone with the sea, and we begin to see how Machado was considering God as being mostly absent from the world for He had been deaf to his pleas, to his pain. The will of God, according to Jesus' teachings in Matthew (6:10), will be done ('Tu voluntad se hizo, Señor'), but Machado questions this idea of abandonment *to* God. Machado counters this idea of abandonment *to* God in the first part of the third verse with one of a personal abandonment *by* God in the last part of the same verse ('contra la mía'). In the first *cantar* of 'Tres cantares enviados a Unamuno en 1913' (three *cantares* Machado sent to Unamuno in 1913 that were never published), he expresses this same sense of infinite solitude before God by once again invoking the symbolic sea:

Señor, me cansa la vida,
tengo la garganta ronca
de gritar sobre los mares,
la voz de la mar me sorda.
Señor, me cansa la vida
y el universo me ahoga.
Señor, me dejaste solo,
solo, con el mar a solas.

In 'Poema de un día', a poem written during this same mournful period, Machado admits that, despite his sincerest efforts, there were times when he did not believe in God. Trapped between reason and bitter despair (Unamuno's 'agonismo' immediately comes to mind), Machado had turned to God in a moment of anguish, he had opened his heart to Him, but He had not responded: 'razón y locura / y amargura / de querer y no poder / creer, creer, creer!' Yet, there are also periods when God brings light to Machado's poetry and closes this distance between self and God. In the poem 'Los olivos I' (CXXXII) written during the 1913–14 period in Baeza, God is portrayed as a generative force capable of alleviating the suffering of 'los benditos labradores'. The poem depicts the dry and sun-drenched olive groves that extend for miles throughout Andalusia, and it reveals the hardships of rural life through telluric images associated with olive production. Machado implores God to bless the olive groves with a bountiful rain: 'Olivares, Dios os dé / los eneros / de aguaceros / los agostos de agua al pie'. Ultimately, he implores God to show Himself and fill the peasants' hearts with hope: '¡Venga Dios a los hogares / y a las almas de esta tierra / de olivares y olivares'. In poem xliv (*NC*) of the *PrCs* written about a decade later, he advises poets to draw their inspiration from God because only His divine word is eternal and transcends the silence and din of the world:

No desdeñéis la palabra;
el mundo es ruidoso y mudo,
poetas, sólo Dios habla.

Much of the confusion surrounding Machado's God derives from the fact that He is a Janus-faced God, both forgiving and merciless, present and absent, and known and unknown. It is an understatement to say that Machado waivered in his idea of God, or what José Luis Aranguren describes as 'un fluctuar entre escepticismo e inconcreta creencia, entre desesperanza y esperanza' (p. 396). Much like the

mystic poet Saint John of the Cross had conceived it, Machado imagined God playing a game of hide-and-seek with him, coming forth
from the darkness into the light one moment, only to withdraw
without a trace the next. And, tragically, it seems the more he desired
Him and the more he wanted to commune with Him in the 'light' of
His love and faith, the more elusive He became:

> 2
> O tú y yo jugando estamos
> al escondite Señor,
> o la voz con que te llamo
> es tu voz.
>
> 3
> Por todas partes te busco
> sin encontrarte jamás,
> y en todas partes te encuentro
> sólo por irte a buscar.[4]

   Through a series of reflections in the *PrCs* that we will turn to in the
following section, Machado constructs what at first glance appears to
be a paradoxical vision of God: He is both absent from life (He eludes
finite human reason and cannot be known by man) and yet He is also
present in life (the *feeling* of God, however, can be known by man in
some way). In a seemingly irreconcilable fashion, the absent God
makes known the present God and both are separate, yet both are one.
Because He is eternal, and because His perfection is unimaginable,
man has little choice but to 'create' Him. In Machado's words: 'Es
cierto que la inteligencia no puede alcanzar la última realidad, mas no
es cierto que haya otro medio de llegar a ella' (1971b: p. 55). By
'create' Machado did not mean a ceremonial or performative act of
devotion, but rather a social act of divine discovery in which God
manifests Himself through the self–Other relation. For Machado,
there was no sentiment more sincere and spiritual of His perfection
than one's love for the Other. In a letter to Unamuno he explained it
as a type of deep fraternal love: '[e]l amor fraternal nos saca de
nuestra soledad y nos lleva a Dios. Cuando reconozco que hay otro yo,
que no soy yo mismo ni es obra mía, caigo en la cuenta de que Dios
existe' (2001b: p. 427). This fraternal love makes God known in
concrete human relations and it gives meaning to existence for the
simple reason that it opens the way to the altruistic self-sacrifice (the
'ley esencial') capable of 'liberating' Him within the limits of man's
understanding.

From this intersubjective idea of God, Machado's theism is brought into sharper focus and begins to reveal its oppositional unity. God is beyond man's finite understanding, but it is precisely this absence of understanding that 'awakens' man's desire for Him. If we consider Machado's fondness for opposites, what appears paradoxical at first glance – His absence and presence – may in fact be a reformulation of a type of Heraclitan Unity of Opposites: the idea that opposites can exist (or are co-instantiated) in the same world, object or thing. Heraclitus appears often in Machado's poetry and prose, and there is no doubt he was fond of his oppositional logic. Willis Barnstone goes so far as to say that 'Heraclitus . . . is for Machado what he is for Borges: an obsession' (p. 119). It is not clear when exactly Heraclitus' ideas first appear in Machado's poetry, but in poem VIII (xliv in *CC*) of the 'Cantares y proverbios, sátiras y epigramas' published in *La Lectura* in 1913, there is a veiled reference to this Unity of Opposites: 'Todo pasa y todo queda / pero lo nuestro es pasar, / pasar haciendo caminos, / caminos sobre la mar'. In the later *PrCs*, and in the *Cancioneros apócrifos*, *Los complementarios*, and Juan de Mairena's *Sentencias*, Heraclitus is a mainstay in his work.[5]

The fundamental idea behind much of Heraclitus' philosophy is contained in his simple dictum 'what opposes unites'. Opposites were essential in preserving a cosmic balance and unity. As it is stated in Heraclitus' philosophical fragments, 'cold warms up, warm cools off, moist parches, dry dampens', and 'the same . . . living and dead, and the waking and the sleeping, and young and the old; for these transposed are those and those transposed again are these' (Kahn, p. 53–71). Other examples Heraclitus uses to illustrate this concept of cosmic balance and unity include cyclical patterns such as night and day and winter and summer. In Hegel's estimation, Heraclitus' Unity of Opposites revealed the logic of Spirit (the rational progression of mind and world), and in his *Lectures on the History of Philosophy* he stated that 'there is no proposition of Heraclitus which I have not adopted in my logic' (p. 279). Considered in conjunction with his complementary Doctrine of Flux (the idea that permanence and change are the universe's governing principles), Heraclitus' Unity of Opposites can be regarded more broadly as dialectical forces of cosmic revelation:

> [O]rder in the cosmos does not arise in spite of tension, conflict, change and chronic transformation, but because of and through conflict. The order of the universe is woven from the warp and woof of *difference* and can only be fully understood as a relational and

configurational field of contraries [. . .] It is not that 'unity' (identity)
assumes 'multiplicity' (difference), but that *unity is constituted through
difference*: 'opposites' unite (the finest harmony stems from things
bearing in opposite directions). (Sandywell, p. 263)

Machado criticizes the absent God in his *PrCs* for He offers man no
real solace or guidance in the concrete here and now. However, the
absent God brings forth the present God, the God in the self, and thus
absence and presence are opposed and united. There is a clear
progression in Machado's idea of God that moves beyond the biblical
Lord, the supreme creator, and the arcane force of absolute transcendence for a collective and present God that could be felt (and thus
known in some way) in the self–Other relation. The absence/presence
opposition and unity, and the tension and resolution it sustains, was
critical in how God manifested Himself in the world. And it is Jesus
who appears as the unifying figure in Machado's theism, since it was
God as man (the divine–earthly paradox of spirit as flesh) who commanded: 'Love your neighbour as yourself'.

The Divine Light Within: Machado's Critique of Organized Religion

Machado never disguised his anticlericalism. In the early article
'Trabajando para el porvenir' published in *Alma Española* in March
1904, he shows his more satirical side by feigning a deep interest for
the new Jesuit seminary that was under construction at the time on
Madrid's *Paseo del Cisne*. The structure's 'beauty' sparks the thought in
Machado of a city wholly entranced in God's rapture. Who would feed
the city, he asks, if its inhabitants were mesmerized by God in such a
way? He also ponders on why it is that only priests have somehow
managed to survive Spain's socio-economic hardships: 'Y en esta tierra
de vividores aborrecemos ya seriamente a los curas, porque ellos son
los únicos que han logrado vivir' (2001b: p. 193). From 1904 onwards,
he consistently railed against organized religion and the Spanish
Church, and in his mind it was terribly ironic and tragic that in a
country filled with churches, monasteries and priests, the individual
was left wanting for a genuine feeling of God.

Machado's anticlericalism must be considered with care since his
criticisms reveal to what extent spiritual meaning was in fact important

in his poetry and thinking. He believed that Spain's social regeneration, as Unamuno had predicted, was really a spiritual problem. 'La
cuestión central es la religiosa', he tells us, 'y ésa es la que tenemos que
plantear de una vez' (2001b: p. 342). Beginning in 1907, he witnessed
firsthand the lasting effects of Spain's spiritual barrenness on the
remote village of Soria. In Baeza, a village even more isolated than
Soria where he lived from 1913 to 1919, he saw how it led the common
man to utter hopelessness and resignation: '[en Baeza] no hay un
átomo de religiosidad . . . Una población encanallada por la Iglesia y
completamente huera' (2001b: p. 340). In the poem 'Los olivos II'
(CXXXII) inspired by Baeza and its surroundings, he shows how
Spanish villages boasting large thriving convents were spiritually desti-
tute. The poem recreates the village as a rubbish dump, and then as
the house of God: 'Esta piedad erguida / sobre este burgo sórdido,
sobre este basurero, / esta casa de Dios'. The speaker exclaims finally:
'¡Dios está lejos!'

Similar criticisms can be found throughout Machado's poetry and
prose and they illustrate his belief that Spain was languishing in a state
of spiritual privation. The individual was in need of spiritual renewal,
Machado believed, yet a spiritual renewal that had to be very personal
('nuestra alma') and have nothing to do with the Church, which was
an institutional 'lazo de hierro . . . que nos asfixia'. He was certain that
a personal spirituality that was capable of exploring the true message
of the Gospel and Jesus' teachings on selflessness and fraternal love
could overcome the Church's long history of injustice: 'Esta Iglesia
espiritualmente huera, pero de organización formidable, sólo puede
ceder al embate de un impulso realmente religioso' (2001b: p. 342).
From his first *PrCs* published in 1909, Machado tackled Spain's spiritual crisis and defined this personal spirituality through mysticism,
which allowed the individual a direct and true feeling of God (the
great age of Spanish mysticism beginning during the first years of the
sixteenth century and extending well into the seventeenth century).
In poem VI (xx in *CC*) published in *La Lectura* in May 1909 he calls
upon the spirits of Saint Teresa and Saint John of the Cross to guide
the country to spiritual renewal:

> ¡Teresa, alma de fuego,
> Juan de la Cruz, espíritu de llama,
> por aquí hay mucho frío, padres, nuestros
> corazoncitos de Jesús se apagan!

As the founders of Spanish mysticism, Saint Teresa and Saint John of the Cross are asked to intervene and help fill the nation's spiritual void (the plural 'nuestros'). The fragile Jesus Hearts – a religious name for geraniums[6] – that are withering away from the spiritual cold ('apagar'), establish a counterpoint to the flames of mystic rapture in the first verses. The symbolic Jesus Hearts, representative of the country's spirit, are dying from spiritual neglect.[7]

Machado held Saint Teresa and Saint John of the Cross in high esteem. To the philosopher Ortega y Gasset he admitted that 'yo preferiría para nuestra patria un ideal dinámico, un misticismo guerrero como el de Teresa de Jesús' (2001b: p. 332). Mysticism could open up a path to spiritual renewal, Machado believed, because it represented a living expression of Jesus' teachings in the Gospel: 'nuestra mística fue un comienzo de reforma religiosa según el espíritu, y una fecunda y vitalísima corriente espiritual opuesta al letrismo inerte de los profesionales y del vulgo' (2001b: p. 353).[8] He even rebukes his alter-ego Martín who equates mysticism with an anachronistic Church: 'Abel Martín tiene muy escasa simpatía por el sentido erótico de nuestros místicos, a quienes llama frailecillos y monjucas tan inquietos como ignorantes. Comete en esto grave injusticia . . . Abel Martín no cree que el espíritu avance un ápice en el camino de su perfección' (1953: p. 16). Machado's interest in mysticism might explain the vivid light–dark imagery in the *PrCs*. Mystics like Saint John of the Cross used light and dark imagery in their poetry to symbolically convey how the soul travelled from the earthly plane of spiritual darkness for the transcendental plane of God's light. This divine ascension was divided into three stages known as the *scala perfectionis*, or 'ladder of perfection', and encompassed the Purgative, Illuminative and Unitive paths. This type of dark–light imagery is well established in the Bible, and there are numerous references to God as light (Genesis 1:4: 'God saw that the light was good; and God separated the light from the darkness'; John 1:5: 'God is Light, and in Him there is no darkness at all'; and Micah 7:8: 'Though I dwell in darkness, the Lord is a light for me'). Yet in poem li (*CC*), Machado suggests that the divine light can lead one astray if it does not originate from within; that is, if it does not arise from a deep spiritual passion within the self:

> Luz del alma, luz divina,
> faro, antorcha, estrella, sol. . .
> un hombre a tientas camina;
> lleva a la espalda un farol.

In the second verse, Machado exteriorizes the soul's divine light in two man-made objects ('faro', 'antorcha'), and two celestial objects ('estrella', 'sol'). Whether from heaven or earth, this divine light originating from outside the self does not illuminate the traveller's symbolic inner path. Unlike mystic symbolism, the progression from darkness to light does not bring about the traveller's divine experience and that ultimate 'rest in God' that Saint Thomas Aquinas proposed in his *Summa Theologica*. On the contrary, the soul's dark night is pervasive and unyielding and the traveller has to grope his way as best he can in spiritual darkness as the external 'luz divina' illuminates the path behind him. It becomes apparent that the spiritually blind traveller is cast into a dark world turned upside down: what should be interiorized is exteriorized, what should be illuminated is enveloped in darkness, and what should be in front of him lies behind him. In poem xii (*CC*), the light that does not originate from within blinds one to genuine spiritual feeling:

> ¡Ojos que a la luz se abrieron
> un día para, después,
> ciegos tornar a la tierra,
> hartos de mirar sin ver!

The verbs 'mirar' and 'ver' represent two different kinds of seeing. The eyes that gaze to the heavens for divine light can look ('mirar') but not see ('ver') the true revelations that come from inner spiritual feeling. As Jordi Doménech points out, this poem could well have been inspired by Unamuno's *Niebla*. In a letter to Unamuno in March 1915, Machado praises *Niebla* but he admits that he did not quite understand one point about the novel: 'Lo que no veo claro es si nos aconseja V. la niebla o la luz, aunque comprendo que todo es niebla, es decir que no vemos con nuestra luz y que, acaso – aquí del riesgo socrático – veamos al cegar' (2001b: p. 392). Yet it seems that what is most significant, particularly for Machado's chiaroscuro imagery and the spiritual traveller, is the seeing that illuminates the inner journey, or that symbolic '*Navigare*' that comes about with 'nuestra luz':

> O rinnovarsi o perire. . .
> No me suena bien.
> Navigare è necessario. . .
> Mejor: ¡vivir para ver![9]

From this inner spiritual light Machado approaches the God question more directly. God makes Himself known in the *PrCs* predominantly in the oneiric realm, yet when He appears He maintains His
distance from the speaker. Machado sharpens his criticism of this
elusive God, and he reiterates the central idea of 'Los olivos II' that
'¡Dios está lejos!' In many ways, the God that appears in the oneiric
realm in the *PrCs* brings to mind the God of Psalm 44. After God
ensured the Jews' triumph over their enemies and had won them their
land, He ignored them, even though they had never wavered in their
love for Him and had been faithful to His covenant. In verses 23–6,
God's absence is symbolically represented in His sleep:

> Awake, O Lord! Why do you sleep?
> Rouse yourself! Do not reject us forever.
> Why do you hide your face
> and forget our misery and oppression?
> We are brought down to the dust;
> our bodies cling to the ground.
>
> Rise up and help us;
> redeem us because of your unfailing love.[10]

Before the *PrCs*, God had appeared in a poem Machado published
in *La Tribuna* in February 1912 that he later included in *SGOP* as poem
LIX: 'Anoche cuando dormía / soñé, ¡bendita ilusión! / que era Dios
lo que tenía / dentro de mi corazón'. Exuberant and hopeful, these
verses suggest that he could discover God on some level in dreams. In
Armand F. Baker's opinion, poem LIX demonstrates that 'the experience of dreaming represents an illusion because the divine reality
cannot be verified rationally, but our non-rational mind can penetrate
the veil of logical concepts in order to reach God' (p. 44). Although
Baker's explanation is germane to poems in Machado's larger work
(especially in his earlier poetry where the non-rational mind is often
capable of penetrating divine mysteries in dreams, particularly those
associated with childhood), God does not offer or announce any
divine revelation in the *PrCs*. On the contrary, He is aloof, indifferent
and silent, as in poem xxi (*CC*):

> Ayer soñé que veía
> a Dios y que a Dios hablaba;
> y soñé que Dios me oía . . .
> Después soñé que soñaba.

The dream's intimate space, almost mystic in its vagueness, brings God and the speaker face to face. The speaker sees and speaks to God, but He does not respond. Ironically, the various preterite and imperfect tenses (all relegated to an indeterminate 'ayer'), and the repetition of 'soñar' (four times), distance Him from the speaker, as if He were little more than an illusion created by the dream itself. The final verse is revealing in this respect, for it can be interpreted in two distinct ways: the verb 'soñaba' that ends the poem can refer to the first or third person singular in the imperfect tense. If Machado intended the verb to be read in the first person singular, the speaker's encounter with God can be interpreted as a dream inspired by a dream (a hopeful, yet unfulfilled wish on the speaker's part to commune with God). If, however, he intended the verb to be read in the third person singular, then God Himself is transformed into a dreamer in the speaker's dream (the speaker dreams of a dreaming God, and His remoteness is much greater). Given that all verbs prior to 'soñaba' except one refer to the first person subject, the first interpretation is more accurate in all probability. Yet interestingly, in poem xlvi (*CC*), God appears in the speaker's dream precisely as a dreamer. Once again, the speaker revisits a past time:

> Anoche soñé que oía
> a Dios, gritándome: ¡Alerta!
> Luego era Dios quien dormía,
> y yo gritaba: ¡Despierta!

God appears in the dream and advises the speaker to be vigilant with the exclamatory '¡Alerta!' (perhaps a word used polysemically to denote wakefulness and spiritual vigilance), but this divine commandment is ironically negated when He falls asleep and requires the speaker to awaken Him. God's '¡Alerta!' is thus vitiated by the speaker's '¡Despierta!', and both words stand in symbolic opposition (the 'luego era' in the third verse establishes a strong division between the first verses that explain God's commandment to man in the dream, and the last verses that explain man's commandment to God *after* waking up and realizing He is asleep). As before, the layers of time ('anoche', 'luego era') and dream reveal God as being not only far from the speaker, but also that He is contradictory. In these poems, Pérez Gago has noted '[que] se inician en un tono religioso, [pero] finalizan con un tinte descreído picando en irreverente. La fe y la razón parecen tener tramados dos combates' (p. 195). And the 'razón'

Gago refers to here is the speaker's doubt in God that comes through in the final verses of each poem.

In poem xxxiii (*CC*), Machado criticized the dreaming God more directly. God is no longer a passive presence that appears in the speaker's dream, but instead He appears as a forge, blacksmith and sword polisher to make the swords for a 'Libertad' and 'Imperio':

> Soñé a Dios como una fragua
> de fuego, que ablanda el hierro,
> como un forjador de espadas,
> como un bruñidor de accros,
> que iba firmando en las hojas
> de luz: Libertad. – Imperio.

While in the previous poems God was a passive presence in the speaker's dreams, He assumes a physicality in three distinct forms that are related to the various stages of sword making: first as a forge (a passive object: 'como una fragua'), then as a blacksmith and a sword polisher (the active 'forjador' and 'bruñidor'). What He signs on the sword blades – the Word of God – is not His promise of compassion or brotherhood among men, but an ambiguous 'Libertad' and 'Imperio'. In light of poems like 'A orillas del Duero' and 'El Dios Íbero', the 'Libertad' and 'Imperio' Machado refers to here conjure up the death and ruin wreaked in His name. In 'A orillas del Duero', Castile's bloody history is described as being dominated by 'la fiebre de la espada'. Machado tells us that 'Sobre sus campos aún el fantasma yerra / de un pueblo que ponía a Dios sobre la Guerra' (and he proceeds to trace the historical trajectory of Spain's socio-economic and moral decline). In 'El Dios Íbero', the man who insults God also uses Him to wage war: '¿No es él quien puso a Dios sobre la guerra . . .?'

Machado could have wanted to use the sword image metaphorically to refer to the liberty and empire God granted his people. In chapters 25 and 26 of the Book of Leviticus, God gives the Jews various commandments after liberating them from bondage, and He warns them not to disobery Him: 'I am the Lord your God, which brought you forth out of the land of Egypt [. . . and] if ye will not hearken unto me, and will not do all these commandments . . . I will bring a sword upon you'.[11] God's sword is capable of both liberty (freedom from bondage and acceptance by God) and empire (His covenant). In the Book of Hebrews 4:12–13, we find more caveats against disobeying God because His word '[is] sharper than any double-edged sword . . .

and judges the thoughts and attitudes of the heart'.[12] Clearly, this is not the God of eternal love or brotherhood, but of Old Testament obedience.[13]

The various oppositions in the *PrCs* (light/dark, sleep/awake, close/far, past/present) are symbolic in terms of God's presence in dreams. While they seem to confine Him to a dream-within-a-dream cycle like in an infinite *mise en abîme* (the dreamer dreams of God, who is in turn dreaming, etc.), they also recreate, from poem to poem, the mythical and poetic space of man's confrontation with God that begins with Jacob's ancient quarrel with Him. This space is articulated in poems xxi and xlvi as a relatively recent past in the temporal markers 'ayer' and 'anoche', while in poem xxxiii the preterite 'soñé' operates much in the same way by conceiving the proximity between God and man through a past–present dualism. When it comes to time, then, God is not found in the 'wakened' reality of the present, but He can only be conceived in the present as an absence (He is relegated to a type of oneiric or past time). God's slumber creates a paradoxical tension in the *PrCs* between His presence in dreams and His absence from reality, and this tension underscores much of Machado's problematical relationship with God in the *PrCs* (He is confined to a past time that is both near and impossibly distant). As in poem xxviii (*CC*), the speaker is forced in dreams to battle God ('tiene . . . que') but awake he battles alone with life's mysteries (the symbolic sea):

> Todo hombre tiene dos
> batallas que pelear:
> en sueños lucha con Dios;
> y despierto, con el mar.

For many readers, God's presence in dreams shows that He listens to man's personal confessions and his most intimate fears and hopes. But in reality, does God listen? In poem xxi (*CC*), the speaker tells us with doubt in his words that 'soñé que Dios me oía', and in poem xlvi (*CC*) he is faced with the sleeping God: 'y yo gritaba: ¡Despierta!' And in poem xxviii above, the speaker confronts the world alone because God is never present other than in dreams. Although God appears to the speaker in dreams, He does not offer any guidance or any type of revelation on life's mysteries.

The duality between dream and reality is a complex and recurring theme in Machado's poetry. In *SGOP*, dreams do open the speaker to promising visions (for instance, poem LIX mentioned earlier 'Anoche cuando dormía. . . ', or poem LXIV that begins 'Desde el umbral de un sueño me llamaron. . . / Era la Buena voz, la voz querida'), but they also reveal more macabre revelations of the wakened world that lies beyond them. In 'Los sueños malos', Spain's rural life is depicted in nightmarish scenes of bones and skulls: 'En toda la tarde brilla / una luz de pesadilla'. In *CC*, Machado dreams in poem CXXII of an encounter with Leonor that kindles hope that he will see her again someday, but this hope stands in stark opposition to the reality presented in the last verse ('¡quién sabe / lo que se traga la tierra!').

Cerezo Galán has identified a progressive 'intención de realidad' in many of Machado's dream sequences. This move towards objective reality from the oneiric realm '[transciende] el propio sueño mismo, adelgaza sus cristales y depura su azogue, de modo que la reflexión en el alma no deforme o violente la realidad, sino que más bien revele su íntima textura' (p. 119). As Machado became more socially aware, dreams became more fragile and they were continually permeated by real-world disruptions, objects and experiences (for example, the intrusion of Soria's harsh countryside in many poems). To dream awake ('el soñar despierto'), as discussed in the last chapter, was an important revelation for Machado that bridged dream and reality as a way to recognize the 'real' Other as an essential part of his poetic metaphysics (as he tells us, 'para arrojar luz sobre el alma de los otros revelando la nuestra'). By 1925, he had misgivings about the illusory nature of dreams:

> No soy ya el soñador, el frenético mimo de mi propio sueño. Tampoco el mundo se viste de máscara para que yo lo contemple. Las cosas están allí donde las veo, los ojos allí donde ven. Lo absoluto será hoy para mí tan inabarcable como ayer. Pero mi relación con lo real también. ¿No equivaldría esto a un despertar? . . . Pero este hombre nuevo, si acaso existe y anda por el mundo, pretende haber despertado. Su mundo se ilumina, quiere poblarse, no de fantasmas, sino de figuras reales. Este hombre no puede ya definirse por el sueño, sino por el despertar. (2001b: p. 525)

In *Cancionero apócrifo de Abel Martín*, Machado expresses a more secular understanding of God that responds to this shift toward the objective world of 'wakened' reality. For Martín, the traditional Christian doctrine that God was the heavenly creator and Lord was absurd, and through Leibniz's monadology, God is conceived as the creator of the 'cero divino', a divine nothingness (also described as 'la nada' and 'el cero integral'):

Dios, como creador y conservador del mundo, le parece a Abel Martín una concepción judaica, tan sacrílega como absurda. La nada, en cambio, es en cierto modo, una creación divina, un milagro del ser, obrado por éste para pensarse en su totalidad. Dicho de otro modo: Dios regala al hombre el gran cero, la nada o cero integral, es decir, el cero integrado por todas las negaciones de cuanto es. Así posee la mente humana un concepto de totalidad, la suma de cuanto no es, que sirva lógicamente de límite y frontera a la totalidad de cuanto es. (1953: p. 33)

God's gift to man ('[Dios] regala al hombre') was the idea of nothingness; in a sense, it was an idea of everything that man was *not*, and it was from this negativity (or absence) from which man could build himself up through his own reason, concepts and ideas. Although critics have written extensively on how Martín's concept of 'nada' is indebted to Leibniz's monadology, I believe its fundamental idea is rather straightforward: God's divine nothingness – which should not be confused with His inexistence – represents the origins of man's existential awareness in the concrete here and now.[14] As Martín remarks in one of his poems, God's nothingness marks the precise moment when '*Fiat umbra!* Brotó el pensar humano' (it is interesting to note how the '*Fiat umbra!*' moment reappears throughout Machado's work beginning with poems xvi (*CC*) and xxxv (*NC*) of the *PrCs*: 'El hombre es por natura bestia paradójica, / un animal absurdo que necesita lógica. / Creó de la nada un mundo y, su obra terminada, / "Ya estoy en el secreto – se dijo –, todo es nada"'; 'Ya maduró un nuevo cero, / que tendrá su corazón: / un ente de acción tan huero / como un ente de razón'. Martín desarrolló su idea de 'nada' en el poema 'Al gran Cero' that conceived God's nothingness as a type of second Genesis: 'Cuando el *Ser que se es* hizo la nada / y reposó, que bien lo merecía, / ya tuvo el día noche, y compañía / tuvo el hombre en la ausencia de la amada. / *Fiat umbra!* Brotó el pensar humano'). God's gift to man, then, can be thought of as a type of thinking about Being. That is, God's gift is a type of reflective consciousness about how He offers no guidance or solace in the present, and how man must live by his own standards of right and wrong and good and evil. In the poem 'Iris de la Noche' in *NC*, Machado makes this point sufficiently clear when he turns to God and asks:

> Y tú, Señor, por quien todos
> vemos y que ves las almas,
> dinos si todos, un día,
> hemos de verte la cara.

It very well could be, following Martín's logic, that the human intellect is incapable of knowing God (thus continuing the long tradition of Christian belief in the suprarational nature of God), but this does little to address why He is so elusive and distant in the present – the feeling of God – as Machado seems to suggest. In many respects, His elusiveness is His nothingness and it leads man to look within and search for God not in the heavens, but in the world. As Machado put it: 'nada hay divino que no sea humano' (2001b: p. 232).

Jesus as Symbol

The presence–absence dualism in the *PrCs* is presented in a paradoxical tension between dreams (His presence) and reality (His absence), and it illuminates Machado's scepticism in God. This was a scepticism that came about after a long and intense period of internal struggle with His nature, and as González Ruiz put it, Machado's theism can be interpreted as 'una actitud escéptica honda y honradamente inquisitiva . . . la actitud humana de la consciencia para situarse en esa zona primordial de la fe es concretamente el *escepticismo*' (p. 28). For Machado, scepticism was not a philosophical system conceived to prove God's inexistence (although it expressed a philosophical character in Mairena's thinking), but rather it was a way to maintain Him present in man's consciousness as both an absence and a presence. Under the subtitle '(Sobre el escepticismo)', Mairena alludes to this scepticism stating 'Dios existe o no existe. Cabe afirmarlo o negarlo, pero *no dudarlo.* / – Eso es lo que usted cree'. And again, 'Un Dios existente – decía mi maestro – sería algo terrible. ¡Que Dios nos libre de él!' (1971a: pp. 45–6). Martín was also sceptical about God:

> Amar a Dios sobre toda las cosas – decía mi maestro Abel Martín – es algo más difícil de lo que parece. Porque ello parece exigirnos: primero, que creamos en Dios; segundo, que creamos en todas las cosas; tercero, que amemos todas las cosas; cuarto, que amemos a Dios sobre todas ellas. En suma: la santidad perfecta, inasequible a los mismos santos. (1971a: p. 49)

Two of Machado's most famous poems on God, 'Desde mi rincón' and 'Profesión de fe', can be examined with this scepticism in mind. These poems speak of God in terms of doubt, and how scepticism required a constant building of God (the verbs 'hacer' and 'crear'):

creo en la libertad y en la esperanza,
y en una fe que nace
cuando se busca a Dios y no se le alcanza,
y en el Dios que se lleva y que se hace.

– – – – – – – – – –

Yo he de hacerte, mi Dios, cual tú me hiciste,
y para darte el alma que me diste
en mí te he de crear.

What this scepticism made clear was that to experience the feeling of God required a larger social awareness of how the self and the Other regarded Him. This independent yet communal understanding of God (the 'comunión de ideas' that Martín and Mairena often refer to), brought to light not only the question of faith as scepticism, but also the ethical dimension of the self–Other relation and its importance in the concrete here and now. God becomes, at least initially, the 'objeto' (the reification) of this communal sentiment: 'El hombre crea en su prójimo, el yo en el tú, y el ojo que ve en el ojo que le mira . . . Y entonces estará Dios en puerta. Dios aparece como objeto de comunión cordial que hace posible la fraterna comunidad humana' (1971a: p. 184). Within this line of thought, Machado believed Jesus was the most compelling and recognizable symbol of spiritual union between the self and Other. Quite simply, Jesus was the embodiment of self-sacrifice and fraternal love, and these qualities granted Him, as a man ('hombre') and as a model of a divine 'communism', a special place in Machado's theism. Jesus was also the embodiment of God's love, and one of his most transcendental tasks as a man was that he revealed a path to the Other: '¿[A] qué vino Cristo al mundo? Él nos reveló valores universales . . . los nuevos caminos de corazón a corazón por donde se marcha tan seguro como de un entendimiento a otro . . . con el inmenso amor que sientes por ti mismo – creo leer en Jesús – ama a tu hermano, que es igual a ti, pero que no eres tú' (2001b: p. 427).[15] In poems xlii and xliii (*NC*), this simple yet profound lesson on love and otherness appears as follows:

Enseña el Cristo: a tu prójimo
amarás como a ti mismo,
mas nunca olvides que es otro.

Dijo otra verdad:
busca el tú que nunca es tuyo
ni puede serlo jamás.

Through Jesus' example, the feeling of God can be known in some way in the self–Other relation. Jesus can awaken that inner spiritual sentiment capable of guiding the self to the divine in the Other, and here we can think of Machado's heterogeneity of Being ('creer en *lo otro* y en *el otro*') as the recognition of otherness. In Jaume Pont's words, 'en la figura de Cristo encuentra Machado el ejemplar ofertorio amoroso de la otredad absoluta. Dios y fraternidad humana coinciden en su fundamental enseñanza' (p. 201). It is Jesus as the son of God – and not as the Church's agonic symbol – who is worthy of Machado's *cantar* in 'La Saeta':

> ¡Cantar de la tierra mía,
> que echa flores
> al Jesús de la agonía,
> y es la fe de mis mayores!
> ¡Oh, no eres tú mi cantar!
> ¡No quiero cantar, ni quiero
> a ese Jesús del madero,
> sino al que anduvo en el mar!

Machado drew a sharp distinction between Jesus pre- and post-crucifixion to show how He had been transformed in His sacrifice. Although the cross established Jesus' victory over death and sin, His substitutionary punishment represented an enduring symbol of not only man's redemption, but also of the broader historic and religious idea of his divineness that has been passed down through the ages.[16] According to Martín, Jesus died on the cross not to imbue a sense of divine agony in his love for others (what in the poem above is presented as 'Jesús de la agonía' / 'Jesús del madero'), but rather to cast it out forever: '[Cristo es] el hijo del hombre que se hizo Dios para expiar en la cruz los pecados de la Divinidad' (1986: p. 122). Words like 'humano' and 'hombre' resurface in Machado's writings on Jesus, not only to distance Him from Church symbolism like in 'La saeta', but also as a reminder of the man who led a relatively uneventful Jewish life until God's spirit roused Him to sacrifice himself for the Other. This is the Jesus 'que anduvo en el mar', the man capable of miracles.

In poem I published in *La Lectura* in February 1909 (ii in *CC*), Machado revisits Jesus' teaching to Peter in the Book of Matthew. In chapter 14:22–34, we read of Jesus walking on water to rescue his disciples:

> Immediately he made the disciples get into the boat and go on ahead to the other side . . . When evening came, he was there alone, but by

this time the boat, battered by the waves, was far from the land, for the wind was against them. And early in the morning [Jesus] came walking toward them on the sea. But when the disciples saw him walking on the sea, they were terrified, saying, "It is a ghost!" [. . . Jesus] said, "Come". So Peter got out of the boat, started walking on water, and came toward Jesus. But when he noticed the strong wind, he became frightened, and beginning to sink, he cried out, "Lord, save me!" Jesus immediately reached out his hand and caught him, saying to him, "You of little faith, why did you doubt me?"[17]

Although Jesus' miracle of walking on water is often interpreted as the symbolic moment He saves the Church, the sea of doubt can be interpreted as both Peter's lack of faith in Jesus (he sinks back into the unbelieving life), as well as his lack of faith in himself (and revealingly, it was Peter who denied Jesus after his death).[18] Like Peter, one's path to belief must begin not only with faith in oneself, but also faith in the Other (and this miracle of walking on water solidifies the disciples' faith in Jesus as the son of God):

> ¿Para qué llamar caminos
> a los surcos del azar? . . .
> Todo el que camina anda,
> como Jesús, sobre el mar.

For Machado, Jesus was also a symbol through which we could reflect upon the concept of wakefulness described earlier: the idea that the sleeping God made it necessary for us to look into the world for the divine. Mairena refers to it as 'una filosofía cristiana del porvenir', a Christian philosophy founded upon the Gospel and Jesus' commandment that 'you shall love your neighbour as yourself'.[19] As Machado points out, this commandment had nothing to do with Catholic doctrines that buried God in Aristotelianism (the proof of a cosmic unmoved first mover), and he references the Gospel of Mark in poem xxxiv (*CC*) to make this point:

> Yo amo a Jesús, que nos dijo:
> Cielo y tierra pasarán.
> Cuando cielo y tierra pasen
> mi palabra quedará.
> ¿Cuál fue, Jesús, tu palabra?
> ¿Amor? ¿Perdón? ¿Caridad?
> Todas tus palabras fueron
> una palabra: Velad

In chapter 13:12–37, Jesus rests on the Mount of Olives and foretells the destruction of Jerusalem. He reveals the signs of its destruction to Peter, James, John and Andrew:

> For nation will rise against nation, and kingdom against kingdom . . . Brother will betray brother to death . . . Heaven and earth will pass away, but my words will not pass away . . . keep awake – for you do not know when the master of the house will come, in the evening, or at midnight, or at cockcrow, or at dawn, or else he may find you asleep when he comes suddenly. And what I say to you I say to all: Keep awake.[20]

In this passage, Machado distinguishes between moral sleep and wakefulness, being that Jesus' admonition to his disciples on the Mount is to stay vigilant of the impending disaster, to 'keep awake' ('velad'), for they do not know when He, the son of God (commonly agreed among theologians to be Jesus' humble self-reference), will return. Jesus' warning 'keep awake', particularly in the fratricidal context of war and Jerusalem's foretold destruction, alludes to the righteous life of the believer who follows His example. According to Warren Carter:

> [T]o keep awake is an active, alert stance of getting on with the tasks at hand. It means being a community . . . of faithful followers who live God's will until God's purposes are completed in Jesus' coming . . . the time of the coming is unknown (sudden; delayed), but the disciples must be ready for it by always living faithfully and obediently to Jesus' teaching. (pp. 481–7)

In the word 'velad', then, we find the spirit of community and of living according to Jesus' teaching. Through an inner vigilance and reflection, one can avoid falling into a moral disregard for the Other and fulfil Jesus' commandment on fraternal love until He returns. Mairena echoes this lesson, referring to God once again as the felt 'objeto' of a collective bond:

> Si eliminamos de los Evangelios cuanto en ellos se contiene de escoria mosaica, aparece clara la enseñanza del Cristo: "Sólo hay un Padre, padre de todos, que está en los cielos". He aquí el objeto erótico transcendente, la idea cordial que funda, para siempre, la fraternidad humana. ¿Deberes filiales? Uno y no más: el amor de radio infinito hacia el padre de todos, cuya impronta, más o menos borrosa, llevamos todos en el alma. (1971a: p. 106)

What has been said so far brings us full circle to the initial question of Machado's concept of 'un impulso realmente religioso', that deep spiritual sentiment required to regenerate the self, the Other, and ultimately the nation. His directed path to explain this 'impulso realmente religioso' has been paradoxical and complex, and it has intersected with organized religion, mysticism, a God of nothingness and the Gospel, and yet it has somehow managed to consolidate all these lines of thinking in the figure of Jesus as the quintessential symbol of otherness. In exploring the feeling of God in the Other, Machado believed that man had to create Him in his day-to-day relation with the Other; or put another way, the feeling of God is made possible in the individual's recognition of and love for the Other. And there is little doubt that he sought to relegate God the Creator – a God not inexistent, but not present as a guiding force – to the oneiric realm where He remained confined in an infinite *mise en abîme* of impossibility.

What makes the *PrCs* so revealing within this discussion is that they disclose, perhaps like no other area of Machado's poetry, the oppositional tensions of his spiritual metaphysics: the appearance of God in the self–Other relation is mediated from the oneiric realm of His impossibility. Or, put more simply, from God's absence comes God's presence. Machado's fondness for opposites and contradictions in the *PrCs* sheds light on the overarching dialectical unity gestured at in his fragment thinking. '[T]he fragment, which carries the contradiction of the infinite and the finite in itself . . . does not avoid stepping into new contradictions with other fragments, which in fact share the tendency toward the infinite, but on the basis of their individuality provoke new reciprocal contradictions' (Frank, p. 213). It is through the oppositions and contradictions in life, as the Romantics well knew, that the complexity of the Absolute can be glimpsed at and comprehended on some level. It was clear for Romantics like Schlegel that 'if one has a sense for the infinite . . . he expresses himself decisively through contradictions' (Frank, p. 214). God's nothingness for Machado clears a path to His divineness in the Other. But we must be clear on this point: the intersubjective experience of God is never completed, but it too is endless and infinite. For God to be present in the self–Other relation, He must remain in the realm of dreams and impossibility as an unrequited desire, and it is this unrequited desire that urges the self to seek Him in the Other. Martín poetized it as follows:

> Al Dios de la distancia y de la ausencia,
> del áncora en la mar, la plena mar. . .
> Él nos libra del mundo – omnipresencia –
> nos abre senda para caminar.
>
> Con la copa de sombra bien colmada,
> con este nunca lleno corazón,
> honremos al Señor que hizo la Nada
> y ha esculpido en la fe nuestra razón.

It must be said, however, that Machado never lost hope of one day communing with the infinite God of Creation. In poem CXLIX of the 'Elogios' he states: 'El alma vence [. . .] / al ángel de la muerte y al agua del olvido'. José Machado understood this hope as an important part of Machado's struggle with his scepticism:

> [S]e entrega Antonio con su ansia de alcanzar algo de la verdad inaccesible. Pero aunque seguro de no lograrlo, no por eso lo dejará de intentar. Y así, en este constante ir y venir suyo, conseguirá el más alto don que Dios parece concederle: el don de no borrar de su corazón la palabra: esperanza de esencia divina. (p. 98)

In the self–Other relation Machado had defined a way to conceive a national model for his idea of Christianity. In 1918, he returned to the Cain and Abel tragedy noting that *cainismo* was ruining the country. 'Sólo los rusos – ¡bendito pueblo!', he declares, 'me parecen capaces de superar [el cainismo] por un sentimiento más noble y más universal' (2001b: p. 427). In Machado's eyes, Russia had effectively united men in a collective ideal through a universal 'impulso realmente religioso', and this ideal was based on a social movement capable of instituting (and institutionalizing) a true spiritual sentiment within the collective: '[L]a santa Rusia, cuyas raíces espirituales son esencialmente evangélicas . . . proclama el Cristo la hermandad de los hombres, emancipada de los vínculos de la sangre y de los bienes de la tierra; el triunfo de las virtudes fraternas sobre las patriarcales' (1971a: p. 60). Russia remained a beacon of hope for Machado because its 'gran Revolución' had demonstrated the individual's potential for a liberating altruism. Once and for all, Russia had released Christianity from what Nietzsche called the Church's 'parasitism', and while Machado concedes that the revolution had its shortcomings, he understood it as a crucial historical moment in which humanity finally 'awoke' to the concept of Other.[21]

Over the years, Machado realized that it was perhaps best to speak of this 'communism' in philosophical rather than religious terms, '[porque] una fe religiosa parece cosa difícil en nuestro tiempo [1934]'. Nevertheless, these ideas retained much of the spiritual vigour they had presented in his early poetry and prose, since they required of the individual, first and foremost, a deep recognition of the Other. In 'Sobre una lírica comunista que pudiera venir de Rusia', he outlines three foundational premises that sum up how he conceived the self–Other relation: '1.ª) que existe un prójimo, una pluralidad de espíritus . . . 2.ª) que estos espíritus no son mónadas cerradas . . . 3.ª) que existe una realidad espiritual, trascendente a las almas individuales, en la cual éstas puedan comulgar' (2001b: p. 750). In the end, Spain was in desperate need of spiritual renewal – one similar to Russia's – if it ever wanted to overcome *cainismo* and liberate God from fear, guilt and melancholia. In a letter to Unamuno in 1918, Machado discussed Spain's spiritual crisis at length and he concluded with this appeal to Christ: '¡Guerra a Caín y viva el Cristo!' As we shall see in the following chapter, the greatest obstacle to Machado's spiritual project was ignorance.

Chapter 5

The Double Bind of Knowledge and Ignorance

Knowledge of ignorance is not ignorance. It is knowledge of the elusive character of truth, of the whole. The whole eludes us, but we know the parts.

Leo Strauss, *What is Political Philosophy?*

For Machado, many of Spain's socio-economic problems were a result of its vast 'problema de cultura'. This was not a term he coined, but he had inherited it from the previous generation of *regeneracionistas* like Joaquín Costa and Lucas Mallada who had witnessed how Spain's poor education, schooling and pedagogy had kept the country divided and in turmoil. 'Lo que llamamos cultura', Machado lamented to Ortega y Gasset in 1912, 'es algo que ni va ni viene ni está más que en el cerebro de unos cuantos solitarios' (2001b: p. 306). In the poem 'El mañana efímero', Machado proposed that Spain's future depended on a unified 'España de la rabia y de la idea', and any unity of this magnitude could not skirt what rested at the heart of the country's spiritual and cultural crisis, namely ignorance. And ignorance, in turn, was symptomatic of epistemological constraints imposed by the Church and State that had become deeply ingrained within Spanish society. Only by coming to know these constraints – and thus bringing an end to the ignorance upon which they depended – could the individual bring about any real social change:

De los dos elementos que nos empujan ... que nos mueven o arrastran a un porvenir más o menos catastrófico, están ausentes las huellas de la ciudadanía. Ambos son campesinos. Estos elementos son la política y la Iglesia, o por decirlo claramente, los caciques y los curas ... y no se trata de combatirlos, sino de conocerlos. (2001b: p. 322)

While several areas of Machado's work explore this difficult relationship between ignorance and knowledge, the *PrCs* provide us with one of the most dynamic spaces in which to consider how it affected his concept of Other. The *PrCs*, examined within the ignorance/ knowledge binarism Machado often employs in tackling Spain's 'problema de cultura', bring to light how he was attempting to explain an infinite knowledge void (poem xxv of *CC*: 'Cantad conmigo a coro: Saber, nada sabemos / [. . .] La luz nada ilumina y el sabio nada enseña'), while at the same time trying to transcend this void (poem lxxxv of *NC*: '¿Tu verdad? No, la Verdad, / y ven conmigo a buscarla. / La tuya, guárdetela'). Both ignorance and knowledge, and the antagonisms they provoke, lead Machado to a sceptical position on what we can and cannot truly know about the world, and they provide him with a critical framework with which to understand better Spain's 'porvenir más o menos catastrófico'. Through various means, he attempts to find some semblance of true knowledge about the world in the *yo* and *tú* relationship in which ignorance plays a pivotal role, as we shall see. It is the face-to-face relation of individuals with other individuals that discloses the complex social practices of 'los conceptos generales' and the ontological 'forma de universalidad' that unites self and Other in knowledge:

> En efecto – decía Mairena –, la cultura vista desde fuera, como si dijéramos, desde la ignorancia . . . puede aparecer como un tesoro cuya posesión y custodia sean el privilegio de unos pocos; y el ansia de cultura que siente el pueblo, como la amenaza a un sagrado depósito, la ingente ola de barbarie que lo anegue y destruya. Pero nosotros, que vemos la cultura desde dentro, quiero decir desde el hombre mismo . . . Para nosotros, difundir y defender la cultura son una misma cosa: aumentar el humano tesoro de conciencia vigilante. (1986: p. 22)

What is illuminating about this approach is how the reader is educated about ignorance in the *PrCs*, and how a knowledge of ignorance (as with Socratic ignorance, explained in this chapter) leads to an awareness of the limits of what we know. The underlying question that motivated Machado in exploring the ignorance/knowledge binarism in the *PrCs* was this: how can any form of collective action, with the ethical and spiritual foundations it demanded from the self–Other relation in 'lo elemental humano', be established if ignorance divided the self from the Other? The self–Other relation had to serve as the primary building block for a larger understanding of knowledge (its claims, uses, power, etc.), an understanding capable of clearing a path to self-examination and, more importantly, to what Mairena called 'un diálogo amoroso'. As we shall see, this lived (and shared) dialogical practice constituted a new type of knowledge, and it was critical to Machado's vision of how intersubjective engagement could effect real social change in Spain.

Ignorance and Spain's 'problema de cultura'

Spain was experiencing difficult and uneven socio-economic transitions in the second half of the nineteenth century with the emergence of the *burguesía*. Between 1875 and 1920, Spain's economy developed on the periphery in the developing industrial centres of Catalonia, Valencia and the Basque provinces, while the central, southern and north-western agricultural regions fell into cycles of recession.[1] Countries like Britain, France, Belgium and Germany solidified their industrial base during this period, yet Spain, save a few key regions, was struggling to maintain a foothold in what Lewis Mumford coined 'the paleotechnic phase' of industrial production, the age when heavy industry becomes an instrumental factor in a country's economy (p. 169). Even taking into account the positive developments brought about by the liberal revolution of 1868, as well as the brief market upsurges in the 1880s and 90s (in large part produced by protectionist tariffs, foreign investment and imported technical know-how), Spain clung to a pre-industrial economy for the most part, and it lagged behind the rest of Europe. The majority of Spaniards, the vast *pueblo*, remained in an ever-worsening state of poverty, while an emerging middle-class slowly began to thrive.[2]

Culturally speaking, Spain experiences dramatic changes during this period. In *La edad de plata (1902–1939)*, José Carlos Mainer has referred to the period between 1902 and 1939 as a cultural 'Silver Age' (what Azorín had previously called Spain's 'Segundo Siglo de Oro') that saw an intellectual middle class come into its own. Spaniards like José Echegaray, Ramón y Cajal and Jacinto Benavente were granted Nobel prizes in 1904, 1906 and 1922 respectively, while Ortega y Gasset founded a 'Spanish philosophy' and became Spain's first best-selling philosopher in Europe and the United States with *La rebelión de las masas* (1930). In 1907, Picasso painted his landmark *Les Demoiselles d'Avignon* (exhibited in Paris in 1916) launching the Cubist movement, and Catalan *modernisme*, with its centre in the bustling city of Barcelona, connected with Impressionism, Futurism, Dadaism and

Surrealism between 1900 and 1936 while at the same time fostering a highly innovative literary scene and revolutionizing the fields of architecture and sculpture at the hands of Antoni Gaudí and Josep Llimona. In Madrid, Ramón Gómez de la Serna had discovered the *greguería* in 1910, and through his gatherings in Café del Pombo he had attracted not only countless foreign intellectuals to Spain, but also inspired Cansinos-Assens, Pedro Garfias, Gerardo Diego and Jorge Luis Borges to develop the Spanish-born *Ultraísmo* movement between 1918 and 1924. The so-called Generation of 1927, with the triumvirate García Lorca, Salvador Dalí and Luis Buñuel at its head (we cannot forget the contribution of the 'mujeres del 27' like Ernestina de Champourcin, Rosa Chacel, Margarita Nelken, Concha Méndez and María Zambrano, among others), connected like no other Spanish generation with the cultural currents in Europe. Spanish theatre, science, pedagogy, and journalism were also developing at a very fast pace, and the number of novels, plays, treatises, poetry books, journals, magazines and manifestos published in Spain during these years was unprecedented.

This cultural renaissance and its *modernidad* have to be considered with care because although Spain's 'Silver Age' was indeed quite unprecedented (and although it owed a great deal to the emergent *burguesía*), it was predominantly localized – in terms of movements, groups and major literary and artistic outlets – in cities like Madrid, Seville, Bilbao and Barcelona. Although economic growth, as the economist and historian Gabriel Tortella relates, did become more pronounced in Spain between 1900 and 1929 in comparison to the final half of the nineteenth century, most of the country did not share in the cultural fruits or the industrial prosperity that stimulated it. In fact, vast areas of Spain's rural regions suffered extreme poverty like never before.[3] No period in modern Spanish history witnessed such widespread impoverishment of the country as during these years of uneven modernization. Between 1898 and 1939, the total number of Spaniards that emigrated abroad or to urban areas is estimated at 5.1 million (Gurría, p. 21). If we take into account that the population of Spain rose roughly from eighteen to twenty-four million during this period, the emigration levels were indeed considerable and, as one would expect, the overwhelming majority of emigrants derived from rural regions like Andalusia, Castile, León, La Rioja and Galicia (Gurría, p. 21). The country's emigration had reached such alarming levels in the early twentieth century that the Maura government passed *La Ley de Colonización y Repoblación Interior* in 1907 in hopes of repopulating peasants to especially hard-hit regions. Its Article 1 reads: 'Tiene por objeto esta ley arraigar en la Nación a las familias desprovistas de medios de trabajo o de capital para subvenir su sustento. Su fin es doble: oponer un dique a la emigración y repoblar el país' (Soldevilla, p. 208). The *Real Orden* issued that same year also sought to curb emigration losses by establishing the Consejo Superior de Emigración, an administrative body that regulated and imposed stricter policies on emigration. In the book titled *Españoles hacia América: La emigración en masa, 1880–1930* (1988), Nicolás Sánchez-Albornoz and other scholars show how significantly this emigration problem affected Spain's socio-economic development, particularly in rural regions.[4] While the causes of emigration were varied and included such factors as the impoverishment of agricultural lands, evading military service and family unity, there is little doubt that the continued pauperization of the country's rural regions was the primary motive behind Spain's emigration problem.

Like nothing else, Spain's emigration losses highlighted the enormous failure of the country's educational system, which Machado, as a rural teacher, knew all about. In a system monopolized by the Church and that had experienced little, if any change throughout the nineteenth century, 'the curriculum prescribed for the lower primary schools . . . aimed at producing docile, useful workers', while 'secondary education . . . was, like the universities, reserved for the social elites' (Boyd, pp. 5–11). The *Decreto de Orovio* of 1875 had handed over the leadership of Spain's universities to the Church, thus ending most of the progressive educational reforms instituted by the 1868 revolution. During this period the 'masa' emerges as a sociopolitical force, and pedagogy, conceived as a way to reinforce State policy, was very much on the minds of liberal and conservative politicians.[5] For the liberal reform movement, the most urgent matter of policy during Spain's *fin de siglo* was precisely 'el tema de la socialización de la cultura y la educación de las masas, como una de las urgencias del momento . . . El tema de la cultura popular está en la conciencia del país porque el peso de las masas en este momento es un hecho innegable' (Gómez Molleda, p. 61). Regardless of the well-intentioned efforts of the Ministerio de Instrucción Pública y Bellas Artes, La Junta para Ampliación de Estudios e Investigación Científicas, and the Residencia de Estudiantes and Residencia de Señoritas, all founded between 1901 and 1915, there would be no major school or university reform in Spain until the Second Republic (the 1919 *Ley Silió* did grant universities greater financial and pedagogical autonomy, but it was repealed in 1922). It is not surprising that sixty-three per cent of Spain's population was illiterate at the turn of the century (in Belgium, by comparison, considered the developed country with the poorest educational record at the time, illiteracy stood at only nine-teen per cent in 1900) (Carr, p. 475; Tortella, pp. 11–12). By 1931, illiteracy in Spain still stood at an alarming forty per cent (Junco, p. 50).

It goes without saying that Spain's ignorance, particularly during a period of so-called cultural renewal, affected Machado deeply. His well-known article 'Nuestro patriotismo y *La marcha de Cádiz*' pub-lished in 1908 shortly after his arrival in Soria (what was then a rural town), addresses Spain's ignorance frontally. The article makes clear his indignation at the sheer enormity of Spain's provincialism: 'Comenzamos a despertar y a mirar en torno nuestro . . . somos los hijos de una tierra pobre e ignorante, de una tierra donde todo está por hacer. He aquí lo que sabemos' (2001b: p. 224). Years later, from the rural austerity of Baeza, he relived this same sense of indignation in a letter to Unamuno when he stated: '[Es] una población rural encallada por la Iglesia y completamente huera. Por lo demás, el hombre del campo trabaja y sufre resignado o emigra en condiciones tan lamentables que equivalen al suicidio' (2001b: p. 340). Yet Machado was not a critic from afar, simply denouncing Spain's igno-rance without actively proposing measures to ameliorate it. Some of his more notable accomplishments in this area include joining Ortega y Gasset's Liga de Educación Política Española in 1913. It was during this period, and with the aid of the Liga's social network, when he most forcefully advocated the establishment of schools in Spain's most impoverished regions. In 1919, he also helped found La Universidad Popular de Segovia, a community-run learning centre that educated the poor working class on everything from 'Higiene del Hogar' to 'Derecho usual y legislación del trabajo' (2001b: pp. 472–3). Years later, in 1931, he fulfilled an important role in the Second Republic's Misiones Pedagógicas, one of Spain's boldest pedagogical enterprises that sought to bring culture (music, theatre, poetry, etc.) to Spain's remotest areas and combat illiteracy through primary education and mobile libraries. The Second Republic had 'placed [its] faith in books as the saviours of the nation' (Holguín, p. 145).

For Machado, Spain was a country stagnated in ignorance. While he believed the *pueblo*'s folklore was an endless spring of 'saber popular' (a type of knowledge, Mairena tells us, much preferred over the limiting 'saber erudito' and 'saber universitario'), he was well aware that the majority of Spaniards were imprisoned in grinding poverty by ignorance. How could any reform programme, Machado often asked, be it social, spiritual, economic or pedagogical, take hold in Spain when an overwhelming majority of its people was hopelessly illiterate and provided with little or no education? This was a question that was hotly debated at the time. In *En torno al casticismo*, Unamuno had already confronted the *pueblo*'s ignorance noting that 'el mal parece que se agrava y cunde; es cada día mayor la ignorancia, y la peor de todas la que se ignora a sí misma' (p. 47). He was so provoked by Spain's ignorance – 'una ignorancia abrumadora', he called it – that he campaigned for liberal educational reform by travelling throughout the country giving lectures and by proselytizing his Europeanized vision of 'una nueva España'.[6] For Ganivet it was also clear that 'la restauración de nuestras fuerzas exige un régimen prudente ... de subordinación absoluta de la actividad a la inteligencia, donde está la causa del mal y adonde hay que aplicar el remedio' (p. 138). Ortega y Gasset founded the Liga de Educación Política, whose members included not only Antonio and Manuel, but also Américo Castro and Ramiro de Maetzu, among others. The Liga adopted many of the pedagogical theories that Ortega y Gasset had outlined in *La pedagogía social como programa político* of 1910, a work inspired by the nineteenth-century German tradition of *Sozialpädagogik*, which believed social renewal depended on improved pedagogical techniques, cultural revitalization, youth work, social networking and adult education. Ortega y Gasset's Liga advocated political change through educational reform, and in *La pedagogía social* he had made it clear that 'todo individuo ha de ser trabajador de la cultura y todo trabajador ha de estar dotado de una conciencia cultural' (Serrano, p. 37). Later figures like Manuel Azaña, responsible for the progressive policies that would give form to the Misiones Pedagógicas between 1931 and 1936, saw how ignorance dominated politics. He often reiterated that 'nada es más urgente en España que el concurso de la inteligencia pura en las contiendas civiles' (p. 633).

The Problem of Empty-Headedness

More than simply a knowledge void, ignorance made concrete Spain's sociohistorical decline for Machado, from its superstitions and aristocratic pomposity (mostly through its rampant 'señoritismo'), to its false sense of grandeur. Like few of his peers, he experienced the full brunt of Spain's ignorance in Soria and Baeza, which left a durable mark on his poetry. As he confessed apologetically to Unamuno from Baeza, 'cuando se vive en estos páramos intelectuales, no se puede escribir nada suave, porque necesita uno de la indignación para no helarse también' (2001b: p. 340). The refrain in 'A Orillas del Duero' captures this sense of national decline: 'Castilla miserable, ayer domi- nadora / envuelta en sus andrajos desprecia cuanto ignora'. Echoing regenerationist educational policies and calls for modernization, Machado conceived Spain as a diseased body in desperate need of rejuvenation: 'Cuando afirmamos que España necesita cultura, deci- mos algo tan incontrovertible como vago, algo que equivale a proc- lamar la salud como una necesidad imprescindible para los enfermos . . . Pero todos sabemos que el enfermo es algo más que la enferme- dad' (2001b: p. 323). And then, alluding to the antiquated science of phrenology to drive home his point, he concluded: 'En suma, es preciso acudir al analfabeto, y no precisamente para medirle el crá- neo, sino para enterarse de lo que tiene dentro . . . ¡Cuántos! que pretenden arrancar secretos a las piedras de España han olvidado interrogar a los hombres' (2001b: p. 323).

It is worth examining this brief phrenological reference more closely. Following the methods of Franz Gall (the Austrian physician who pioneered the science of phrenology in the early 1800s), nineteenth-century phrenologists measured the circumference of the head to calculate approximately one's brain size, which was one of several measurements used to ascertain a person's intelligence and so-called 'mental powers' (memory, perception, etc.). In this offhand phrenological remark, Machado is most likely censuring the State's passive outlook when it came to Spain's 'problema de cultura': simply examining it from the 'exterior' – from afar – was ineffective (as ineffective as a phrenologist measuring the circumference of a per- son's head for signs of intelligence), since what was required was a detailed knowledge of the socio-economic conditions that generated it and, just as importantly, a detailed knowledge of ignorance itself. He goes on to explain: 'También sabemos que el cerebro de un ignorante no es, ni mucho menos, una página en blanco. Atrevámonos a afirmar que tampoco hay una ignorancia, sino muchas, y que es preciso descender al ignorante para conocerlas' (2001b: p. 323). In his 'Discurso' for Antonio Pérez de la Mata of 1910, Machado had previ- ously used the word 'cráneo' in relation to ignorance stating that intelligence cannot be ascertained by appearances alone since this would lead to error: 'Un hombre mal vestido, pobre y desdeñado, puede ser un sabio, un héroe, un santo; el birrete de un doctor puede cubrir el cráneo de un imbécil' (2001b: p. 244). In the *PrCs*, however, the 'cráneo' is symbolically represented in the hollowed 'calavera', which conjures up the grimmer side of Spain's ignorance in a type of deathly empty-headedness. In the poetic cycle 'Del pasado efímero', 'El mañana efímero', 'A Orillas del Duero', 'Una España joven', and 'Desde mi rincón', Machado had depicted to what degree Spain had become stagnated by ignorance, and indeed, the theme of hollowness – from the country's desolate landscapes to the sterile 'mañana vacío' of 'El mañana efímero' – is a symbolic leitmotif throughout these poems. In poem X of the 'Proverbios y cantares' published in *España* in 1923, he admits that Spain's empty-headedness comes in many forms, some of which smell like death:

> Pero esa filosofía
> de carroña y gusanera
> tan sombría,
> o, si queréis, tan ibera,
> no me gusta: huele a cera
> y a calavera vacía.

From Machado's *Unicaja* workbooks, we know that poem X once included three initial verses that were published separately as poem IX in *España* in 1923: '¡Gloria a Valdés que pintara / el fondo del alma huera / de Don Miguel de Mañara!'[7] It is clear, then, that the Iberian philosophy Machado speaks of here refers to the devout and pietistic religiosity of Miguel de Mañara (1627–79). In the mid-seventeenth century, Mañara was one of Seville's wealthiest residents who renounced his extravagant lifestyle after his wife's death from the plague in 1661 to serve the indigent and sick in the Brotherhood of the Holy Charity (a lay fraternity founded in 1565 to provide burials for paupers). Mañara broadened the Brotherhood's socio-religious agenda by erecting an impressive church on the site of its old chapel. The church is remembered mostly for its decorated walls because they are adorned near the entrance with two gruesome pieces by the artist Valdés Leal titled *Finis Gloriae Mundi* and *In Ictu Oculi* dedicated to Mañara's philosophy of life. Mañara's philosophical views can be summed up in the simple idea that the certainty of death and final judgement should dictate one's actions on earth (*Finis Gloriae Mundi* depicts a stigmatized hand holding a balance representing equal measures of sin and charity directly above two rotting corpses that are being eaten by insects; *In Ictu Oculi* represents the triumph of death in the figure of an imposing skeleton that tramples a globe and symbols of worldly power to snuff out the candle of life). In Mañara's *Discurso de la verdad* (1671), he admonished his reader, much in the vein of the *ubi sunt* motif in medieval and baroque literature, of the nothingness of life, the futility of hope and the inescapability of the grave. Throughout his work, Mañara describes in detail how corpses decompose and are devoured by worms to convey how the mere thought of death and divine judgement can bring clarity of mind to why we must never stray from the devout life:

> Si tuviéramos delante la verdad, ésta es, y no hay otra, la mortaja que hemos de llevar ... Y si consideramos los viles gusanos que han de comer este cuerpo cuán feo y abominable ha de estar en la sepultura ... Los más de los hombres de este miserable siglo no se acuerdan de volverse a Dios, si no es cuando el mundo los deja, y entonces, a más no poder, lo hacen porque la muerte los deja el tiempo. (pp. 13–19)

Much like the 'calavera', Mañara's soul is hollow in Machado's eyes, and what is more, Valdés Leal had captured its terrible emptiness in a collection of *memento mori* populated with skulls and lifeless corpses. The comparison between Mañara's philosophy (described as 'tan ibera' and bringing to mind extreme pietism and death) and a hollowed 'calavera', reveals not only how Machado linked the country's ignorance to the Church and religious institutions more generally, but how a preoccupation with death (in a sense, a death philosophy) did nothing to remedy the country's socio-economic realities. If anything, it promoted a withdrawn, ascetic way of life in which social action was mediated by the Church or religious doctrine and subject, in the end, to God's final judgment. In poem xlviii (*CC*), Machado poetizes a different kind of 'calavera', that of Yorick in Shakespeare's *Hamlet*:

> Mirando mi calavera
> un nuevo Hamlet dirá:
> he aquí un lindo fósil de una
> careta de carnaval.

After his father's murder, Hamlet is overcome by thoughts of death (the murder of old King Hamlet, Ophelia's apparent suicide, the many corpses rotting in the cemetery). Hamlet's quest for meaning in life punctuates these thoughts on death, since death's nearness serves as a symbolic frame to his questions concerning truth, revelation, the afterlife and knowledge. However, the 'calavera' in poem xlviii – what in *Hamlet* leads to the famous contemplation of Yorick's skull, 'Alas, poor Yorick!' in Act V – provokes no such existential search for meaning, but it undergoes a type of tragicomic transformation into a festive carnival mask (Machado often presented the carnival theme in the context of decay and degeneration, as in the poem 'Una nueva España': 'A España toda, / la malherida España, de Carnaval vestida / nos la pusieron, pobre escuálida y beoda').[8] The 'nuevo Hamlet' that looks upon the 'calavera' is not a prince in search of the meaning of life, but a nameless Pandolfo. As this new Hamlet regards the skull, he does not ask the hard questions about life and death and sees only its emptiness:

> ¡O calavera vacía!
> ¡Y pensar que todo era
> dentro de ti, calavera!,
> otro Pandolfo decía.[9]

Poem 1 (*CC*) explores this emptiness of the 'calavera' further. A doctor examines a typical, apathetic Spaniard (perhaps the nameless Pandolfo alluded to above), and his final diagnosis is that he suffers from empty-headedness:

> – Nuestro español bosteza.
> ¿Es hambre? ¿Sueño? ¿Hastío?
> Doctor, ¿tendrá el estómago vacío?
> - El vació es más bien la cabeza.

In a songlike manner, Machado adds an existential despair to the theme of the 'calavera' in poem xv (*CC*). The speaker leads a choir in song:

> Cantad conmigo a coro: Saber, nada sabemos,
> de arcano mar venimos, a ignota mar iremos. . .
> Y entre los dos misterios está el enigma grave;
> tres arcas cierra una desconocida llave.
> La luz nada ilumina y el sabio nada enseña.
> ¿Qué dice la palabra? ¿Qué el agua de la peña?

The poem is an accumulation of unknowns in which the symbolic 'luz' and the old sage reveal nothing about man's origins or destiny capable of illuminating the why of existence ('el enigma grave'). The long *alejandrino* verse, with its strong caesura, only strengthens this oscillation between unknowns. Finally, the speaker asks: who or what can ameliorate the mystery of life and death? Without any clear answer, the final two questions of the poem remain purposefully unanswered.

Cucaña Logic

In the 1905 article 'Divagaciones (En torno al libro último de Unamuno)', Machado praises Unamuno for his treatment of madness in his recently published *Vida de Don Quijote y Sancho*. On this subject of madness, he asks Unamuno: '¿Necesita maestros de cordura esta tierra de vividores, de fríos y discretos bellacotes? Locos necesitamos, que siembren para no cosechar. Cuerdos que talen él árbol para alcanzar la fruta, abundan, por desdicha' (2001b: p. 207).[10] The nuanced reference to altruism ('[sembrar] para no cosechar') is set in counterpoint to a simple tree-cutting metaphor that illustrates to what extent ignorance is often disguised as good judgement. In his tree symbolism, Machado broached the theme of empty-headedness by showing how ignorance and knowledge had somehow become inverted in Spain; that is, ignorance had become the sociopolitical norm and was more valued than knowledge. In poems xci and xcii (*NC*), for example, he develops the tree metaphor by imagining a dialogue between a living tree and a *cucaña* on the subject of Spain's regeneration. Poem xci reads as follows:

> Siempre en alto, siempre en alto,
> ¿Renovación? Desde arriba.
> Dijo la cucaña al árbol.[11]

The *cucaña* was a regular fixture in Spanish *ferias*. It was a tall and smooth log that was lathered with soap, bacon grease or oil, and at its top sat a prize. In a display of strength and agility, young men would scale the slippery log in hope of claiming the prize. With this festive image serving as a backdrop, Machado questions, and clearly criticizes, the ill-fated logic behind any type of renewal that favours, symbolically speaking, only the treetops at the expense of the whole tree ('¿Renovación? Desde arriba'). In the following poem xcii (*NC*), the tree responds to the *cucaña*:

> Dijo el árbol: Teme al hacha,
> palo clavado en el suelo:
> contigo la poda es tala.

The idea of 'renovación desde arriba' presented in these poems alludes to president Antonio Maura's concept of a revolution from above, from the government downward to the people. During his second premiership between 1907 and 1909, Maura had sought to institute various government reforms at local and state levels that would – in theory – do away with the widespread problems of *caci-quismo*, yet he soon encountered great opposition from both liberal and republican parties, which rallied against him with the emphatic cry '*¡Maura, no!*' Like the ignorance–knowledge inversion, Machado believed Maura's revolution from above was flawed. The tree metaphor and the illogical revolution from above (as far as the *cucaña* is concerned, the 'prize' rests at the top) resurface in *Los complementarios* in far more ominous terms when Machado speaks of Maura's misguided 'mentalidad arcaica y hueca': 'El reino de las sombras, infierno de la vida nacional, empezó hace ya tiempo a empedrarse de buenas intenciones. Recordemos a Maura – ¿existe aún? – que habló de una revolución desde arriba, es decir, desde el ápice de la cucaña' (p. 37). However, it is Mairena who outlines a 'logical' revolution by the people for the people in which culture and knowledge would play an emancipatory role for the individual. Once again, Machado returns to his tree symbolism: 'También la cultura . . . necesita ser podada, en beneficio de sus frutos, como los árboles demasiado frondosos. Y a falta de una poda consciente y sabia, bueno es el huracán' (1986: p. 163).[12] The hurricanes and blustery winds of revolution prune the symbolic 'tree of culture' of its yellowed leaves, and in the end allow it to bear new fruit. It is no wonder why Mairena warns his reader: 'Nunca peguéis con lacre las hojas secas de los árboles para fatigar al viento. Porque el viento no se fatiga, sino que se enfada, y se lleva las hojas secas y las verdes' (1986: p. 13). This warning had appeared years before in poem lxii (*NC*) in the dictum:

> Por dar al viento trabajo
> cosía con hilo doble
> las hojas secas del árbol.

The *cucaña* is a symbol of Spain's inverted sociopolitical logic. The State-sponsored ignorance of razing a tree to reach its fruit is equated not only to Maura's revolution from above, but also to a type of ill-conceived renewal that symbolically privileged only the top foliage of society while ignoring its roots and trunks. In Mairena's words: '¡Revolución desde arriba! Como si dijéramos . . . renovación del árbol por la copa . . . Revolución desde abajo me suena mejor . . . Porque no se trata de renovar el árbol por la copa, sino ¡por la corteza!' (1986: p. 21). In poems xcvi and xcvii (*NC*), the *cucaña*, and the disastrous ignorance it brings to mind, is to be feared:

¿Ya sientes la savia nueva?
Cuida, arbolillo,
que nadie lo sepa.

Cuida de que no se entere
la cucaña seca
de tus ojos verdes.

By referring to Maura's revolution from above, Machado's symbolic *cucaña* speaks to how the entire 'social tree' requires renewal. To look after the foliage (the upper crust of society) to the detriment of the rest of the tree (the majority) is not only illogical, but it invites the winds of revolution (and as the tree informs the *cucaña*: 'Teme al hacha / [. . .] / contigo la poda es tala'). As we shall see in the following section, Machado believed that only through critical thinking on the ignorance/knowledge dualism would it be possible to overcome *cucaña* logic. He knew all too well that in a world turned on its head, 'se admira a todo pillo que logra encaramarse en el ápice de la cucaña' (2001b: p. 408).

The Collective Meaning of 'saber'

Si me tengo que morir
poco me importa aprender
y si no puedo saber
poco me importa vivir.

As the *redondilla* above suggests (poem II of the 'Apuntes, parábolas, proverbios y cantares' published in *La Lectura* in 1916), it is from the darkest abyss of ignorance that Machado begins to reflect upon 'saber'. To be sure, 'saber' is a complex term in his work that hinges on the idea that reason and logic can establish a deeper collective understanding between self and Other. 'Saber' was not simply knowledge in the classic sense (facts, truths, principles, etc.), but a type of revealing of the self to the Other through honest dialogue. Machado realized that 'saber' would be deprived of its collective meaning if it served the interests of a religious or political agenda, a point that he made clear in the previous examples of Mañara's pietism and Maura's State-sponsored revolution from above. Before any religion or political ideology, 'saber' had to concern the individual. Mairena explains why this had to be so:

Nosotros pretendemos fortalecer y agilitar nuestro pensar para aprender de él mismo cuáles son sus posibilidades, cuáles sus limitaciones; hasta qué punto se produce de un modo libre, original, con propia iniciativa, y hasta qué punto nos aparece limitado por normas rígidas, por hábitos mentales inmodificables, por *imposibilidades* de pensar de otro modo. (1971a: p. 149)

Only the individual's self-examination of knowledge was capable of revealing its constructedness and limitations, and this type of self-examination is presented most symbolically in Machado's work in the apocryphal Escuela Popular de Sabiduría Superior. The Escuela Popular, made famous by Mairena, had little to do with providing a standard education but rather with elevating the *pueblo* from ignorance by teaching scepticism as a constructive way of analysing how knowledge is produced, used and circulated:

Porque la finalidad de nuestra escuela ... consistiría en revelar al pueblo, quiero decir al hombre de nuestra tierra, todo el radio de su posible actividad pensante, toda la enorme zona de su espíritu que puede ser iluminada y, consiguientemente, obscurecida; en enseñarle a repensar lo pensado, a desaber lo sabido y dudar de su propia duda. (1971a: pp. 196–9)

It is not by accident that Mairena's meditations include inquiries into the impossibility of absolute knowledge; inquiries that, borrowing from the maieutic method, were published in popular outlets like *Hora de España* and *La Vanguardia* in the 1930s with this didactic end in mind. The role of language in knowledge is significant in this respect, since Mairena often reflects upon the nature of truth ('verdad') by trying to demarcate its limits through how discourse reflects and is influenced by power structures. Perhaps for this reason it was necessary to carry out an epistemological *tabula rasa* and 'repensar lo pensado ... desaber lo sabido'. Doubt could serve as a yardstick for truth because it allowed the individual to examine knowledge claims in order to reveal a different reality. Machado's doubt is not Cartesian doubt in its methodology, nor does it advocate nihilism or resignation, but it is a revelatory 'duda poética' that questions what knowledge actually is and does. Paul Aubert has explained this 'duda poética' as a pedagogical instrument '[que] pretende orientar al hombre descaminado mediante una práctica razonable de la sofística que empieza por el recuerdo de algunas verdades elementales' (p. 318). Only through the interrogative act – by doubting what we know or think we know – is the self truly open to 'saber'. Mairena often insisted that this doubt represented the foundation of his thinking: 'yo os enseño, o pretendo enseñaros, a que dudéis de todo . . . yo os enseño una duda sincera, nada metódica . . . yo os enseño una duda integral, que no puede excluirse a sí misma' (1986: pp. 71–2). In poem xciii (*NC*), Machado shows how knowledge claims, particularly those that are derived from so-called truths, are relative to their methods of production. He draws inspiration from the Heraclitan and Eleatic schools of thought to pose two rhetorical questions about the nature of truth: is truth variable, relative and time-dependent? Or is truth immutable and timeless?:

> ¿Cuál es la verdad? ¿El río
> que fluye y pasa
> donde el barco y barquero
> son también del agua?
> ¿O este soñar del marino
> siempre con ribera y ancla?

In poems xlvi and xlix (*NC*), Machado examines falsity to illustrate to what degree truth is caught up between competing claims to knowledge:

> Se miente más de la cuenta
> por falta de fantasía:
> también la verdad se inventa.
>
> ¿Dijiste media verdad?
> dirán que mientes dos veces
> si dices la otra mitad.

For Machado, scepticism was a useful pedagogical tool to educate the individual on how to examine and question his knowledge, in particular any knowledge that was considered 'lugar común'. Ignorance had an important role to play in this regard but to understand exactly why, we must take a moment and consider why Machado argued, as did Socrates, that knowledge of ignorance could lead to self-enlightenment. Like Socrates, Machado embraces his ignorance: 'no toméis demasiado en serio nada de cuanto oís de mis labios, porque yo no me creo en posesión de ninguna verdad' (1971a: p. 244).[13] For Socrates and Machado, ignorance was critical in bringing about knowledge. The structure of Socrates' dialectical question/answer logic, his concern with questions of the nature of truth and falsity, and the scepticism of his interrogative thinking (all mainstays in Machado's poetry and prose), brought about an awareness of what one did not know, and thus of ignorance itself. In *Meno*, for instance,

Socrates questions one of Meno's slave boys on a geometrical problem: how does one go about conceiving a square with an area twice that of a given square? How the slave boy 'awakens' to his ignorance through a series of inquiries represents one of the most significant passages in Plato's works on Socratic ignorance:

> SOCRATES: Observe, Meno, the stage he has reached on the path of recollection. At the beginning he did not know the side of the square of eight feet. Nor indeed does he know it now, but then he thought he knew it and answered boldly, as was appropriate – he felt no perplexity. Now, however, he does feel perplexed. Not only does he not know the answer; he does not even think he knows.
>
> MENO: Quite true.
>
> SOCRATES: Isn't he in a better position now in relation to what he didn't know?
>
> MENO: I admit that too.
>
> SOCRATES: So in perplexing him and numbing him like a sting-ray, have we done him any harm?
>
> MENO: I think not.
>
> SOCRATES: In fact, we have helped him in some extent toward finding the right answer, for now not only is he ignorant of it, but will be quite glad to look for it. (p. 38)

Socrates believed it was possible to attain a knowledge of ignorance that was capable of leading the self to what he called 'human wisdom'. In the *Apology* he referred to 'human wisdom' to answer questions regarding his tarnished reputation among Athenian citizens who believe him a corruptor of youngsters and a worshipper of false gods. 'I have gained this reputation, gentlemen,' Socrates says, 'from nothing more or less than a kind of wisdom. What kind of wisdom do I mean? Human wisdom, I suppose. It seems that I really am wise in this limited sense' (p. 43). Throughout the *Apology*, and all the way up to Socrates' final sentencing, he will explain in different ways how this wisdom arises from truthfully recognizing his ignorance. Hugh Benson explains further:

> Not to be aware of one's ignorance is the most blameworthy ignorance ... not because of the hubris of thinking one can obtain what is reserved for the gods, but because it hinders one in the quest for what is truly valuable. Those who have not achieved human wisdom – the

recognition of their ignorance – will not seek what they already think they have. (p. 183)

Poems viii (*CC*) and iv (*CC*) explore this question of Socratic ignorance and 'human wisdom'. Machado echoes Socrates' teaching on ignorance when he suggests that keen self-examination is the indispensable first step in attaining an awareness of what one does not know:

> En preguntar lo que sabes
> el tiempo no has de perder. . .
> Y a preguntas sin respuesta
> ¿quién te podrá responder?
>
> Nuestras horas son minutos
> cuando esperamos saber,
> y siglos cuando sabemos
> lo que se puede aprender.

While Socratic ignorance is more than simply an awareness of ignorance, one of its fundamental aims in regards to 'human wisdom' is that it draws others into a dialogue, and here is where it intersects with Machado's poetic-philosophical thinking. Although the very idea of dialogue for Socrates comprised such things as desire (*eros*), rhetoric, speech, and various moral concepts like virtue, justice and courage, it was only through the dialogic encounter with the Other, and the resulting dialectical openness it established between self and Other, that one's ignorance could be more fully revealed. From this knowledge of ignorance, the self–Other dialogue is brought to bear on the very meaning of existence. In his dialogues with others, Socrates did not intend to teach anything specific, except perhaps that 'I know that I know nothing'. However, through the dialogical experience, Socrates lived up to his guiding Delphic maxim 'know thyself' (he himself gazed inwards at his ignorance on all sorts of subjects), but more significantly he allowed his interlocutors to truthfully examine their inner self. For Kenneth Seeskin, the interpersonal structure of Socratic dialogue 'requires . . . that the people whose voices we hear be intimately connected with the positions they take . . . Socrates insists that the respondent not say anything short of what he truly believes' (pp. 1–2). After an exchange with Socrates, Alcibiades reports in *The Symposium* how significantly this type of self-examination had altered his thinking: 'My soul wasn't in turmoil, and I wasn't disturbed by the thought that I was a slave to my way of living. But after listening to this

Marsyas here I was very often reduced to thinking that being as I was, my kind of life was not worth living' (p. 56). For Machado, this self-examination, if sincere, reflected directly upon the Other in that it offered the self a way to conceive the self–Other relation in ethical terms:

> Cuando un hombre reflexivo . . . se mira por dentro, comprende la absoluta imposibilidad de ser juzgado con mediano acierto por quienes lo miran por fuera, que son todos los demás, y la imposibilidad en que él se encuentra de decir cosa de provecho cuanto pretende juzgar a su vecino. (1971a: p. 162)

Dialogue thus opens a space for intersubjective communion, and what is essential about the self–Other exchange is not what is said exactly, but the face-to-face contact. For Pierre Hadot, 'the dialogue itself . . . already constitutes a moral and existential experience, for Socratic philosophy is not the solitary elaboration of a system, but the awakening of consciousness, and accession to a level of being which can only be reached in a person-to-person relationship' (p. 163). Both Socrates and Machado proposed that the self and Other live differently, and treat one another differently, when they are 'awakened' to their ignorance through dialogue. In other words, the very language and presence dialogue requires enacts the relational I–Thou structure of intersubjective experience in what Martin Buber called a 'life of dialogue':

> [T]he life of dialogue is no privilege of intellectual activity like dialectic. It does not begin in the upper story of humanity. It begins no higher than where humanity begins. There are no gifted and ungifted here, only those who give themselves and those who withhold themselves . . . Dialogue is not an affair of . . . spiritual luxuriousness, it is a matter of creation, of the creature, and he is that, the man of whom I speak. (p. 203)

Poem ii (*NC*) is perhaps one of Machado's most profound and Socratic poems on this intersubjective experience of dialogue. In a type of minimalist *tercetilla*, the imperatives 'preguntad' and 'escuchad', neatly divided by two temporal markers 'primero' and 'después', reveal the essence of the dialogical encounter:

> Para dialogar,
> preguntad primero;
> después. . . escuchad.

This dialogical encounter informs Machado's 'saber' in various ways, perhaps the most important one being that it facilitates a search for existential meaning in the presence that Levinas termed simply 'the Other before me'. The need for dialogue may appear rather straightforward on the surface – without it there is no discussion, no sociopolitical consensus and so on – but it is much more than opening a line of communication between self and Other for Machado (although this was clearly the essential first step: 'En España no se dialoga porque nadie pregunta, como no sea para responderse a sí mismo. Todos queremos estar de vuelta, sin haber ido a ninguna parte') (1971a: p. 233). It was through dialogue that the self embarks on what Benson calls 'the quest for what is truly valuable', which for Machado had to do with social belonging (the 'fraternidad humana') and conceiving a communal reason (the 'razón humana'):

> La razón humana no es hija, como algunos creen, de las disputas entre los hombres, sino del diálogo amoroso en que se busca la comunión por el intelecto en verdades, absolutas o relativas, pero que, en el peor caso, son independientes del humor individual. (1971a: p. 67)

> La razón humana es pensamiento genérico. Quien razona afirma la existencia de un prójimo, la necesidad del diálogo, la posible comunión mental entre los hombres ... Quien dialoga, ciertamente, afirma a su vecino, al otro yo ... Pero no basta la razón, el invento socrático, para crear la convivencia humana; ésta precisa también la comunicación cordial, una convergencia de corazones en un mismo objeto de amor. (1971a: p. 35)

> Es la razón la facultad de los conceptos generales, de las ideas; en ellas hay una forma de universalidad ... El hombre libre opina, discute, polemiza, conversa, dialoga, contrasta su propio pensar con el de su prójimo y averigua por sí mismo – no acepta como dogma – que las normas y categorías de su entendimiento, no son individuales, sino específicas, que revelan la común estructura del espíritu humano. (1971b: pp. 90–1)

Logic was also conceived as a type of collective understanding: 'Nuestra lógica pretende ser el pensar poético, *heterogeneizante, inventor* o descubridor de lo real ... Mas si éste se lograse algún día, nuestra lógica pasaría a ser la lógica del sentido común' (1971a: p. 147). It was regarded more broadly as a communal consciousness: 'la lógica es ...

la gran rueda de molino con que comulga la Humanidad entera a través de los siglos' (1971a: p. 226). Machado developed this idea of communal consciousness in logic over the years, often elaborating on specific philosophical points (the pitfalls of circular logic, for instance), yet he never strayed too far from the fundamental idea that 'por nuestra lógica vamos siempre de lo uno a lo otro' (1971a: p. 147).

Reason and logic, anchored by the Socratic principle of self-examination, laid the foundation of Machado's idea that 'saber' was a collective knowledge born from dialogue. As in other parts of his poetry and thinking, he is exploring knowledge beyond the margins of the transcendental idealist tradition (its critique of empiricism and rationalism) by advocating what can be understood as an intersubjective structure to the process of knowing itself. In his criticisms of Kantian idealism, he often alluded to this important point by reiterating that 'lo que Kant demuestra, y sólo a medias . . . es que él no cree en más intuición que la sensible, ni en otra existencia que la espacio-temporal' (1971a: p. 102). Reason and logic depend on the Other's presence, yet we must not infer from this that knowledge is somehow set adrift in a sea of intersubjective relativity (what each self and each Other might ultimately make of knowledge), but rather that it is dynamic and transformed in the individual's web of social interactions with other individuals.

When confronted with ignorance, then, Machado understood that the self cannot conceive the Other, at least not in the ethical terms the self–Other relation demanded in the Spanish context, without self-examination and dialogue. Without the self interrogating given knowledge (a sceptical method of de/constructive inquiry that consisted of 'repensar lo pensado' and 'desaber lo sabido y dudar de [la] propia duda'), empty-headedness and *cucaña* logic would prevail. What is more, the epistemological constraints imposed by the Church and State presented in this chapter would further divide the country in a 'régimen de iniquidad'. In a letter to Juan Ramón Jiménez in 1913, Machado summed it all up by saying:

> Pero no se puede hacer nada inmediato y directo. Hay un ambiente de cobardía y mentira que asfixia . . . Cuanto he escrito hasta ahora ha tenido más éxito del que yo creía merecer. No es cuestión de amor propio, sino amor al prójimo. Este régimen de iniquidad en que vivimos empieza a indignarme . . . Hoy quiero trabajar, humildemente, es cierto, pero con eficacia, con verdad. Hay que defender a la España que surge, del mar muerto, de la España inerte y abrumadora que amenaza anegarlo todo. (2001b: pp. 328–9)

The Infinity of Knowledge and Ignorance

Given the revelatory character of Machado's 'saber', many of the *PrCs* provide the reader with the groundwork to understanding the type of self-examination and dialogue that was needed to challenge 'los dos elementos que nos empujan . . . a un porvenir más o menos catastró-fico . . . la política y la Iglesia'. Much in the spirit of the Romantic fragment, Machado's sententious poems serve as open conceptual forms with which to doubt not only systems of thought, be they religious or political, but also the so-called 'truths' of Spain's narra-tives of progress (culture, education, economic development, etc.). Considered critically, the *PrCs* offer a miscellany of guiding principles that invite the reader to begin a journey of self-examination capable of generating an awareness of his ignorance, as well as an awareness of the seemingly infinite relativity of knowledge itself. We need only consider how the *PrCs* illuminated Machado's own practice of self-examination:

> Todos creerán que mis epigramas están escritos contra alguien. Tras ellos se pondrá un nombre ¿quién sabe de quién? Tal vez de aquel a quien menos haya yo querido aludir. Nadie comprenderá que estos epigramas están escritos contra mí mismo. ¿Y por qué no? Yo soy Tartarín, yo soy el grillo, el burro de la flauta ronca, el caracol y todo lo demás. ¿Por qué no ha de sorprender al hombre su triste figura? ¿Hemos de escribir para exaltarnos y jalearnos? O lo contrario. (1971b: p. 45)

One of the key conclusions Machado adopts from Socratic philoso-phy is that knowledge is endlessly deferred in the dialogical face-to-face moment itself. For Socrates, there was no end to what one did not know. To truly know one's ignorance was a lifelong venture of continu-ally striving toward truth, and fittingly all the Socratic dialogues end with no definitive answer on any given matter. Knowledge can never be a closed system, a wholeness or completion, but rather it encompasses an infinite progression from ignorance to understanding, from doubt to truth, and from self to Other. For Machado, knowledge was both produced and facilitated in dialogue, which provided the self with the insight – the intersubjective reason and logic that comes with the Other's presence – to interrogate knowledge and reveal what Karl Marx called the 'demon' of ignorance (p. 130).

Clearly, there are many facets to Machado's 'saber'. Again echoing Socrates' teachings (particularly in *Meno* and *Phaedo*), he often consid-ered 'saber' in relation to immutable and guiding truths. Mairena tells

us, 'cuando el hombre deja de creer en lo absoluto, ya no cree en
nada' (1971a: p. 95). Ironically, it was often in folklore and its 'saber
popular' where this type of knowledge emerged, and while it was
dynamic and complex ('nuestro *folklore*. . . es saber vivo en el alma del
pueblo'), it also revealed those ideas and truths that were eternal in
man's thinking: 'hay verdades que todos los hombres pueden elevarse,
porque son fruto del pensar de todos' (1971b: p. 91). Poem xxx (*CC*),
for instance, uses a popular proverb to address these types of immutable and guiding truths:

> El que espera desespera,
> dice la voz popular.
> ¡Qué verdad tan verdadera!
> La verdad es lo que es,
> y sigue siendo verdad
> aunque se piense al revés.

The *PrCs* also demonstrate to what degree Machado's 'saber' was
indebted to Romantic anti-foundationalism. In broad terms, the
Romantics considered the Enlightenment's concept of reason too
restrictive, where reason alone, through the methods of observation
and logic, could do away with the darkness of superstition, speculation
and error that had stranded human understanding in theological
modes of thought. Without a doubt, Enlightenment methodologies
for explaining experience required ever more rigorous philosophical
systems that could categorize and order knowledge and make it
accessible. In *Fichte Studies*, Novalis criticized the 'closedness' of these
types of systems of knowledge. He proposed that philosophy had to
expand its horizons and regard things like faith and love in questions
of subjectivity, for instance, since '[t]he borders of feeling are the
borders of philosophy' (p. 13). The shift we find with the Romantics
has to do with conceiving knowledge as something actively made
rather than passively observed, documented or hypothesized through
systematic cogitation. To put it differently, the distance between the
thing-in-itself in the world, and our knowledge of it, all but disappears
with the Romantics, in that the language and feeling of the self's
creative spirit could unite inner and outer worlds in new and inexplicable ways:

> The typical romantic was inclined to conceive the infinite totality
> aesthetically, as an organic whole with which man felt himself to be
> one, the means of apprehending this unity being intuition and feeling

rather than conceptual thought. For conceptual thought tends to fix
and perpetuate defined limits and boundaries. (Copleston, p. 18)

If we take Schlegel as our guide, we find that he criticized the
Enlightenment doctrine that all philosophy required self-evident first
principles upon which to build systems of knowledge. 'Our philosophy
does not begin', he proclaimed, 'like the others with a first principle –
where the first proposition is like the centre or first ring of a comet –
with the rest of the tail of mist – we depart from a small but living seed –
our centre lies in the middle' (Frank, p. 89). His underlying argument
was that it is inconceivable to approach knowledge from any point of
certainty. In his estimation, all knowledge required a conceptual
'middle' that took into account the larger history of ideas. Like the
seed metaphor suggests, knowledge was organic, it grew and developed, and understanding this historical development meant acknowledging how any knowledge was full of gaps and contradictions.
Undeniably, this process fostered a critical awareness and scepticism
concerning the claims of knowledge (what exactly was excluded and
why), and from this perspective, Schlegel, like many Romantics, 'was
anti-foundationalist through and through', since he attempted 'to
capture the inherent incompleteness of . . . knowledge' (Frank, p. 10).
This project provided the foundation for his ideas on the fragment
and irony, among other things, in which the continual striving toward
an absolute knowledge revealed its very impossibility.

This same concern about the incompleteness of knowledge is
apparent in Machado's *PrCs*, and it grounds significant portions of his
poetry and thought, as we have seen. Yet what sets him apart from the
Romantics is that he examined the interpersonal dimension of knowledge much more deeply. It was a mix of experiencing the hardships
and solitude in Soria and Baeza, as well as delving deeper into Kant
and transcendental idealism (and through Kant, philosophy itself as
an epistemological practice) that led him to understand knowledge as
a way to 'awaken' the self to the Other. Mairena's pedagogy is founded
upon this premise: 'Enseñad al que no sabe; despertad al dormido;
llamad a la puerta de todos los corazones, de todas las conciencias'
(1986: p. 63). We unearth in his *PrCs* the organizing thesis that the
Other is not a construct, a proposition, or a set of philosophical claims,
but a way of experiencing the world in an ethical manner. If we accept
this view, then the dialogical encounter examined earlier informs
Machado's concept of otherness in a most crucial way: it puts into play
the idea that the Other is irreducible to any act of knowing. In the

dialogical face-to-face moment, the Other cannot be objectified by knowledge, the Other cannot be reduced, confined, explained or subjugated by the objective event presented to the self. As Machado had said it: 'Toda revelación del espíritu humano . . . es revelación de lo otro, de lo esencialmente otro, la equis que nadie despeja . . . no por inagotable, *sino por irreductible en calidad y esencia a los datos conocidos*, no ya como lo infinito ante lo limitado, sino como lo otro ante lo uno' (1971a: p. 185).

We return once again to the uneasy relationship between ignorance and knowledge. As the *PrCs* make clear, the infinite knowledge void can never be adequately 'filled', so to speak, but it is the attempt to transcend it, to *know* it, that constitutes a way of understanding reality. With this proposition Machado connects with the ontological phenomenology that takes root with Heidegger's *Being and Time* and continues to this day. Although Machado's otherness shares significant insights with Heidegger (the temporal aspect of *Dasein* and the individual who questions the nature of Being), Martin Buber (the I–Thou relationship) and Merleau-Ponty (the potential reversibility of self and Other in a chiasmic ontology), it is with Emmanuel Levinas where we can conceive it within a much larger sociophilosophical frame of reference. We will find that Machado's concept of Other explored questions concerning the experience of otherness that, in its fundamental arguments, anticipated some of the major philosophical discoveries of the twentieth century.

Conclusion

The Infinite Inquiry

No es fácil que pueda yo enseñaros a hablar ni a escribir, ni a pensar correctamente, porque yo soy la incorrección misma, una alma siempre en borrador, llena de tachones, de vacilaciones y de arrepentimientos.

Antonio Machado, *Juan de Mairena*

From his early *modernista* period to the writings of Juan de Mairena of the 1930s, the *PrCs* connect with various aspects of Machado's work. The basic argument that I have presented in this book has been that they articulate a distinct poetics that reveals how Machado tackled the problem of subjectivity that came about with post-Kantian modernity. This poetics represents a reflexive poetic and philosophical undertaking, one that opened new discursive spaces in the folkloric *proverbio* and *cantar* in which Machado could explore his evolving sense of self and Other. When considered within this framework, the *PrCs* never gesture toward a grand interpretation of otherness. On the contrary, they show how the Other, particularly regarded in the face-to-face moment of dialogue, continually resists any form of conceptual wholeness. With the theory of the fragment in particular, I have wanted to underscore this practice of *resistance* in Machado's *PrCs* as one of the productive ways he articulated the self–Other relation in the oppositional part/whole, singular/universal and individual/collective relationships (all of which lead, as we have seen, to an affirmative scepticism and to the idea of infinite and dialogic possibility). These types of 'ironic' structures make clear what Schlegel, Bécquer and Nietzsche regarded in their own ways as the impossibility and necessity of a complete communication. In Machado's *PrCs*, the oppositional 'cainismo' and 'diálogo amoroso', like two organizing paradigms striving for reconciliation where poetry and philosophy converge, can be said to sustain this type of ironic tension. Overall, however, there are three ideas that are essential in Machado's concept of Other in the *PrCs* and his work in general: firstly, the idea that concepts of self, if anchored upon 'un solipsismo extremado', will inevitably lead to a social 'callejón sin salida'; secondly, when we gaze into the world, we must acknowledge the Other as Other without any form of violence and without imposing limitations to the experience of difference (concepts of self depend on the Other, thus enacting an ethical bond, or 'comunión cordial', which can be deeply spiritual and enriching); and finally, the dialogical structure of the self–Other relation itself – the presence of the Other and his speaking – makes clear how otherness transcends any form of conceptual closure.

Machado's Trajectory Toward Otherness

If I have insisted on the Romantic influences on Machado's concept of Other it is only to emphasize how his struggle with the legacy of Romanticism not only reflected the complex philosophical discussions of his time (Demófilo's idea of *Volk* and *pueblo*; the Krausist 'hombre'; *fin de siglo* irrationalism; neo-Kantian idealism; scepticism; the absence of God, etc.), but also opened a path to conceiving the Other beyond Romantic models of self and world. In light of the various contradictions and antagonisms that we find lurking in his idea of Other, it becomes apparent that he used the great Romantic discoveries as a foothold to explore his own ideas on the nature of the world. If we consider, for example, some of the tenets of Romantic inwardness like the belief in a boundless imagination or the sanctity of the artist's inner truth, we find that he embraces and rejects them at various stages in his work, yet they are always present somehow, always exerting an oppositional influence on his thinking. For this reason, poet and critic Luis Jiménez Martos believes that 'la poesía de Antonio Machado pertenece más al siglo XIX que al XX' (p. 15), yet Cerezo Galán is right to caution us not to read Machado's work exclusively through this Romantic lens, for clearly this type of reading will never yield an adequate picture of the 'post-Romantic' sensibility of his work:

> La interpretación de Machado en clave exclusivamente romántica no
> da cuenta ni del proceso de crisis interior de su obra ni de su esfuerzo
> por desembarazarse del yo interior especular y sus secretas galerías de
> fantasmas, para abrirse a lo real, buscándose afanosamente el lugar de

los ojos . . . Machado ha sufrido la quiebra del yo romántico y se ha
enzarzado en una lucha intestina con el romanticismo. Ya se le llame
'desubjetivización' (despertar del sueño) o apertura cordial a la
alteridad, o ambas cosas conjuntamente, es innegable que se trata de
un dato consustancial al espíritu machadiano. ('Lo apócrifo', p. 188)

With that said, Machado's concept of Other in the *PrCs*, given this
ever-present 'lucha intestina' with Romanticism, has to be reinscribed
within a broader critical framework. Often repeated is that his concept
of Other, aside from a handful of key poems mostly from *Cancionero
apócrifo* and *NC*, really takes form in the more philosophical problems
presented in Martín's and Mairena's prose. While there is no doubt
that Martín and Mairena are indispensable in this respect, the origins
of Machado's idea of *el/lo otro* date from his earliest formative years. It
was his father Demófilo who initially brought the problem of subjectivity to Machado's attention. He educated the young Antonio on folklore's social significance, defining it in the Romantic *Volk* tradition, at
least during his Krausist period, as 'el sentir popular', and by showing
him that it was the ideal medium to explore concepts of self and world
(something that Bécquer had already demonstrated in his *Rimas*).
During his years in Madrid, Machado learned to what extent certain
Romantic models of poetry had fallen short in accommodating social
experience. He gravitated towards the *tablaos* and the *cante hondo* and
connected with poets like Salvador Rueda and Enrique Paradas, the
latter being crucial in how Machado understood the intersubjective
nature of *cantares*. And although the popularity of the *cantar* owed a
great deal to a type of Romantic populism, it could poetize, particularly with a skilled poet like Paradas, a social reality that directly
involved the subjective poetic self. The Institución Libre de Enseñanza
was also crucial during these years. In the Institución, Machado
learned Krause's 'ideal de la humanidad', a Romantic rationalism
reminiscent in parts of his own idea of 'lo elemental humano' in which
the self was conceived as continually striving to harmonize with the
world and the Absolute beyond it through various ethical obligations
to the collective. Also important is Eduardo Benot, whose *tertulias* and
works on grammar and philosophy could have very well served
Machado to acquaint himself with the major philosophical discussions
of the nineteenth century.

We can say, then, that before Machado began seriously writing
poetry he was familiar with the idea of Other as a poetic and philosophical question. From these early years, his idea of Other, while

clearly inchoate, begins to emerge with more clarity in his discussions with Unamuno between 1903 and 1905. After the publication of *Soledades*, he sought to pare down his poetry and rid it of its ornamentation and stylistic excesses in order to 'tear' his verses from lived experience ('la obra del verdadero artista; la cual se arranca directamente de la vida'). This poetic distillation came about through his evolving social awareness that he articulated in the Life/Art distinction: the idea that artists, and the 'bohemios' he so criticized in the 1890s, cannot sit idly by in their ivory towers and disregard the world of social engagement. Of this he tells Juan Ramón: 'Neguemos, pues, la divinidad del arte y arrinconemos su ritual retórico, mas no caigamos en divinizar la vida y levantarla sobre nuestras cabezas con loores e inciensos' (2001b: p. 179). The 'otro' that surfaces in his letters to Unamuno is expressed rather abstractly at first, but this changes when he experiences Soria's harsh rural life. 'Orillas del Duero', published in 1907, demonstrates that Spain's socio-economic crisis had sharpened his concept of Other in a broad, spiritually-based collectivity that he identified in 'el pueblo' (what he would call 'lo elemental humano'). It is precisely during this period in Soria that he speaks of writing a new poetry and begins a considerable 'existential' shift in his thinking that sought to acknowledge 'los otros'.

Machado's passion for philosophy also brought him into contact with the problem of subjectivity. From his early letters to Unamuno and Juan Ramón we know that before arriving in Paris in 1911 to study in the Collège de France with Henri Bergson, he was well acquainted with modern European philosophy. In 1913, he had stated that 'ahora me dedico a leer obras de Metafísica. Ésta ha sido siempre mi pasión y mi vocación' (2001b: p. 336). The works he studied so avidly during these years dealt predominantly with the subject–object paradigm of post-Kantian philosophy. Ancient Greek philosophy was important during this time, and so was the work of rationalists such as G. W. Leibniz, yet it was Kant's *Critique of Pure Reason* that was most influential. The German philosopher was a wellspring of inspiration for Machado, since he had brought to light one of the most fundamental questions nineteenth-century philosophy had to contend with after the long reign of Enlightenment scientism: how do we know the world? Over the years, Machado lauded and criticized Kant (and sometimes he did both in one fell swoop), yet there was one issue that remained a source of fascination for him: 'he de deciros que la . . .

revolución copernicana . . . me pareció siempre una ocurrencia maravillosa para saltarse a la torera y dejar intacto el problema del conocimiento' (1971a: p. 278). This epistemological problem of the Copernican revolution (what Machado recognized as the problem of the unknowable thing-in-itself), and the wedge it had forced between self and world, pushed him further toward understanding the nature of objectivity ('lo real') and, concomitantly, otherness ('un *otro* real'). Over the years, it also allowed Mairena to perfect his sceptical attitude toward any type of philosophical exegesis that attempted to explain, reduce or confine otherness with systems of thought:

> ¿Puedo yo saber lo que pasa en el alma de mi vecino?
> ¿Sé yo, acaso, si existe el alma de mi vecino?
> ¿Cómo puedo saber si existe el alma de mi vecino?
> ¿No pudiera ser mi vecino un cuerpo sin alma?
> Y, en último término ¿quién me asegura que existe mi vecino?
> Seguid preguntando, nunca os canséis de preguntar, sin preocuparos demasiado de las respuestas. (1986: p. 254)

The idea of Other for Machado, then, had a long and complex history. The shift we witness in his poetry and thinking between 1903 and 1913 toward a more direct rapport with the world is indicative of how he was labouring through the 'doble espejismo' of the subject–object paradigm in Western metaphysics. Clearly, the *PrCs* were one of the ways he explored this paradigm throughout most of his life.[1] Simply put, the poet should never do away with a type of Romantic inwardness in his work, but it is the acknowledgment of 'un *otro* real' that allows him to find his true lyrical voice. This idea remained mostly unchanged throughout Machado's poetry, and if anything it provided the foundation for Martin's and Mairena's thinking on otherness.

From Machado to Levinas

If there is one thing that the *PrCs* make clear it is to what extent Machado transcended Romantic inwardness and conceived the Other and 'lo real' as an indispensable part of his thinking on subjectivity. What he considered more generally as 'lo esencialmente otro', as we have seen, always called into question Romantic self-sufficiency, and it compelled the self to look beyond the solitude of the inner life and enter into a concrete social relationship with the world. This relationship defined the self, and in face-to-face encounters with the Other, it

brought about a collective awareness through dialogue of the human
condition. And at a time when Edmund Husserl was setting into
motion the phenomenological turn with his *Idea of Phenomenology* in
1907, Machado, with the idea of the Other's irreducibility, was slowly
giving form to some of the core epistemological propositions that
would characterize the larger shift towards a phenomenology of otherness in Europe in the 1930s. To better understand the relevance of his
work within this larger European framework, and to see how exactly he
connected with a transnational philosophical discussion on alterity
through some of the discoveries present in the *PrCs*, it suffices to
highlight a few points of convergence between his thinking and that of
Emmanuel Levinas, one of the foremost twentieth-century philosophers on the subject of ethical alterity.

Much like Machado, Levinas believed Western metaphysics had
somehow enclosed itself in the world of immanence. It had negated
the Other's 'realness' and limited ontology to the subject–object
paradigm. This skewed vision of difference had reduced otherness to
concepts of sameness, or the idea that the Other is really a self like me,
and thus conceives the world much as I do. To overcome this reduc-
tionism, Levinas wanted to insert philosophy into a distinctly ethical
sphere in which Being would be rethought as Being-for-the-other, a
shift that would bind the self in an ethical obligation to the Other.
What this meant was that the Other's difference – what he called 'the
absolutely other' – had to be acknowledged and safeguarded from
concepts of sameness. As Peperzak explains it, 'Levinas insists forcefully on the irreducible moments of heteronomy. Instead of seeing all
realities as unfolding or surrounding elements of one basic instance
called 'the Same' . . . the irreducibility of all Otherness must be
recognized' (p. 19). While Machado does not theorize the Other's
difference to the extent that Levinas does (the Other as existing in a
wholly different experiential world that is foreign to the self), he is also
very attentive in his concept of otherness to those 'irreducible
moments of heteronomy'. In Mairena's words, '¿cómo he de atreverme . . . a degradar a mi prójimo tan profunda y substancialmente
que le arrebate el ser en sí para convertirlo en mera representación, en
un puro fantasma mío?' (1971a: pp. 214–15). There is a constant
mindfulness, or 'conciencia', of acknowledging difference and awakening the self to '[una] intuición de *otredad*' as a way of safeguarding
otherness from sameness.

As the title of his book *Totality and Infinity: An Essay on Exteriority*
(1961) suggests, Levinas tackles the sameness/otherness dichotomy by

distinguishing between concepts of totality and infinity. Totality dominates Western metaphysics according to Levinas. With the atrocities of the Second World War fresh in his mind, he defines it as a tradition of philosophical thinking in which 'individuals are reduced to being bearers of force that commands them unbeknown to themselves . . . The meaning of individuals (invisible outside of this totality) is derived from the totality. The unicity of each present is incessantly sacrificed to a future appealed to bring forth its objective meaning' (p. 22). This totality is best represented as man's future desire for unity and ultimate objective meaning, and it urges him to forfeit the present for an indefinite historical 'completion' and broach difference within the teleological framework of sameness. Infinity, on the other hand, challenges this totalization in that it calls for a 'relation with being *beyond the totality* . . . it is a relationship with a surplus always exterior to the totality, as though the objective reality did not fill out the true measure of being' (p. 23). What is most important in this concept of infinity is man's relationship to the 'surplus' of meaning; that is, all that lies beyond totality and cannot be contained by it. What mediates this transition between totality and infinity, and 'where totality breaks up . . . is the gleam of exteriority or of transcendence in the face of the Other' (p. 24). The Other's presence for Levinas is concretized in the 'nudity' of the face, which brings about dialogue and makes us aware of what he called 'the radical heterogeneity of the other' (p. 36), a term that is reminiscent of Machado's own 'radical heterogeneidad del ser'. And both Machado and Levinas converge on this idea of heterogeneity as the cornerstone to the 'infinite' experience that is opened up with the Other's presence. Regarding this dialogue that comes with infinity, Levinas adds:

> Conversation, from the very fact that it maintains the distance between me and the Other, the radical separation asserted in transcendence which prevents the reconstitution of totality, cannot renounce the egoism of its existence; but the very fact of being in conversation consists in recognizing in the Other a *right* over this egoism, and hence in justifying oneself. (1969: p. 40)

What Machado termed 'el diálogo amoroso' involves a similar exercise of thinking beyond totality and transcending 'lo individual humano' to acknowledge this distance between self and Other in which dialogue is possible. In the *PrCs*, and in particular parts of his work, the concept of infinity reveals itself with the Other's presence as if it were an experiential surplus that is irreducible and unexplainable (for instance, the feeling of God in the self–Other relation). What is more, Levinas's words above bring to mind what Mairena tells us about his own approach to otherness: 'Yo os enseño – en fin –, o pretendo enseñaros el amor al prójimo y al distante, al semejante y al diferente y un amor que *exceda* un poco al que os profesáis a vosotros mismos, que pudiera ser insuficiente' (1986: p. 72). We arrive at the idea that the concept of self as a contained and independent locus of experience is called into question by the Other in dialogue, and for Levinas 'this calling into question of my spontaneity by the presence of the Other [is] ethics' (1969: p. 43). With this proposition, he intended to over-come the Other's reduction to sameness, since it is the ethical sphere of dialogue that precedes ontology and where the question of Being can be taken up. In the following excerpt from the 'Foreword' to *Humanism of the Other* (1972), Levinas alludes to the totality/infinity distinction and examines the irreducibility of this relation in dialogue. Not only is his philosophical language similar to that of Machado, but he also refers to the same collectivity that Machado knew as 'la fraternidad humana':

> Between the one that I am and the other for whom I answer gapes a bottomless difference, which is also the non-difference of responsibility, significance of signification, irreducible to any system whatsoever. Non-difference, which is the very proximity of one's fellow, by which is profiled a base of community between one and the other, unity of the human genre, owing to fraternity of men. (p. 6)

Where Machado's thinking on otherness perhaps comes closest to that of Levinas is the ethical dimension described above that Levinas simply called one's 'responsibility for others'. This responsibility con-nects on various levels with Machado's humanism in 'cainismo' and 'el diálogo amoroso', and it underscores most of Levinas's ethical philoso-phy. In 'On Intersubjectivity: Notes on Merleau-Ponty', Levinas sum-marized this responsibility for others as '[b]eginning with the face – in which the other is approached according to his or her ineradicable difference in ethical responsibility – sociality, as the human possibility of approaching the other, is signified – that is commanded' (1994: p. 102). Levinas is well aware that the self could refuse to answer this 'command' of the Other: 'one can do the opposite of what the face demands. The face is not a force. It is an authority. Authority is often without force' (Wright, p. 169). In Machado's poetry and thought, this refusal is where the question of ignorance, self-knowledge and 'awakening' to otherness comes into play: it is through the acknowledgement of the Other (the thirsting brother in the Cain and Abel tragedy, for example) that the ethical is aroused in the individual. This 'command' also had a divine dimension to it, and Machado and Levinas conceive of the divine as 'revealed' in the ethical responsibility that comes about with the self–Other relation. While there are clearly significant differences in their ideas of God, they discern the clearest evidence of His existence when the self accepts responsibility for the Other. For Machado, 'cuando reconozco que hay otro yo, que no soy yo mismo ni es obra mía, caigo en la cuenta de que Dios existe' (2001b: p. 427). As Levinas understood it, 'it is in the human face that . . . the trace of God is manifested, and the light of revelation inundates the universe' (1996: p. 95).

Levinas was writing of the Other after living the traumatic events of the Second World War in a French prisoner of war camp near Hanover, Germany. This experience drastically affected his philosophy, and his ethics derived from a different world view than that of Machado, which cannot be obviated. Yet, given the limited examples presented here, we can appreciate that their point of departure in understanding the Other – the subject–object paradigm of Western metaphysics – is indeed very similar. Machado connected with a larger European discussion of alterity in that he had intuited, like Levinas after him, the 'gaps' in thinking that had reduced the Other to distinct epistemic categories of sameness within contemporary philosophy. The *PrCs* demonstrate how conscious Machado truly was of the reductionist assumptions underlying philosophy's grand narratives in which difference was often simplified, treated with incomprehension or, worse yet, forced to conform to systems of knowledge. The point for Machado is that one needed to transcend 'totalizing' thinking and embrace the infinite inquiry between oneness and difference. From this perspective, the *PrCs* remain as relevant today to our understanding of the concept of Other as they were during Machado's lifetime.

Works Cited

Abellán, José Luis (1995). *El filósofo Antonio Machado*. Valencia: Pre-Textos.
— (1996). *Historia del pensamiento español (de Séneca a nuestros días)*. Madrid: Espasa-Calpe, S. A.
Adorno, Theodor W. (2001). *Negative Dialectics*, tr. Dennis Redmond. Frankfurt: Suhrkamp Verlag.
Aguirre, J. M. (1973). *Antonio Machado, poeta simbolista*. Madrid: Taurus.
Albornoz, Aurora de (1970). *Antonio Machado. Antología de su prosa*. Madrid: Cuadernos para el Diálogo, S. A.
— (1968). *La presencia de Miguel de Unamuno en Antonio Machado*. Madrid: Editorial Gredos.
— (1961). *La prehistoria de Antonio Machado*. Puerto Rico: Ediciones La Torre.
— (1994). 'Rubén Darío en Antonio Machado', in Paul Aubert (ed.), *Antonio Machado Hoy (1939–1989)*. Madrid: Casa de Velázquez, pp. 71–84.
Alonso, Dámaso (1962). *Cuatro poetas españoles: Garcilaso, Góngora, Maragall, Antonio Machado*. Madrid: Editorial Gredos.
Alvar, Manuel (1975). 'Antonio Machado y la lírica de tipo tradicional', in *Homenaje a Machado*. Málaga: Diputación Provincial de Málaga, pp. 151–70.
— (1976). *De Galdós a Miguel Ángel Asturias*. Madrid: Cátedra.
— (2001). 'Introducción', in *Poesías completas de Antonio Machado*. Madrid: Austral, pp. 9–69.
— (1989). *En torno a Antonio Machado*. Madrid: Ediciones Júcar.
Álvarez Junco, José (1995). 'Education and the Limits of Liberalism', in Graham, H. and Labayni, J. (eds), *Spanish Cultural Studies: An Introduction*. New York: Oxford University Press.
Andreu Rodrigo, Agustín (2004). *El cristianismo metafísico de Antonio Machado*. Valencia: Editorial Pre-Textos.
Aparicio, Antonio (1958). 'Antonio Machado, poeta andaluz'. *Revista Nacional de Cultura*, 133, 34–43.
Aranguren, José Luis (1949). 'Esperanza y desesperanza de Dios en la experiencia de la vida de Antonio Machado'. *Cuadernos Hispanoamericanos*, 11–12, 383–96.
Aristotle (1976). *The Nicomachean Ethics*, tr. J. A. K. Thomson. New York: Penguin.

Arrebola, Alfredo (1975). 'Poesía y cante', in *Homenaje a Machado*. Málaga: Diputación Provincial de Málaga, pp. 139–49.

Arrellano, Ignacio (1997). 'Notas sobre el refrán y la fórmula coloquial en la poesía burlesca de Quevedo'. *La Perinola*, 1, 15–37.

Aubert, Paul (1994). '"Gotas de sangre jacobina": Antonio Machado republicano'. In Paul Aubert (ed.), *Antonio Machado Hoy (1939–1989)*. Madrid: Casa de Velázquez, pp. 309–62.

Azaña, Manuel (1966). *Obras completas Vol. I*, Juan Marichal (ed.). (4 vols). México D.F.: Ediciones Oasis, S. A.

Baker, Armand F. (1985). *El pensamiento religioso y filosófico de Antonio Machado*. Sevilla: Ayuntamiento de Sevilla.

Barnstone, Willis (1993). *Six Masters of the Spanish Sonnet: Essays and Translations*. Carbondale: Southern Illinois University Press.

Barjau, Eustaquio (1975). 'Antonio Machado: Idealismo – Solipsismo – "Salto al otro" (Entre la poesía y la filosofía)'. In *Antonio Machado: Teoría y práctica del Apócrifo*. Barcelona: Ariel.

Baudelaire, Charles (1966). *Oeuvres Complètes Vol. I*. (3 vols) Paris: Le Club Français du Livre.

Bécquer, Gustavo Adolfo (1993). *Rimas*, José Carlos de Torres (ed.). Madrid: Castalia.

Belaunde Moreyra, Antonio (2005). *Alcance filosófico en César Vallejo y Antonio Machado*. Lima: Instituto de Investigación para la Paz, Cultura e Integración de América Latina.

Benot, Eduardo (1888). *Breves apuntes sobre los casos y las oraciones preparatorias para el estudio de las lenguas*. Madrid: Librería de la Viuda de Hernando y Compañía.

— (1889). *En el umbral de la ciencia*. Madrid: Librería de la Viuda de Hernando y Compañía.

— (1901). 'Prólogo'. In Ramón León, *Cervantes y su época*. Jérez de la Frontera: Litografía jerezana.

Benson, Hugh (2000). *Socratic Wisdom: The Model of Knowledge in Plato's Early Dialogues*. New York: Oxford University Press.

Bernheimer, Charles (2002). *Decadent Subjects: The Idea of Decadence in Art, Literature, Philosophy, and Culture of the Fin de Siècle in Europe*. Baltimore: The Johns Hopkins University Press.

Betz, Hans Dieter (1998). *Antike und Christentum*. Tübingen: Mohr Siebeck.

Blanchot, Maurice (1993). *The Infinite Conversation*. Minneapolis: University of Minnesota Press.

Bloom, Harold (1969). *Shelley's Mythmaking*. Cornell: Cornell University Press.

Bordoli, Domingo L. (1965). *Rubén Darío. Sus mejores Poemas*. Montevideo: Ediciones de la Banda Oriental.

Boyd, Carolyn P. (1997). *Historia Patria: Politics, History, and National Identity in Spain, 1875–1975*. Princeton: Princeton University Press.

Blanch, Juan Lope (2001). 'Introducción'. In Eduardo Benot, *Breves apuntes sobre los casos y las oraciones*. México: Universidad Nacional Autónoma de México.

Brotherston, Gordon (1964). 'Antonio Machado y Álvarez and Positivism'. *Bulletin of Hispanic Studies*, XLI, 223–9.

— (1968). *Manuel Machado: A Revaluation.* London: Cambridge University Press.

Bruner, Frederick Dale (2004). *Matthew: A Commentary.* Grand Rapids: Eerdmans Publishing.

Buber, Martin (2002). *The Martin Buber Reader: Essential Writings*, Asher D. Biemann (ed.). New York: Palgrave Macmillan.

Bürger, Peter (1984). *Theory of the Avant Garde.* Minneapolis: University of Minnesota Press.

Callahan, William James (2000). *The Catholic Church in Spain, 1875–1998.* Washington D. C.: Catholic University of America Press.

Campoamor, Ramón de (1902). *Obras completas Vol. III.* (8 vols) Madrid: González Rojas.

Cardwell, Richard (1990). 'Antonio Machado, la institución y el idealismo finisecular'. in *Antonio Machado Hoy.* (4 vols) Sevilla: Ediciones Alfar, I, pp. 381–401.

Carnero, Guillermo (1978). *Los orígenes del romanticismo reaccionario español: El matrimonio Böhl de Faber.* Valencia: Universidad de Valencia.

Carr, Raymond (1982). *Spain 1808–1975.* Oxford: Clarendon Press.

Carter, Warren (2005). *Matthew and the Margins: A Socio-political and Religious Reading.* London: Continuum International Publishing Group.

Carvalho-Neto, Paulo de (1975). *La influencia del folklore en Antonio Machado.* Madrid: Ediciones Demófilo.

Castro, Isabel de (1989). 'Antonio Machado y Enrique Paradas'. In *Cincuentenario de la muerte de Antonio Machado. A Distancia.* Madrid: UNED.

Cerezo Galán, Pedro (1975). *Palabra en el tiempo: poesía y filosofía en Antonio Machado.* Madrid: Gredos.

— (1994). 'Lo apócrifo machadiano: "un ensayo de esfuerzos fragmentarios"'. In Paul Aubert (ed.), *Antonio Machado Hoy (1939–1989).* Madrid: Casa de Velázquez, pp. 187–207.

Chicharro, Dámaso and Miguel Cruz Giráldez (1993). 'Demófilo en el teatro de los Machado'. In *La Andalucía de Demófilo.* Madrid: Sociedad Editorial Electa, S. A., pp. 74–81

Chomsky, Noam (2006). *Language and Mind.* Cambridge: Cambridge University Press.

Cicero, Marcus Tullius (2005). *The Academic Questions: Treatise De Finibus and Tusculan Disputations*, tr. Charles Duke Yonge. New York: Cosimo.

Cobos, Pablo A. (1971). *El pensamiento de Antonio Machado en Juan de Mairena.* Madrid: Ínsula.

Coplestone, Frederick Charles (1977). *History of Philosophy: Maine de Biran to Sartre, Vol. 7.* (9 vols) New York: Bantam Doubleday.

Cossío, José María de (1960). *Cincuenta años de poesía española I.* (2 vols) Madrid: Espasa-Calpe, S. A.

Costa, Joaquín (1964). *Ideario de Joaquín Costa*, José García Mercadel (ed.). Madrid: Aguado.

— (1998). *Oligarquía y caciquismo*, introduction by José Várela Ortega. Madrid: Biblioteca Nueva.

— (1888). *Introducción á un tratado de política sacado textualmente de los refraneros, romanceros y gestas de la península.* Madrid: Librería de Fernando Fé.

Cruz Giráldez, Miguel (1975–6). 'Elementos lírico-populares en el teatro machadiano'. *Cuadernos Hispanoamericanos*, 304–7, 1083–94.

Darío, Rubén (1901). *Prosas profanas.* Paris: C. Bouret.

Del Vecchio, Eugene (1989). 'Schlegelian Philosophical and Artistic Concept of Irony in Bécquer'. *Hispania*, 72 , 220–6.

De Man, Paul (1996). *Aesthetic Ideology,* ed. Andrezj Warminski. Minneapolis: University of Minnesota Press.

Díez-Canedo, Enrique (1924). 'Antonio Machado, poeta japonés'. *El Sol,* 142, 6.

Domènech, Jordi (1996). 'Sobre la publicación de *Campos de Castilla'. Ínsula,* 594, 3–7.

Eco, Umberto (1989). *The Open Work.* Cambridge: Harvard University Press.

Esdaile, Charles J (2000). *Spain in the Liberal Age: From Constitution to Civil War, 1808–1939.* Indianapolis: Wiley-Blackwell.

Fernández-Ferrer, Antonio (1982). *Campos de Castilla. Antonio Machado.* Barcelona: Guías Laia de Literatura.

Flitter, Derek (1992). *Spanish Romantic Literary Theory and Criticism.* Cambridge: Cambridge University Press.

Frank, Manfred (2004). *The Philosophical Foundations of Early German Romanticism,* tr. Elizabeth Millan-Zaibert. Albany: SUNY Press.

Friedrich von Hardenberg 'Novalis', Georg Philipp (2003). *Fichte Studies,* ed. Jane Kneller. Cambridge: Cambridge University Press.

Fuente Ballesteros, Ricardo de la (1990). 'El haiku en Antonio Machado'. In *Antonio Machado Hoy.* (4 vols) Sevilla: Ediciones Alfar, II, pp. 393–405.

Ganivet, Ángel (1981). *Idearium español. El porvenir de España.* Madrid: Espasa-Calpe S. A.

García Bacca, Juan David (1975). 'Antonio Machado ¿Poeta o filósofo?' *Cuadernos para el diálogo,* XLIX, 350–7.

— (1984). *Invitación a filosofar según espíritu y letra de Antonio Machado.* Barcelona: Anthropos.

Gasché, Rodolphe (1991). 'Foreword'. In *Friederich Schlegel. Philosophical Fragments.* Minneapolis: University of Minnesota Press.

Gibson, Ian (2006). *Antonio Machado. Ligero de Equipaje.* Madrid: Santillana Ediciones.

Giménez Caballero, Ernesto (1928). 'A Occidente por Oriente. Valor proverbial de Antonio Machado'. *La Gaceta Literaria,* mayo 15, 1–2.

Giner de los Ríos, Francisco (1969). *Ensayos.* Madrid: Alianza Editorial.

— (1899). *Estudios y fragmentos sobre la teoría de la persona social.* Madrid: Imprenta de Federico Rojas.

— (1876). *Estudios de literatura y arte.* Madrid: Librería Victoriano Suárez.

Gómez Molleda, Dolores (1977). *Guerra de ideas y lucha social en Machado.* Madrid: Narcea.

Gómez-Pablos, Jacinta Cremades (2002). 'La imagen de la fuente de Verlaine en Antonio Machado'. In *Actas del Congreso Internacional sobre Antonio Machado. Vida y Obra (Segovia, 6, 7 y 8 de abril de 2000).* Segovia: Junta de Castilla y León, pp. 193–200.

González, Ángel (1982). *Aproximaciones a Antonio Machado.* México D. F.: UNAM.

González-Ruiz, José María (1975). *La teología de Antonio Machado*. Madrid: Editorial Fontanella.

Guadalajara Solera, Simón (1984). *El compromiso en Antonio Machado (a la ética por la estética)*. Madrid: Emiliano Escolar.

Guignon, Charles B. (2004). *On Being Authentic*. New York/London: Routledge.

Gullón, Ricardo (1958). *El último Juan Ramón Jiménez*. Madrid: Taurus.

— (1970). *Una poética para Antonio Machado*. Madrid: Gredos.

— (1994). 'Antonio Machado modernista'. In Paul Aubert (ed.), *Antonio Machado Hoy (1939–1989)*. Madrid: Casa de Velázquez, pp. 23–69.

Gurría García, Pedro (2002). *Tener un tío en América. La emigración riojana a ultramar (1880–1936)*. Logroño: Gobierno de la Rioja, Instituto de Estudios Riojanos.

Gutiérrez-Girardot, Rafael (1989). *Machado: reflexión y poesía*. Bogotá: Tercer Mundo Editores.

— (1969). *Poesía y prosa de Antonio Machado*. Madrid: Guadarrama.

Habermas, Jürgen (1990). 'Modernity's Consciousness of Time and Its Need for Self-Reassurance'. In *The Philosophical Discourse of Modernity*, tr. Frederic G. Lawrence. Cambridge, Mass.: MIT Press, pp. 3–22.

Hadot, Pierre (1995). *Philosophy as a Way of Life: Spiritual Exercises from Socrates to Foucault*, ed. Arnold I. Davidson. New York: Blackwell Publishing.

Hasker, William (1983). *Metaphysics: Constructing a World View*. Downers Grove: Inter Varsity Press.

Hecht, Paul (1979). 'La copla flamenca en la poesía de Antonio Machado y Federico García Lorca'. Unpublished Ph.D. dissertation, CUNY.

Hegel, Georg Wilhelm Friedrich (1995). *Lectures on the History of Philosophy: Greek Philosophy to Plato. Volume I*, tr. E. S. Haldane. (3 vols) Lincoln: University of Nebraska Press.

— (1998). *The Hegel Reader*, Stephen Houlgate (ed.). Oxford: Blackwell Publishing.

Helmstadter, Richard (1997). *Freedom and Religion in the Nineteenth Century*. Stanford: Stanford University Press.

Henderson, Andrea K. (2006). *Romantic Identities – Varieties of Subjectivity 1774–1830*. Cambridge: Cambridge University Press.

Hierro, José (1971). 'Prólogo'. In *Antonio Machado: Antología poética*. Barcelona: Ediciones Marte, p. xx.

Holguín, Sandie Eleanor (2002). *Creating Spaniards: Culture and National Identity in Republican Spain*. Madison: University of Wisconsin Press.

Iglesia, José Luis (1989). *Antonio Machado y la filosofía*. Madrid: Orígenes.

Jiménez Martos, Luis (1976). *Informe sobre poesía española (siglo XX)*. Madrid: Magisterio.

Jrade, Cathy L. (1998). *Modernismo, Modernity and the Development of Spanish America*. Austin: University of Texas Press.

Jutglar, Antoni (1963). *La era industrial de España*. Barcelona: Ediciones Nova Terra.

Kant, Immanuel (2000). *Critique of Pure Reason*, tr. and ed. Paul Guyer and Allen W. Wood. Cambridge: Cambridge University Press.

Karagiorgos, Panos (1999). *Greek and English Proverbs*. Corfu: Ionian University.

Khan, Charles H. (1981). *The Art and Thought of Heraclitus.* Cambridge: Cambridge University Press.
Kirkpatrick, Gwen (1989). *The Dissonant Legacy of Modernismo: Lugones, Herrera y Reissig, and the Voices of Modern Spanish American Poetry.* Berkeley: University of California Press.
Klein, Melanie (2003). *Envy and Gratitude: A Study of Unconscious Sources.* New York: Routledge.
Kofman, Sarah (1993). *Nietzsche and Metaphor,* tr. Duncan Large. Stanford: Stanford University Press.
Krause, Karl Christian Friedrich (1871). *Ideal de la humanidad para la vida,* tr. Julián Sanz del Río. Madrid: Martínez García.
Lacoue-Labarthe, Phillipe and Jean-Luc Nancy (1978). *The Literary Absolute: The Theory of Literature in German Romanticism,* tr. Philip Barnard and Cheryl Lester. Albany: State University of New York Press.
Laín Entralgo, Pedro (1963). *La generación del noventa y ocho.* Madrid: Espasa-Calpe S. A.
Levinas, Emmanuel (1969). *Totality and Infinity: An Essay on Exteriority,* tr. Alphonso Lingis. Pittsburgh: Duquesne University Press.
— (1994). *Outside the Subject,* tr. Michael B. Smith. Stanford: Stanford University Press.
— (2003). *Humanism of the Other,* tr. Nidra Poller. Champaign: University of Illinois Press.
— (1996). *Proper Names,* tr. Michael B. Smith. Stanford: Stanford University Press.
Levinson, Marjorie (1986). *The Romantic Fragment Poem. A Critique of Form.* Chapel Hill: University of North Carolina Press.
López Álvarez, Juan (1996). *El krausismo en los escritos de Antonio Machado y Álvarez, 'Demófilo'.* Cádiz: Universidad de Cádiz.
— (1968). 'Antonio Machado: ética y poética'. *Ínsula,* 23, 256, 1–12.
López-Morillas, Juan (1972). *Hacia el 98: Literatura, sociedad, ideología.* Barcelona: Ariel.
— (1971). 'Giner: De la setembrina al desastre'. In *Actas del Cuarto Congreso Internacional de Hispanistas,* I, pp. 37–55.
Lukács, Georg (1974). *Soul and Form.* Cambridge, Mass.: MIT Press.
Lyotard, Jean-François (1992). *The Lyotard Reader,* ed. Andrew Benjamin. Oxford: Blackwell Publishers.
Machado y Álvarez, Antonio (1947). *Cantes flamencos.* Buenos Aires: Colección Austral.
— (1887). 'Terminología del Folk-Lore'. In *Boletín de la Institución Libre de Enseñanza,* XI, pp. 280–3.
— (1884a). 'Introducción'. *Biblioteca de las Tradiciones Populares.* Madrid: Librería deFernando Fe.
— (1884b). *Estudios sobre literatura popular.* Madrid: Librería de Fernando Fe.
— (1886). 'El Folk-Lore del niño. Juegos de niños de ambos sexos'. *Revista de España,* CXI, 260–81.
Machado y Ruiz, Antonio (1953). *Abel Martín. Cancionero apócrifo de Juan de Mairena. Prosas Varias.* Buenos Aires: Editorial Losada, S. A.
— (1971a). *Juan de Mairena. Sentencias, donaires, apuntes y recuerdos de un profesor apócrifo. 1936,* ed. José María Valverde. Madrid: Clásicos Castalia.

— (1986). *Juan de Mairena II (1936–1938)*, ed. Antonio Fernández Ferrer. Madrid: Cátedra.

— (1971b). *Los complementarios*. Madrid: Taurus Ediciones, S. A.

— (2001a). *Poesías completas*, ed. Manuel Alvar. Madrid: Espasa Calpe S. A.

— (2001b). *Prosas dispersas*, ed. Jordi Domènech. Madrid: Páginas de Espuma.

Machado, José (1977). *Últimas soledades del poeta Antonio Machado. Recuerdos de su hermano José*. Madrid: Forma Ediciones.

Machado, Manuel (1942). *Poesía*. Madrid: Editora Nacional.

Machado, Antonio and Manuel Machado (2005). *Colección Unicaja. Manuscritos de los Hermanos Machado*. (10 vols) tr. and ed. Rafael Alarcón Sierra, Pablo del Barco and Antonio Rodríguez Almodóvar. Málaga: Servicio de Publicaciones de Unicaja.

Macrí, Oreste (1989). *Antonio Machado – Poesías completas I*. (4 vols) Madrid: Espasa Calpe, S. A.

Mañara, Miguel de (1878). *Discurso de la verdad dedicado a la imperial majestad de Dios*. Madrid: Imprenta de Alejandro Gómez Fuentenebro.

Marichal, Juan (1990). *El intelectual y la política española (1898–1936)*. Madrid: Publicaciones de la Residencia de Estudiantes.

Martínez Ruiz, José (1980). *Política y literatura*. Madrid: Alianza.

Marx, Karl (1997). *Writings of the Young Marx on Philosophy and Society*, tr. Loyd David Easton and Kurt H. Guddat. Indianapolis: Hackett Publishing.

McGann, Jerome (1985). *The Romantic Ideology: A Critical Investigation*. Chicago: University of Chicago Press.

Melero Ruiz, Domingo (1990). 'Proverbios y cantares de Antonio Machado'. In *Antonio Machado Hoy*. (4 vols) Sevilla: Ediciones Alfar, IV, 325–41.

Mesa, Joaquín (1986). 'Arte de hablar y pragmática: Notas sobre el pensamiento lingüístico de Eduardo Benot (1822–1907)', in Antonio Quilis, Hans-Josef Niederehe and E. F. K. Koerner, *The History of Linguistics in Spain*. Amsterdam/Philadelphia: John Benjamins, pp. 341–66.

Mizrahi, Irene (1994). 'El fragmento en Bécquer'. *El Gnomo – Boletín de Estudios Becquerianos*, 3, 49–63.

— (1998). *La poética dialógica de Bécquer*. Amsterdam: Rodopi.

Mumford, Lewis (1938). *The Culture of Cities*. New York, Harcourt.

Murillo Zamora, Roberto (1981). *Antonio Machado (ensayo sobre su pensamiento filosófico)*. San José: Editorial Universidad Estatal a Distancia.

Nietzsche, Friedrich (1974). *The Gay Science*. New York: Vintage Books.

— (1997). *Beyond Good and Evil*. New York: Dover Publications.

Nora, Eugenio de (1949). 'Machado ante el futuro de la poesía lírica'. *Cuadernos Hispanoamericanos*, 11–12, 583–92.

Pageard, Robert (1990). *Bécquer, leyenda y realidad*. Madrid: Espasa-Calpe.

Pascal, Blaise (2004). *Pensées*, tr. W. F. Trotter. Whitefish: Kessinger Publishing.

Payne, Stanley (1984). *Spanish Catholicism: An Historical Overview*. Madison: University of Wisconsin Press.

Pedro Díaz, José (1964). *G. A. Bécquer. Vida y poesía*. Madrid: Editorial Gredos.

Peperzack, Adrian Theodor (1993). *To the Other: An Introduction to the Philosophy of Emmanuel Levinas*. Lafayette: Purdue University Press.

Pérez Ferrero, Miguel (1973). *Vida de Antonio Machado y Manuel*. Madrid: Espasa-Calpe.

Pérez Gago, Santiago (1984). *Razón, 'sueño' y realidad en Antonio Machado.* Salamanca: Ediciones Universidad de Salamanca.

Pineda Novo, Daniel (1991). *Antonio Machado y Álvarez 'Demófilo' – Vida y obra del primer flamencólogo español.* Madrid: Editorial Cinterco.

Pippin, Robert B. (2005). *The Persistence of Subjectivity – On the Kantian Aftermath.* Cambridge: Cambridge University Press.

Plato (1961). *Great Dialogues of Plato,* tr. W. H. D. Rouse. New York: New American Library.

— (1971). *Meno,* tr. W. K. C. Guthrie. New York: Harper and Row.

— (2003). *Apology,* tr. Hugh Tredennick and Harold Tarrant. London: Penguin Classics.

— (2008). *Symposium,* tr. M. C. Howatson. Cambridge: Cambridge University Press.

Pont, Jaume (1989). 'La juventud como tema en los escritos de guerra de Antonio Machado'. In *Antonio Machado: El poeta y su doble.* Barcelona: Edicions Universitat Barcelona, pp. 195–206.

Rabassó, Francisco J. (1992). 'Antonio Machado entre la tradición del haiku y el vitalismo lírico de su poesía breve', in Antonia Vilanova (ed.), *Actas del X Congreso de la Asociación Internacional de Hispanistas (1989),* Barcelona: PPU, pp. 201–8.

Ribbans, Geoffrey (1975). 'Prólogo'. *Antonio Machado. Soledades. Galerías. Otros Poemas.* Barcelona: Labor.

— (1989). 'Introduction'. In Antonio Machado, *Campos de Castilla (1907–1917).* Madrid: Cátedra.

— (1957). 'Unamuno and Antonio Machado'. *Bulletin of Hispanic Studies,* XXXIV, 10–28.

— (1958). 'Unamuno and the Younger Writers in 1904'. *Bulletin of Hispanic Studies,* XXXV, 83–100.

Rosales Juega, Elisa (1998). *Comportamiento ético de la poesía de Antonio Machado.* Delaware: Juan de la Cuesta.

Rotker, Susan (2000). *The American Chronicles of José Martí. Journalism and Modernity in Spanish America,* tr. Jennifer French and Katherine Semler. Hanover: University Press of New England.

Sánchez Barbudo, A. (1969). 'El Dios de Antonio Machado'. In *Homenaje a Antonio Machado.* Montevideo: Fundación de Cultura Universitaria, pp. 144–54.

— (1967). *Los poemas de Antonio Machado. Los temas. El sentimiento y la expresión.* Barcelona: Editorial Lumen.

— (1968). *Estudios sobre Galdós, Unamuno y Machado.* Madrid: Ediciones Guadarrama.

— (1974). *Miguel de Unamuno.* Madrid: Taurus.

Sánchez Romeralo, Antonio (1995). '"Folklore" y "Creación popular" en Antonio Machado y Juan Ramón Jiménez'. In *Oral Tradition and Hispanic Literature.* New York: Garland, pp. 598–620.

Sandywell, Barry (1996). *Presocratic Reflexivity: The Construction of Philosophical Discourse c. 600–450BC.* New York/London: Routledge.

Schlegel, Friedrich (1991). *Philosophical Fragments,* tr. Peter Firchow. Minneapolis: University of Minnesota Press.

— (1968). *Dialogue on Poetry and Literary Aphorisms*, tr. Ernst Behler and Roman Struc. University Park and London: Pennsylvania State University.

Schlegel, August W. (2007). *Lectures on Dramatic Art and Literature*, tr. John Black. Whitefish: Kessinger Publishing.

Seeskin, Kenneth (1987). *Dialogue and Discovery: A Study in Socratic Method*. Albany: SUNY Press.

Serrano, Gloria Pérez (1984). *Pedagogía social, educación social*. Madrid: Narcea Ediciones.

Serrano Poncela, Segundo (1962). *Del Romancero a Machado*. Caracas: Universidad Central de Venezuela.

Sesé, Bernard (1980). *El hombre. El poeta. El pensador*. Madrid: Gredos.

Sinclair, Alison (2001). *Uncovering the Mind: Unamuno, the Unknown, and the Vicissitudes of Self*. Manchester: Manchester University Press.

Siskin, Clifford (1988). *The Historicity of Romantic Discourse*. Oxford: Oxford University Press.

Sobejano, Gonzalo (1967). *Nietzsche en España*. Madrid: Gredos.

— (1976). 'La verdad en la poesía de Antonio Machado: de la rima al Proverbio'. *Journal of Spanish Studies: Twentieth Century*, 4, 47–73.

Soldevilla, Fernando (1908). *El año político – 1907*. Madrid: Imprenta de Ricardo Rojas.

Stevens, Shelley (1986). *Rosalía de Castro and the Galician Revival*. Suffolk: Boydell & Brewer.

Such, Francisco (1982). *Lectura ética de Antonio Machado*. Murcia: Editora Regional de Murcia.

Tatarkiewicz, Wladyslaw (1973). *Nineteenth-Century Philosophy*. Belmont: Wadsworth Publishing.

Tillich, Paul (1975). *Systematic Theology: Existence and the Christ*. (2 vols) Chicago: University of Chicago Press.

Tortella, Gabriel (1994). *El desarrollo de la España contemporánea. Historia económica de los siglos XIX y XX*. Madrid: Alianza Editorial.

— (1995). 'Patterns of economic retardation and recovery in south-western Europe in the nineteenth and twentieth centuries'. In Pablo Martín-Aceña and James Simpson (eds) *The Economic Development of Spain since 1870*. Vermont: Edward Elgar Publishing, pp. 3–23.

Tuñón de Lara, Manuel (1967). *Antonio Machado, poeta del pueblo*. Madrid: Taurus.

Turk, H. C. (1959). *German Romanticism in Gustavo Adolfo Bécquer's Short Stories*. Lawrence: The Allen Press.

Unamuno, Miguel de (1996). *En torno al casticismo*. Madrid: Editorial Biblioteca Nueva.

— (1995). *Niebla*, ed. Armando F. Zubizarreta. Madrid: Clásicos Castalia.

— (1971). *Obras completas, Vol IX*. Madrid: Escelicer.

— (1970). *Diario íntimo*. Madrid: Alianza.

— (1968). *Mi religión y otros ensayos breves*. Madrid: Espasa-Calpe.

— (1967). *Del sentimiento trágico de la vida*. Madrid: Espasa-Calpe.

— (1951). 'Arte y cosmopolitismo'. *Ensayos II*. Madrid: Aguilar, pp. 1187–95.

Urbano, Manuel (1982). *El cante jondo en Antonio Machado*. Córdoba: Ediciones Demófilo.

Urrutia, Jorge (2002). 'El inicio de *Soledades*. Una lección de simbolismo'. In *Actas del Congreso Internacional sobre Antonio Machado. Vida y Obra (Segovia, 6, 7 y 8 de abril de 2000)*. Segovia: Junta de Castilla y León, pp. 109–29.

Vázquez Medel, Manuel and Ángel Costa Medel (1990). '"Demófilo", Antonio Machado y la poesía popular'. In *Antonio Machado Hoy*. (4 vols) Sevilla: Alfar, I, 151–60.

Vicens Vives, Jaime (1965). *Manual de historia económica de España*. Barcelona: Editorial Vicens Vives.

Vilanova, Antonio (1989). 'La metafísica poética de Antonio Machado'. In *Antonio Machado: Intervenciones del Simposium celebrado en la Universidad de Barcelona los días 14, 15 y 16 de marzo de 1989*. Edicions Universitat de Barcelona, pp. 61–99.

Villacañas Berlanga, José Luis (2006). *Kant en España: El neokantismo en el siglo XIX*. Madrid: Verbum.

Wiedemann, Emilio García (1994). *Concordancias y frecuencias en el léxico poético de los 'Proverbios y cantares' de Antonio Machado*. Granada: Universidad de Granada.

— (2001). 'Bohemia y folklore en Antonio Machado'. In *Andalucía y la bohemia literaria*, Manuel Galeote López (ed.), Málaga: Ediciones Arguval, pp. 173–240.

— (1990). 'Los Proverbios y cantares de Antonio Machado'. In *Antonio Machado Hoy*. (4 vols) Madrid: Ediciones Alfar, IV, pp. 299–313.

Woolf, Stuart Joseph (1996). *Nationalism in Europe, 1815 to the present*. New York/London: Routledge.

Wood, Allen W. (2005). *Kant*. Oxford: Blackwell Publishing.

Wright, Tamara, Peter Hughes and Alison Ainely (1988). 'The Paradox of Morality: An Interview with Emmanuel Levinas'. In Robert Bernasconi and David C. Wood (eds), *The Provocation of Levinas: Rethinking the Other*. New York/London: Routledge, pp. 168–81.

Zavala, Iris M. (1989). *Rubén Darío bajo el signo del cisne*. Rio Piedras: Universidad de Puerto Rico.

Notes

Introduction: Beyond the Lyrical and Proverbial: Antonio Machado's Poetic Thinking

[1]   The first 'Proverbios y cantares' appeared in *La Lectura: Revista de ciencias y de arte* in February (no. 98) and May (no. 101) 1909. The February publication includes poems ii to xi of the 'Proverbios y cantares' in *CC* (my numbering of poems derives from the 1936 edition of *Poesías completas*). The poems published in May include i and xii to xx of *CC* (under the subtitle *Apuntes*, Machado also included the poem 'Amanecer de otoño' and 'Pascua de resurrección'). These initial twenty poems of 1909 plus an additional eight new poems (xxi to xxvi, and li and lii) appeared in the first edition of *Campos de Castilla* in 1912. In August 1913, eighteen more poems were published in *La Lectura* (no. 149) under the title 'Cantares, proverbios, sátiras y epigramas'. This publication is divided in two sections: the first section includes poems numbered i to xv – of these only xlii, xliii, xliv, xlv, xlvi, xlvii, and xlix (which is divided into two poems in *La Lectura*) appear in *CC*; in the second section that appears under the subtitle 'Sátiras y epigramas', Machado published three poems numbered I, II, and III corresponding to xlviii, l, and 'El mañana efímero' respectively of *CC*. Under the title 'Apuntes, parábolas, proverbios y cantares', nine more poems appeared in *La Lectura* in 1916 (the poems appeared without numbering, and the only one that was included in the 'Proverbios y cantares' of *CC* is xxviii; the remainder include CXXVII 'Otro viaje', CXXXVII 'Parábolas' poems I and III, as well as the poems 'Si hablo suena', 'Si me tengo que morir', '¿Qué es amor?, me preguntaba' and 'Pensar el mundo es como hacerlo nuevo' that were not included in *Poesías completas*). In January 1917, Machado used the original title 'Proverbios y cantares' to publish ten more poems without numbering in *Lucidarium* (nos 2 and 3) that included from *SGOP* poem LX, and from *CC* poems xxvii, xxx (divided into two poems: verses 1–3, and 4–6), xxxi, xxxii, xxxvi, cxxxvii (this poem includes 'Parábolas' VII and VIII, the latter divided into two poems consisting of verses 8–13 and 14–19). By the time the 1917 edition of *Campos de Castilla* was published in *Poesías Completas*, the section had expanded to fifty-three poems. Also in 1917, Machado

published *Páginas escogidas* that included fourteen poems numbered i to
xiv: ii, iii, xii, xiii, xxi, xxviii, xli, xlii, xliv, xlvi, li, poem II of *SGOP*'s
'Consejos' ('Moneda que está en la mano'), CXXXVII 'Profesión de fe'
and CXXXVIII 'Mi bufón'. In the journal *España* (no. 360) on 10 March
1923, Machado published fifteen poems numbered I to XV under the title
'Proverbios y cantares' that included the poems lviii–lxii, lxix, lxx, lxxiii,
lxxi, lxxii, lxiii, lxxiv and lxxv of *NC*. Also in *España* (no. 363) on 31 March
1923, he published fourteen poems numbered I to XIV that included the
poems xliv, xlvi, xlviii, xlvii, xlix, l, li, lii, lv, and lvi of *NC*. In *Revista de
Occidente* (no. III), he published twenty-six more poems in September
1923 numbered I to XXVI. Those poems that were included in *NC* are i, ii,
vi–xiii, xviii, xxviii, xxix, xxxi, xxxiv, xxxv, xxxvi, lxvi, lxxvi, and lxxxi. In
1924, the 'Proverbios y cantares' in *NC* consisted of one hundred and
three poems. Finally, in the second edition of *Poesías completas* published in
1928, Machado edited the section and deleted four poems (xliv, lvii, lxxxv
and lxxxvi). His interest in the 'Proverbios y cantares' continued in Juan
de Mairena's writings, where he references and alludes to them often. For
more detailed information on the various alterations in numbering of the
'Proverbios y cantares', see Emilio J. García Wiedemann's excellent introductory note in his book *Concordancias y frecuencias en el léxico poético de los
'Proverbios y cantares' de Antonio Machado* (Granada, 1994). Also by
Wiedemann, *Para una edición crítica de los Proverbios y cantares de Antonio
Machado* (Granada, 1990).

2   All the 'Proverbios y cantares' in *Campos de Castilla* and *Nuevas canciones*
numbered with lower-case Roman numerals are the definitive versions
published in his collected works (as per Manuel Alvar's *Antonio Machado –
Poesías completas*, Madrid, 2001). I have used lower-case Roman numerals
for this purpose to eliminate the potential confusion resulting from the
various numbers and numerals Machado used for the 'Proverbios y
cantares' that he published with edits and variations over the years.

3   Echo clarifies further that 'the comprehension of the original artifact is
always modified by [one's] particular and individual perspective. In fact,
the form of the work of art gains its aesthetic validity precisely in propor-
tion to the number of different perspectives from which it can be viewed
and understood. These give it a wealth of different resonances and echoes
without impairing its original essence' (p. 3).

4   J. M. Aguirre, *Antonio Machado, poeta simbolista* (Madrid, 1973), p. 183;
Giménez Caballero, 'A Occidente por Oriente: Valor proverbial de
Antonio Machado', *La Gaceta Literaria*, 36 (1928), 1–2; Francisco Javier
Rabassó, 'Antonio Machado entre la tradición del haiku y el vitalismo
lírico de su poesía breve', in *X Congreso AIH – Actas* (1989), 201–8; Ricardo
de la Fuente Ballesteros, 'El Haiku en Antonio Machado', in *Antonio
Machado Hoy*, 4 vols, II, 393–405. Fuente Ballesteros remarks on how the
Guatemalan poet and writer Enrique Gómez Carrillo may have sparked
Machado's curiosity for haikus during his visits to Paris in 1899 and 1902.
In a short article titled 'Antonio Machado, poeta japonés' in *El Sol*, 142
(1924), 6, Díez-Canedo was the first to suggest that the haiku's syllabic
structure as well as its impressionistic style could have influenced
Machado's *cantares* in *NC*. Díez-Canedo references a poem from 'Hacia la

tierra baja' ('A una japonesa / le dijo Sokán [. . .]') of *NC* to comment on the poet's Far East influences and their possible influence on his poetry.

5   See Eugenio de Nora's 'Machado ante el futuro de la poesía lírica', *Cuadernos Hispanoamericanos*, Sept–Dec, 11–12 (1949), 59. Sánchez Barbudo also adds to this argument: 'Es evidente, sin embargo, que al llegar a *Nuevas canciones* se advierte una decadencia. O más bien podría decirse que sigue la decadencia, ya que ésta es bien visible al final de *Campos de Castilla*' (1968: p. 318).

6   'Los Proverbios y cantares de Antonio Machado', *Antonio Machado Hoy*, 4 vols, IV (Madrid, 1990), pp. 305–24. The Girardot reference derives from *Machado: reflexión y poesía* (Bogotá, 1989), p. 79.

7   See Antonio Aparicio, 'Antonio Machado, poeta andaluz' in *Revista Nacional de Cultura*, 133 (1958); Alfredo Arrebola, 'Poesía y cante', *Homenaje a Machado* (Málaga, 1975); Paulo de Carvalho-Neto, *La influencia del folklore en Antonio Machado* (Madrid, 1975); Paul Hecht, *La copla flamenca en la poesía de Antonio Machado y Federico García Lorca* (unpublished Ph.D. thesis, City University of New York, New York, 1979); Manuel Alvar, 'Antonio Machado y la lírica de tipo tradicional', *Homenaje a Machado* (Málaga, 1975); also by Manuel Alvar, 'Introducción', *Poesías completas de Antonio Machado* (Madrid, 2001), and *En torno a Antonio Machado* (Madrid, 1989); Manuel Urbano, *El cante hondo en Antonio Machado* (Córdoba, 1982); Sánchez Romeralo, 'Folklore y creación popular en Antonio Machado y Juan Ramón Jiménez', *Oral Tradition and Hispanic Literature* (New York, 1995).

8   'Al final de *Campos de Castilla* había unos Proverbios y cantares que significaban la aparición de un nuevo Machado, el que se logrará definitivamente en las *NC*. Pero conviene aclararlo inmediatamente: la continuidad no lo es en cuanto a espíritu, sino en cuanto a forma. Los *cantares* no son lo mismo que las *canciones*. Esta es la cuestión. Por más que cantares (¿hace falta recordar a Manuel?) fueran el alma de Andalucía, Antonio escribe – a la manera castellana – canciones' (1976: p. 129).

9   As Shelley Stevens points out, 'although Rosalía de Castro was not familiar with the Galician-Portuguese *Cancioneros* of the thirteenth and fourteenth centuries, she was firmly convinced of the inherent literary qualities of the rural songs and certainly sensed the presence of tradition that had survived many generations' (pp. 13–14).

10 González adds: 'Sin embargo, deducir de todo ello que Machado es un poeta romántico, y nada más que eso, me parece excesivo . . . Para ser verdad romántica, a la obra de Machado le ha faltado eso: el tiempo propicio. Además, tampoco Machado pretendió ser romántico, sino vencer la atracción del romanticismo sin coincidir con la órbita descrita por el simbolismo' (p. 35).

11 The philosophical interpretations of certain poems in the *PrCs* are too numerous to cite here. The books that contain valuable references to philosophy in the *PrCs* include: Bernard Sesé, *El hombre. El poeta. El pensador* (Madrid, 1980); Roberto Murillo Zamora, *Antonio Machado (ensayo sobre su pensamiento filosófico)* (San José, 1981); Juan David García Bacca, *Invitación a filosofar según espíritu y letra de Antonio Machado* (Barcelona, 1984); José Luis Abellán, *El filósofo 'Antonio Machado'*

(Valencia, 1995); Geoffrey Ribbans, *Campos de Castilla* (Madrid, 1989); Andreu Rodrigo, *El cristianismo metafísico de Antonio Machado* (Valencia, 2004); Belaunde Moreyra, *Alcance filosófico en César Vallejo y Antonio Machado* (Lima, 2005). Also of interest is the collection of essays titled *Antonio Machado y la filosofía* (Madrid, 1989).

[12] *Colección Unicaja Manuscritos de los Hermanos Machado,* Introduction, transcription and notes by Rafael Alarcón Sierra, Pablo del Barco and Antonio Rodríguez Almodóvar, 10 vols (Málaga, 2005).

[13] The astrological sign Aries Machado references in poem ix corresponds to the months of March and April.

Chapter 1: The Problem of Subjectivity: How to Know the Self and Other

[1] Although he was selected for the Real Academia Española de la Lengua in 1927 (he was granted the post left vacant by the death of Miguel de Echegaray), Machado never formalized his relationship with the academy. The clues as to why he distanced himself from this honour reside in the *Proyecto de un discurso* itself: 'No creo poseer las dotes específicas del académico. No soy humanista, ni filólogo, ni erudito. Ando muy flojo de latín, porque me lo hizo aborrecer un mal maestro. Estudié el griego con amor, por ansia de leer a Platón, pero tardíamente y, tal vez por ello, con escaso aprovechamiento. Pobres son mis letras en suma, pues aunque he leído mucho, mi memoria es débil y he retenido muy poco. Si algo estudié con ahínco fue más de filosofía que de amena literatura. Y confesaros he que, con excepción de algunos poetas, las bellas letras nunca me apasionaron' (2001b: pp. 690–1).

[2] All the citations of Machado's poetry, unless otherwise stated, derive from Manuel Alvar's edition of *Antonio Machado – Poesías completas* (Madrid, 2001).

[3] Machado often referred to Plato when discussing Kant's philosophy. In *Los complementarios,* he considers them both as innovators of a certain philosophical discourse that summarized key stages of Western thought: 'Fue Kant el último filósofo de gran estilo. Para encontrarle su igual, es preciso recordar a Platón. Pero ni Platón ni Kant crearon ningún tema esencial de la filosofía. Platón reasume la filosofía helénica, desde los jonios a los sofistas; Kant reasume la filosofía renacentista. Ni uno ni otro vinieron al mundo a poner fin a las disputas filosóficas, sino a enseñarnos a filosofar. Después de leer a Platón, no disminuye nuestra admiración por Protágoras; después de leer a Kant, aumenta nuestra afición a Hume' (p. 46).

[4] In 'Sobre poesía. Fragmentos de lecciones', Mairena refers again to Plato's and Kant's dove to make a point about the type of so-called lyric poetry that fails to be lyrical because it ignores time (that which sustains it): 'El poeta pretende elevar su corazón hasta ponerlo fuera del tiempo, en el "topos uranios" de las ideas . . . Si leyeráis a Kant . . . os encontraríais con

aquella su famosa parábola de la paloma que, al sentir en las alas la resistencia que le opone el aire, sueña que podría volar mejor en el vacío' (1971a: p. 70).

5 In a letter to Unamuno in 1914, Machado mentions Kant's 'Críticas' for the first time: '¿no es La vida es sueño obra tan filosófica como las Críticas de Kant?' (2001b: p. 368).

6 Machado tells Ortega y Gasset in 1919 that '[n]ingún [libro] me agradó tanto como Kant, cuya *Crítica de la razón pura* he releído varias veces con creciente interés. El libro de Morente, recientemente publicado, y algunas páginas de Cassirer y Natorp me han dado alguna luz para una comprensión relativamente clara de la obra de Kant en sus líneas generales' (2001b: p. 437). As Doménech explains, Machado is referring to Manuel García Morente's *La filosofía de Kant* of 1917 (Morente also translated Kant's *Critique of Practical Reason* in 1913, and the *Critique of Judgement* in 1914). 'Quizá leyera [Machado] el "epílogo" de Cassirer en Kant, *Prolegómenos a toda metafísica del porvenir que haya de poder presentarse como una ciencia*, traducción y prólogo de Julián Besteiro (Madrid, Jorro, 1912); y de Natorp la obra citada, *E. Kant y la escuela filosófica de Marburgo* (1915)' (2001b: p. 437).

7 Emmanuel Levinas theorizes a very similar intersubjective responsibility in *Totality and Infinity: An Essay on Exteriority* that begins with the Other's presence: 'It is only in approaching the Other that I attend to myself. This does not mean that existence is constituted in the thought of the others. An existence called objective, such as is reflected in the thought of the others, and by which I count in universality, in the State, in history, in the totality, does not express me, but precisely dissimulates me. The face I welcome makes me pass from phenomenon of being in another sense: in discourse I expose myself to the questioning of the Other, and this urgency of the response – acuteness of the present – engenders me for responsibility; as responsible I am brought to my final reality . . . When I seek my final reality, I find that my existence as a "thing in itself" begins with the presence in me of the idea of Infinity. But this relation already consists in serving the Other' (pp. 178–9). The conclusion deals more at length with the points of contact between Levinas's philosophy and Machado's concept of otherness.

8 Jerome McGann argues for a Romantic 'consciousness industry' in *The Romantic Ideology: A Critical Investigation* (Chicago, 1984), emphasizing how romantic discursivity contained and portrayed 'the idea that poetry, or even consciousness, can set one free of the ruins of history and culture is the grand illusion of every Romantic poet. This idea continues as one of the most important shibboleths of our culture, especially – and naturally – at its higher levels' (p. 91). Clifford Siskin shows to what extent such concepts such as inwardness or imaginative truth were historically constructed in *The Historicity of Romantic Discourse* (Oxford, 1988). His core idea of 'generic history' seeks to use 'genre to construct history rather than the other way around. Understood as a family concept, genre can address both change *and* continuity' (p. 10). In *Romantic Identities – Varieties of Subjectivity 1774–1830* (Cambridge, 2006), Andrea K.

Henderson aims to 'historicize Romantic subjectivity [through] competing models of the self that were produced during the [Romantic] period.
The depth model, which criticism has, in effect, canonized as *the* Romantic
view of subjectivity, was, during the Romantic period itself, only one
available model among many . . . these models are to be found in not only
non-canonical writings but even in the works of the period's canonized
authors' (p. 2).

9   In 'Modernity's Consciousness of Time and Its Need for Self-Reassurance',
Habermas argues that 'in the fundamental experience of aesthetic modernity, the problem of self-grounding becomes acute, because here the
horizon of temporal experience contracts to the decentered subjectivity
that splits away from the conventions of everyday life . . . The actual
present can no longer gain its self-consciousness from opposition to an
epoch rejected and surpassed, to a shape of the past. Actuality can be
constituted only as the point where time and eternity intersect' (pp. 8–9).

10   In *Los complementarios*, he continues his critique stating: 'En el siglo XIX ha
habido una tendencia a la cobardía y a la inmunidad filosófica.
Llamémosle positivismo, aceptando el término en su acepción más gener-
alizada . . . Refutando el positivismo la filosofía recobra su vuelo y parte
nuevamente de Kant; se reanuda la reflexión filosófica, en aquel
momento en que quedó interrumpida' (p. 47).

11   Machado expressed his fondness for gypsy paradoxes through Mairena as
well: 'Dos formas hay de enunciar las paradojas, que recomiendo a vuestra
reflexión . . . La primera es la dogmática y rotunda, cínicamente engas-
tada entre silogismos, la calderoniana, siempre impresionante . . . La
segunda es popular, más graciosa y sutil, que ni siquiera parece paradójica,
la del gitano . . . Si me preguntáis cuál de estas dos maneras de expresar lo
paradójico es la más poética, os contestaré: eso va en gustos; para mí,
desde luego, la del gitano' (1986: p. 36).

12   For more on how the Böhl de Faber and Joaquín de Mora dispute opened
a critical space in early nineteenth-century Spanish politics and historiog-
raphy for German Romantic thought, it is worth reviewing Chapter IV of
Guillermo Carnero's *Los orígenes del romanticismo reaccionario español: El
matrimonio Böhl de Faber* titled 'La polémica y la mitología reaccionaria de
su época' where he discusses 'la corriente reaccionaria que surge en
nuestro país como respuesta dictada por el inmovilismo contra todo
aquello que pone en peligro la pervivencia del Antiguo Régimen, es decir:
la Ilustración, la Revolución Francesa y las Cortes de Cádiz' (p. 247).

13   See Paul de Man's *Aesthetic Ideology*, edited and with an introduction by
Andrezj Warminski (Minneapolis, 1996), pp. 178–9.

14   In a letter to Juan Ramón Jiménez, Machado says: 'V. continua a Bécquer,
el primer renovador del ritmo interno de la poesía española' (2001b: p.
200).

15   Albornoz also comments briefly on the possible influence of Machado's
sentenious poetry on Miguel de Unamuno's *Cancionero* (an area that still
today is relatively unexplored): 'Así como de los poemas de hombres y
tierras de *Campos de Castilla* volvió a ocuparse Unamuno en repetidas
ocasiones, no creo que volverá a hablar de los 'Proverbios y cantares', salvo
excepcionalmente. Sin embargo, no cabe duda de que el género le

interesaba profundamente, y acaso no sea exageración el apuntar que la presencia de los de Machado se deja ver muchos años más tarde en varios poemas del *Cancionero*' (1968: p. 98).

16   The Valera-Campoamor debate began in December 1888 when in the prospectus of the newly formed journal *El Ateneo. Revista Científica, Literaria y Artística*, the editors added the note: 'Se insertará toda producción referente a cualquier rama de la ciencia, sin desdeñar la poesía'. Shortly thereafter, Campoamor published '¿La poesía desdeñada por la ciencia?', a short piece that argued how positivist science wanted to do away with metaphysics and eliminate everything in poetry that was, in his opinion, poetic. Valera responded stating that prose was to be valued above metaphysics and poetry, since in terms of utility, 'la metafísica es ciencia *inútil* y arte *inútil* la poesía'. As expected, Campoamor retorted: 'La metafísica consiste en pensar sobre el pensamiento y, al declarar el señor Valera su inutilidad, hace retroceder al hombre a la categoría de mono sabio, que aunque hace cosas de *entendimiento*, no sabe hacer cosas de *entendimiento entendido* . . . la metafísica, no sólo no es *inútil*, sino que es de *necesidad absoluta* . . . ¡Desengáñese el señor Valera: por más que se burle de mis pretensiones, de llevar la filosofía a la poesía, ya Lessing demostró que la obra de arte consiste en elevar lo individual a la categoría de lo general'. Prose was an imperfect form of art, Campoamor argued: 'la prosa no es arte' (391–8).

17   Machado's uncle Agustín Durán had studied what he considered was a 'Spanish' folklorism by 1832, the year the last of his five-volume *Romances castellanos anteriores al siglo XVIII* was published (volumes that later appeared in the *Romancero general* of 1849 and 1851).

18   Manuel Machado, *Poesía* (Madrid, 1942), p. 14.

19   Ibid., p. 45.

Chapter 2: Towards Conceiving the Other: The Formative Years

1   'Edward B. Tylor, to whom [Demófilo] considered Spenser [*sic*] indebted, exercised a still greater influence. Machado had read, in English, the two sizeable volumes of *Primitive Culture* (1871) within eight years of their publication, and from then on references to Tylor and partial translations and reviews of his work were frequent. Largely for financial reasons he did publish, in 1888, a translation of *Anthropology* (1881), a smaller, mainly repetitive work. Just as Spenser's [*sic*] elucidation of opaque social custom gratified Machado's sense of being at odds with the values of Spanish society, so Tylor's eloquent derivation of religion from animism gave welcome support and renewed vigour to a rather stale traditional anticlericalism . . . Reassured that the hostility of the Church served only to prove him right, he continued to reproduce and expand Tylor's demonstrations of the origins of the Adams of the various Genesis myths; of baptism, common to most savages in some form; of the rosary, a rose abacus from

India, and so on', Gordon Brotherston, 'Antonio Machado y Álvarez and Postivism' (Brotherston, pp. 224–5).

2   Demófilo also defined folklore in *Cantes flamencos* as 'esa ciencia niña sin nombre todavía, aunque conocida en toda Europa bajo el nombre de Folklore, de la cual forma parte importantísima el estudio del *sentir popular,* correspondiente y paralelo al *saber* y al *querer* del pueblo dentro de la división, quizá algo convencional, que hacemos de las facultades de espíritu humano' (p. 313).

3   In the introduction to the first volume of his *Biblioteca de las tradiciones populares españolas* (Madrid, 1884), Demófilo also stated: 'A los hombres científicos, en cambio, toca más especialmente ocuparse en analizar e incorporar a la ciencia los conocimientos relativos a los fenómenos naturales y sociológicos que el pueblo ha aprendido en su larga experiencia' (p. x).

4   See Juan López Álvarez's *El krausismo en los escritos de Antonio Machado y Álvarez, 'Demófilo'* (Cádiz, 1996), pp. 55–69.

5   See Dámaso Chicharro and Cruz Giráldez, '"Demófilo" en el teatro de los Machado', *La Andalucía de Demófilo* (Madrid: Sociedad Editorial Electa, S. A., 1993), pp. 74–81; Cruz Giráldez, 'Elementos lírico-populares en el teatro machadiano', *Cuadernos Hispanoamericanos,* 304–7 (1975–6): 1083–94.

6   See José María Valverde, 'Introducción' in *Juan de Mairena* (Madrid, 1971), p. 53.

7   As Wiedemann points out, 'Cipriano Álvarez Durán llegó a publicar cinco cuentos en *El Folk-Lore Andaluz*: "La mano negra", "Una rueda de consejos", "La serpiente de las siete cabezas", "Las velas", y "Las tres Marías". También colaboró en la colección de su hijo Machado y Álvarez, titulada *Cuentos populares españoles,* aportándole los cuentos "El barquito de oro, plata y seda", y "La sirena". En 1885 publicó sus *Cuentos extremeños* y un estudio acerca de la "Culinaria popular extremeña"' (2001: p. 188).

8   In a 1903 letter to Juan Ramón Jiménez, Machado clearly echoes Giner's example: 'Yo procuro calcar la línea de mi sentimiento y no me asusto de que salga en el papel una figureja extraña y deforme, *porque eso soy yo*' (2001b: 181).

9   Manuel explains how he and Antonio came into contact with Paradas for the first time: '[Paradas] vino a buscarnos a mi hermano Antonio y a mí, y a decirnos que si queríamos ayudarle levantaríamos hasta las nubes el periódico y se alcanzaría un magnífico negocio. Ni que decir tiene que nosotros ayudábamos absolutamente *gratis et amore* . . . Formamos, pues, con él la Redacción fija de *La Caricatura*' (2001b: p. 113.

10   The volume has no page numbers.

11   *Colección Unicaja Manuscritos de los Hermanos Machado,* Introduction, transcription and notes by Rafael Alarcón Sierra, Pablo del Barco and Antonio Rodríguez Almodóvar, 10 vols (Málaga: Servicio de Publicaciones de Unicaja), II, p. 123.

12   The volume has no page numbers.

13   In 'Arte de hablar y pragmática: Notas sobre el pensamiento lingüístico de Eduardo Benot (1822–1907)', Joaquín Mesa states: 'la obra gramatical de Benot no puede encuadrarse dentro de la lingüística Histórica y

Comparada, que nuestro gramático conoció . . . sino en el programa de investigación anterior, la Gramática filosófica, como señala Sarmiento. De adscripción a la Gramática filosófica no presenta dificultades. De acuerdo con los caracteres básicos de la gramática ideológica que Brigitte Schlieben-Lange (1990:p. 549) determina, en la obra benotiana se advierte claramente la perspectiva genética del lenguaje (lenguaje de acción y lenguaje artificial) . . . trazos de la teoría sensualista del conocimiento . . . las relaciones entre lenguaje y pensamiento, y otros muchos aspectos' (p. 342).

14   Antonio Vilanova also provides evidence that Machado's eye metaphor could have derived from Plato's *Alcibiades I*. In 'La metafísica poética de Antonio Machado', Vilanova believes that this text by Plato represents 'el verdadero punto de partida de la machadiana búsqueda del otro' (p. 83).

15   I do not discount that Béquer's 'Rima IV' could also have been a source of inspiration for these poems: 'Mientras haya unos ojos que reflejen / los ojos que los miran [. . . /] ¡habrá poesía!'

16   For the Unicaja workbook references to Hamlet, see *Cuaderno 1* {fol. 8r}, {fol. 12r}, {fol. 13r}, {fol. 19r}, {fol. 34r}, {fol. 35r}, and {fol. 36r}.

17   'Publiqué un libro de versos *Soledades* en 1903, refundido más tarde en 1907 *Soledades, Galerías, otros poemas* con aumento de muchas composiciones y otro libro *Campos de Castilla* en 1912. Los versos que van insertos en los primeros libros están en su gran mayoría escritos en época anterior a su publicación' (2001b: p. 334).

18   In the prologue to Ayuso's *Helénicas* of 1914, Machado explains the water–thirst relationship further: 'Desdeñar una porcelana de Sèvres cuando se necesita un cántaro con agua es, tal vez, más disculpable que desdeñar el vaso en que se bebe cuando está saciada la sed. Sin embargo, yo pregunto: ¿sabéis vosotros para que sirve el vaso en que se bebe? Si me decís que sirve para beber, nada me respondéis, porque yo seguiré preguntando: ¿para qué sirve el beber?' (2001b: p. 364).

19   *The New Oxford Annotated Bible* (New York, 1991), p. 842.

20   Ibid., p. 844.

21   In his 'Discurso en el homenaje a Antonio Pérez de la Mata', Machado returns once again to the Book of Ecclesiastes to propose a similar interior/exterior dualism: 'Y no es sólo el espíritu escéptico, tan viejo como el pensar de los hombres y que en remotos tiempos produjo aquel universal, formidable bostezo salomónico del vanitas vanitatum et omnia vanitas sub sole, el enemigo del pensador y del filósofo. Contra este espíritu escéptico bien puede reaccionar el amor de la vida que, si en la mayoría de los hombres se manifiesta por una necesidad y un placer de nutrirse y de acrecentar la especie, es también, en los hombres de fuerte mentalidad, la necesidad de pensar y exteriorizar el propio pensamiento' (2001b: p. 240).

Chapter 3: From Art to Life: Critical Inquiries and a New Poetry

1   The year 1913 is significant since it marks the end of Machado's intense period of writing and publishing his first *PrCs*. In February and May 1909, he published the first twenty *PrCs* in *La Lectura: Revista de ciencias y de arte*. In the 1912 edition of *CC*, he published all twenty of the 1909 poems that appeared in *La Lectura*, as well as an additional eight poems written between 1910 and 1912. In 1913, he published eighteen more *PrCs* in *La Lectura* under the title 'Cantares, proverbios, sátiras y epigramas'. The next intense writing period of the *PrCs* begins in 1916 and stretches to 1924 with the publication of *NC*.

2   Aurora de Albornoz suggests that Machado and Unamuno may have met before this first exchange of letters: 'Según el doctor Álvarez Sierra, amigo de juventud de don Antonio, el poeta conoció a don Miguel antes de 1900. Afirma Álvarez Sierra que Machado estuvo presente en unos Juegos Florales, celebrados en Bilbao, en los que don Miguel fue el orador principal. Según Alice Mc Van, en 1903 Unamuno visitó a Antonio Machado en su casa para darle las gracias por el envío de *Soledades*. Añade esta escritora que, en agradecimiento, Machado dedicó a don Miguel el poema *Luz*' (1968: p. 23).

3   Machado would discuss this topic with Ortega y Gasset in 1912 and reiterate the importance of extracting Art from life experience: 'Paréceme a mí que el lírico español no ha nacido aún, acaso no nazca nunca. Sin embargo, ningún momento tan propicio como el actual en que nos proponemos crear la patria. Preciso es que tengamos en cuenta para crear la lírica: [. . .] 8.º Que es preciso buscar el poema fundamental nuestro que no está ni en la historia, ni en la tradición, sino en la vida' (2001b: p. 310).

4   In his article 'Antonio Machado, la institución y el idealismo finisecular', Richard Cardwell analyses Machado's early years to demonstrate the various influences that affected his aestheticism (Giner's Krausism, Darío's *modernismo*, the pedagogical question, folklorism etc.). Ultimately, however, it was the pursuit of an aesthetic ideal based on social change and renewal – and symbolically represented in the publication of *Helios* – that defined Machado's poetry during his early years according to Cardwell: 'Es esto el idealismo de *Helios*, de la generación finisecular. Es esto lo que emprendió Machado en su arte poética, es esto también lo que anhelaron hacer sus mentores y sus amigos, los intelectuales de fin de siglo' (p. 400).

5   See for example: Geoffrey Ribbans, 'Prólogo', *Antonio Machado. Soledades. Galerías. Otros poemas* (Barcelona, 1975), pp. 21–2; Jorge Urrutia, 'El inicio de *Soledades*. Una lección de simbolismo', *Actas del Congreso Internacional sobre Antonio Machado. Vida y Obra (Segovia, 6, 7 y 8 de abril de 2000)* (Segovia, 2002), pp. 109–29; Jacinta Cremades Gómez-Pablos, 'La imagen de la fuente de Verlaine en Antonio Machado', *Actas del Congreso Internacional sobre Antonio Machado. Vida y Obra (Segovia, 6, 7 y 8 de abril de 2000)* (Segovia, 2002), pp. 193–200.

6   Years later when Machado resided in Baeza, he confided in Unamuno:

'comprendo ... su repulsión por esa *mandangas y garliborleos* de los modernistas cortesanos. A esos jóvenes los llevaría yo a las Alpujarras y los dejaría un par de años allí. Creo que esto sería más útil que pensionarlos en la Soborna. Muchos seguramente desaparecerían del mundo de las letras, pero acaso alguno encontraría acentos más hondos y verdaderos' (2001b: pp. 340–1).

7   See the chapter titled 'Decadent Diagnostics' in Charles Bernheimer's *Decadent Subjects: The Idea of Decadence in Art, Literature, Philosophy, and Culture of the Fin de Siècle in Europe*, pp. 139–62.

8   This proposition demonstrates, I believe, to what degree Machado was further reorienting his poetry towards folklore during these years. Demófilo had already articulated this point in his *Cantes flamencos*. According to Demófilo, the *copla* was the most universal and lyrical poetry, since it was capable of reaching the collective while still maintaining its deeply intimate character. In the prologue to the 1917 edition of *CC*, Machado returns to this concept of subjective/objective balance in his poetry: 'Somos víctimas de un doble espejismo. Si miramos afuera y procuramos penetrar en las cosas, nuestro mundo externo pierde en solidez, y acaba por disipársenos cuando llegamos a creer que no existe por sí, sino por nosotros. Pero si, convencidos de la íntima realidad, miramos adentro, entonces todo nos parece venir de afuera, y es nuestro mundo interior, nosotros mismos, lo que se desvanece' (2001a: p. 78–9).

9   Machado believed both the 1903 and 1907 editions constituted in essence one book: '[*Soledades*] fue refundida en 1907, con adición de nuevas composiciones que no añadían nada sustancial a las primeras ... Ambos volúmenes constituyen en realidad un solo libro' (2001a: p. 78). In a 1913 biography, he worded it as follows: 'Publiqué un libro de versos *Soledades* en 1903, refundido más tarde en 1907 *Soledades, Galerías, otros poemas* con aumento de muchas composiciones' (2001b: p. 334). Machado distanced himself even further from *Soledades* by only including eight of its poems in his *Poesías escogidas* of 1917.

10 Ricardo Gullón, 'Antonio Machado modernista', in *Antonio Machado Hoy (1939–1989)*, ed. Paul Aubert (Madrid, 1994), pp. 23–67; Aurora de Albornoz, 'Rubén Darío en Antonio Machado', in *Antonio Machado Hoy (1939–1989)*, ed. Paul Aubert (Madrid, 1994), pp. 71–84. In the 'Introducción' to Machado's *Poesías completas* (Madrid, 2001), Manuel Alvar opines that: 'Decir que Antonio no es poeta modernista no es decir gran cosa, pues también podría defenderse lo contrario. A mi modo de ver, hay algo diferente de escribir poemas en un sentido u otro: es el talante de la inclinación, la voluntad de ser. Y Antonio Machado no quiso ser modernista por más que se puedan rastrear, y encontrar, en él influencias de la escuela' (p. 12).

11 It is important to note how Darío finishes this paragraph in his *Prosas profanas*. After expressing his admiration for Spanish authors, he continues with the famous phrases: 'Después exclamo: Shakespeare! Dante! Hugo! (Y en mi interior: Verlaine. . . !). Luego al despedirme: – "Abuelo, preciso es decirlo: mi esposa es de mi tierra; mi querida de París"' (p. 49).

12 In this excerpt Zavala explains Darío's intricate usage of alexandrines in the poem 'Cisnes I'.

13   Kirkpatrick adds further: 'While working within patches of this *modernista* discourse, later poets allow us to sense the absences, rather than the accumulations, which make us feel that we are in new territories . . . The tear Lugones made in *modernismo*'s fabric of social and sexual dynamics is still being rewoven by contemporary poets. Lugones' intrusiveness created a lingering discordance, and no amount of dispassionate criticism can gloss over the uneasy spaces he created' (pp. 10–11).

14   See my article 'The Modern Self as Subject: The Structure of Crisis in José Asunción Silva's *De Sobremesa*', *Latin American Literary Review*, Vol. 68 (2006): 59–82.

15   Simón Guadalajara Solera, *El compromiso en Antonio Machado (a la ética por la estética)* (Madrid, 1984); Francisco Such, *Lectura ética de Antonio Machado* (Murcia, 1982); Elisa Rosales Juega, *Comportamiento ético de la poesía de Antonio Machado* (Delaware, 1998).

16   *The New Oxford Annotated Bible* (New York, 1991), p. 64.

17   Ibid., pp. 40–1.

18   Ibid., p. 776.

19   The poem 'Coplas elegíacas' in *SGOP* presages Machado's preoccupation with thirst: '¡Ay del que llega sediento / a ver el agua correr, / y dice: la sed que siento / no me la calma el beber! / ¡Ay de quien bebe y, saciada / la sed, desprecia la vida'. In poems xxi and xlv in *NC*, Machado pondered further on the symbolic and moral implications of thirst: '. . . Pero yo he visto beber / hasta en los charcos del suelo. / Caprichos tiene la sed'; '¿Todo para los demás? / Mancebo, llena tu jarro, / que ya te lo beberán'.

20   Machado returned to the honeybee trope in *Juan de Mairena*: 'Esa abeja que liba en la miel y no en las flores, es más ajena a toda labor creadora que el humilde arrimador de documentos reales, o que el consabido espejo de lo real, que pretende darnos por arte la innecesaria réplica de cuanto no lo es' (1986: p. 45). In the weekly journal *La Internacional*, Machado published an article in 1920 where he revisited many of these core themes: 'El artista no puede crear *ex nihilo* como el Dios bíblico. No puede tampoco ser un copista de la obra divina ni un plagiario de la naturaleza. El artista crea a la manera del hombre: transformando una cosa en otra, o, si queréis, dando una forma a una materia'. In the second part of this article he returns to the honeybee metaphor: "Si vino la primavera, / volad a las flores; / no chupéis cera"' (2001b: pp. 447–8).

Chapter 4: The God of Intersubjectivity

1   For Sánchez Barbudo, 'Machado es de los fideístas que, más propiamente, o con más claridad al menos, podríamos llamar ateos, aunque ciertamente ateos insatisfechos: hombres que sienten la falta de Dios' (1969: p. 146); Pedro Laín Entralgo considers Machado an agnostic whose 'idea de Dios . . . insita en el hombre' (pp. 66–7); Armand F. Baker proposes: 'No cabe duda de que la metafísica de Antonio Machado se basa sobre una concepción panteísta' (p. 16); for Pablo Cobos, 'no hay poema, ni en Machado, ni en Mairena, ni en Martín, que no se pueda inscribir en esquema

panteísta, o panenteístia' (p. 236); and in González Ruiz's opinion, 'el poeta sevillano insiste machaconamente en el hecho de que en el ámbito de su creencia aparecía Dios como algo esencial e insustituible'(p. 34).

2   Stanley G. Payne refers to the period between 1875 and 1898 as a 'Catholic revival', a period that witnessed 'a new work of evangelism and the expansion of religious devotion'. However, 'the revival was limited by its increasingly close dependence upon the newly dominant political and social sectors, and failed to recapture the complete popular dimension of the traditional religion' (p. 97).

3   In *Del sentimiento trágico* Unamuno declares: 'Y si cada cual de nosotros, en el empuje de su amor, en su hambre de divinidad, se imagina a Dios a su medida, y a su medida se hace Dios para él, hay un Dios colectivo, social, humano, resultante de las imaginaciones todas humanas que le imaginan. Porque Dios es y se revela en la colectividad. Y es Dios la más rica y más personal concepción humana' (p. 130). Yet, how is each imagined concept of God effectively articulated in a social context? And, what of the differences in our personal concepts of God, how do they affect the Idea of God, and are they meaningful? These questions are crucial considering that for Unamuno, 'mi idea de Dios es diferente cada vez que la concibo' (1967: p. 73).

4   These poems are the second and third *cantares* of 'Tres cantares enviados a Unamuno en 1913'. Albornoz notes that these *cantares* refer to Unamuno's mention of Pascal in *Del sentimiento trágico*. For Pascal, God hides from those who are not interested in finding Him, while He reveals Himself to those with open hearts ready to receive Him. In *Pensées* he writes: 'That God has willed to hide Himself – If there were only one religion, God would indeed be manifest . . . If there were no obscurity, man would not be sensible of his corruption . . . Thus, it is not only fair, but advantageous to us, that God be partly hidden and partly revealed; since it is equally dangerous to man to know God without knowing his wretchedness, and to know his own wretchedness without knowing God' (p. 143).

5   In *Los complementarios* Machado draws an analogy between Bergson and Heraclitus and he considers antieleatic Cartesianism the defining note of nineteenth-century philosophy: '*Henri Bergson* es el filósofo definitivo del siglo XIX . . . Lo característico de su obra es su antieleatismo, el motivo heraclitano de su pensamiento. El péndulo del pensamiento filosófico marca con Bergson la extrema posición heraclitana. Así termina, en filosofía, el siglo XIX, que ha sido, todo él una reacción ante el eleatismo cartesiano' (pp. 23–4). Heraclitus reappears in *Cancionero apócrifo de Abel Martín* in a passage on lyrical poetry. Machado alludes in this passage to Heraclitus' famous river metaphor ('No one steps into the same river twice') to explain the Doctrine of Flux in light of the oppositional Eleatic idea of the permanent unity of being: 'Necesita, pues, el pensar poético una nueva dialéctica, sin negaciones ni contrarios, que Abel Martín llama lírica y, otras veces, mágica, la lógica del cambio sustancial o devenir inmóvil, del ser cambiando o el cambio siendo. Bajo esta idea, realmente paradójica y aparentemente absurda, está la más honda intuición que Abel Martín pretende haber alcanzado' (pp. 31–2). In poem xciii of the

PrCs of *NC,* Machado touches upon the eleatic and Heraclitan discussion once again to broach life and death (and the river in this poem brings to mind not only Heraclitus' river, but also that of Jorge Manrique): '¿Cuál es la verdad? ¿El río / que fluye y pasa / donde el barco y barquero / son también ondas del agua? / ¿O este soñar del marino / siempre con ribera y ancla?' In *Juan de Mairena,* Machado digresses on the porous boundaries that separate poetry and philosophy, and he refers once again to Heraclitus' river: 'El escepticismo de los poetas puede servir de estímulo a los filósofos. Los poetas, en cambio, pueden aprender de los filósofos el arte de las grandes metáforas: Ej. El río de Heráclito' (p. 267).

6   The begonia – *Begonia fuchsioides* – is sometimes called a Jesus Heart (or Heart of Jesus).

7   Machado's 'corazoncitos de Jesús' reappear in 'Divagaciones – En torno al último libro de Unamuno' as early as 1905. Unamuno reminded Machado of Saint Teresa and Saint John of the Cross in his relentless pursuit of spiritual transcendence: 'Continúa Unamuno a los místicos españoles, almas de fuego. ¡Pobres corazoncitos de Jesús, no os asustéis! . . . A él acudimos en demanda de auxilio espiritual y él siempre, en amable maestro, nos acoge' (2001b: pp. 206–7). In the poem 'Desde mi rincón' published in *El Porvenir Castellano* on 27 November 1913, Machado added the following verses after verse 69 (later deleted from the 1917 version of the poem): 'Malgrado de mi porte jacobino, / Y mi asco de las juntas apostólicas / Y las damas católicas, / Creo en la voluntad contra el destino. / A pesar de la turba milagrera / Y sus mastines fieros, / Y de esa clerigalla vocinglera / ¡corazoncitos de Jesús tan hueros!, / Creo en tu Dios y en el mío' (2001a: p. 255).

8   He continues, stating: 'Nuestra mística representa el gran momento introspectivo de la raza, en que llegó ésta, por la vía intuitiva, a expresar, aunque de un modo balbuciente, su yo fundamental. Y ¿adónde hubiera llegado esta reforma, ahogada en germen por la Inquisición o malograda por sí misma, a no haber sido ahogada o malograda? . . . Pero nosotros ahogamos el ascua en la ceniza. Cuando cesó para la Iglesia todo peligro de reforma, el sentimiento religioso [se] asfixiaba' (2001b: p. 353). This mention of the 'ascua' and 'ceniza' in this mystical context brings to mind poem lviii (*NC*): 'Creí mi hogar apagado, / y revolví la ceniza. . . / Me quemé la mano'. Perhaps what Machado is saying is that one needs only to look below the surface (the 'hogar' alluding to the *pueblo*) to find a burning spiritual desire.

9   Poem xxxiv (*NC*). Although often attributed to Mussolini, the first verse '*O rinnovarsi o perire*' ('Renew oneself or perish') is perhaps a motto that originated with D'Annunzio. The third verse of the poem derives from Gnaeus Pompeius Magnus (106–48BCE): 'Navigare è necessario, vivere non è necessario'.

10 *The New Oxford Annotated Bible,* pp. 711–12.

11 Ibid., pp. 158–60.

12 Ibid., p. 320.

13 In poem XXV published in *Revista de Occidente* in 1923 ('Enemigo / que por el amor me hieres / brazo de Dios. ¡Dios contigo!'), Machado may allude once again to the Old Testament God. The 'arm of God' appears

often in the Old Testament and refers broadly to both God's wrath and salvation (see Isaiah 40:10, 52:10, 59:15–16; also Psalm 98: 1–2, and Job 40:9).

14 Sánchez Barbudo's foundational *Estudios sobre Galdós, Unamuno y Machado* tackles 'El ser y la nada' and serves as a good point of departure to understand the various studies dedicated to Machado's idea of God and nothingness over the years. In fact, many of Sánchez Barbudo's core arguments and conclusions are still valid today. Agustín Andreu Rodrigo's *El cristianismo metafísico de Antonio Machado* (Valencia, 2004) proposes a very similar line of thought on Machado's idea of God and nothingness: 'La idea de la creación de la nada (*ex nihilo*), de que el Universo haya salido de la nada, se le puede ocurrir solamente a un Dios insuficiente que convierte la distancia entre Él y su criatura, en planteamiento de entrada . . . El poeta, descubridor de ser mediante intuiciones, sabe estar en el ser y no tiene ningún problema con ese no-ser que es propiamente lo que Dios ha hecho por nosotros y para nosotros' (pp. 198–201).

15 Machado goes on to say: 'Me parece, más bien, la fraternidad el amor al prójimo por amor al padre común. Mi hermano no es una creación mía ni trozo alguno de mí mismo; para amarlo he de poner mi amor en él y no en mí, el es igual a mí, pero es otro que yo' (2001b: p. 427). Years later, Mairena sought to define Jesus through love and otherness: 'Y reparad ahora en que el "ama a tu prójimo como a ti mismo y aún más, si fuera preciso", que tal es el verdadero precepto cristiano, lleva implícita una fe altruista, una creencia en la realidad absoluta, en la existencia en sí del otro yo . . . ¿cómo he de atreverme, dentro de esta fe cristiana, a degradar a mi prójimo tan profunda y substancialmente que le arrebate el ser en sí para convertirlo en mera representación, en un puro fantasma mío?' (1971a: pp. 214–15).

16 In a letter sent to Unamuno in June 1913, Machado expresses this same concern for the figure of Jesus pre and post-crucifixion, and he alludes to Unamuno's poem 'El Cristo yacente de Santa Clara (iglesia de la Cruz) de Palencia' that was published in *Los Lunes del Imparcial* that previous month of May: 'Tenía intención de escribirle cuando leí su soberbia composición sobre el Cristo de Palencia . . . También aquí [Baeza] el Cristo precristiano y postcristiano milagrea por los cabellos y las uñas y en cuanto al Cristo del cielo de que V. habla, no hay cuestión todavía' (2001b: p. 338). As far as Jesus' death and resurrection, this moment is crucial to the foundation of the Church. As Tillich explains it: 'In the moment in which Jesus was called the Christ and the combination of his messianic dignity with an ignominious death was asserted – whether in expectation or in retrospection – the application of the idea of resurrection to the Christ was almost unavoidable. The disciples' assertion that the symbol had become an event was dependent in part upon their belief in Jesus, who, as the Christ, became the Messiah. But it was affirmed in a way which transcended the mythological symbolism of the mystery cults, just as the concrete picture of Jesus as the Christ transcended the mythical pictures of the mystery gods. The character of this event remains in darkness, even in the poetic rationalization of the Easter story. But one thing is obvious. In the days in which the certainty of the Resurrection grasped the small, dispersed, and

despairing group of his followers, the church was born, and, since the
Christ is not the Christ without the Church, he has become the Christ'
(p. 154).

17   *The New Oxford Annotated Bible*, p. 22.
18   '[Matthew 14:22–33] is a miracle story with two acts, each six verses long,
one centred on Jesus (14:22–7) and one centred on Peter (14:28–33) – a
tableau of Christ and his church. In the first act the Lord approaches his
troubled church astride the waves and speaks to her in epiphany,
"Courage! I am! Don't be afraid!" – commands worthy of inscription in
churches, homes, and hearts. In the second act a believing disciple and an
enabling Lord do the impossible, master the elements, and for a brief
moment give the church a glimpse of her unearthly possibilities in the
world. But in the second scene of the second act the believer becomes an
unbeliever, sinks back into the natural life, cries out to the Lord and is
saved. This act and the play itself end with a confession of faith in the Son
of God, who mounts water, supernaturalizes believing disciples, and then
saves barely-believing-yet-praying disciples from death' (Bruner, p. 73).
19   'Para mi es evidente . . . que el Cristo trajo al mundo, entre otras cosas, un
nuevo tema de reflexión, sobre el cual no hemos meditado bastante
todavía. Por esta razón, creo yo en una filosofía cristiana del porvenir, la
cual nada tiene que ver – digámoslo sin ambages – con esas filosofías
católicas, más o menos embozadamente eclesiásticas, con que hoy, como
ayer, se pretende enterrar al Cristo en Aristóteles . . . Nosotros partiríamos
de una investigación de lo esencialmente cristiano en el alma del pueblo,
quiero decir en la conciencia del hombre, impregnada de cristianismo'
(1986: pp. 29–30).
20   *The New Oxford Annotated Bible*, pp. 68–59. The last lines in Spanish read:
'Velad, pues, porque no sabéis cuándo vendrá el señor de la casa. Para que
cuando venga de repente, no os halle durmiendo. Y lo que a vosotros digo,
a todos lo digo: Velad'.
21   In 'Sobre la Rusia actual' Machado states: 'Moscú, en cambio – resumamos
en este claro nombre toda la vasta organización de la Rusia actual –
aunque salude con el puño cerrado, es la mano abierta y generosa, el
corazón hospitalario para todos los hombres libres, que se afanan por
crear una forma de convivencia humana, que no tiene sus límites en las
fronteras de Rusia. Desde su gran revolución, un hecho genial surgido en
plena guerra entre naciones, Moscú vive consagrado a una labor construc-
tora, que es una empresa gigante de radio universal . . . La Rusia actual
nace con la renuncia a todas las ambiciones del Imperio, rompiendo todas
las cadenas, reconociendo la libre personalidad de todos los pueblos que
la integran' (2001b: p. 721).

Chapter 5: The Double Bind of Knowledge and Ignorance

1   In *La era industrial de España* (Barcelona, 1963), Antoni Jutglar notes that
from 1876 onwards, Catalonia's cotton industry developed at a fast pace
and reached its peak in 1898 with eleven million kilograms in exports.

Basque mining also developed quickly during this period. Between 1864 and 1913, the production of iron soared from 280,000 tons to 9,860,000 tons, while the production of copper and carbon jumped from 213,000 tons to 2,268,000 and 387,000 to 3,700,000 respectively (pp. 198–9). One of the key factors that allowed Catalonia and the Basque Country to develop so rapidly were the State's protectionist measures that shielded Spanish markets from foreign imports.

2   Although it is true that the country's defeat in the Spanish–American War stimulated the economy in the long run, most of the capital was reallocated to the already proven industrial sectors: 'There were promising new departures [after 1900]: the growth of heavy industry in the north (in Biscay and to a lesser extent in Guipúzcoa) where the laws of industrial concentration and the availability of raw materials were working against the industrial primacy of Catalonia; later the beginnings of a light industry based on hydro-electric power redressed the balance in favor of the older industrial complex. But these developments, limited by an imperfect system of rail communication which was to collapse under the strains of the Great War, failed to stimulate the stagnant center. In so far as Spain experienced a minor industrial and agricultural revolution it was confined, for the most part, to the periphery' (Carr, pp. 398–9).

3   For a brief summary of Tortella's main ideas on this period, see his article 'Patterns of Economic Retardation and Recovery in South-Western Europe in the Nineteenth and Twentieth Centuries' in *The Economic Development of Spain since 1870*, pp. 3–23. What Tortella sets out to prove is that '[r]elative to the British-French norm, the Latin economies [of Spain, Portugal and Italy] appear to have declined dramatically during the first half of the nineteenth century, almost held their own during the second half, begun a halting recovery from 1900 to 1930, sunk again – Spain especially – in 1930–50, and partially caught up since then' (p. 3).

4   Of particular interest in this book is Rafael A. Álvarez's 'La gran emigración asturiana' (pp. 33–52) and Antonio M. Bernal's 'La emigración de Andalucía' (pp. 143–65). Álvarez and Bernal show how emigration losses affected the rural regions of Asturias and Andalusia specifically.

5   In *Historia Patria: Politics, History, and National Identity in Spain, 1875–1975* (Princeton, 1997), Carolyn Boyd discusses at length how conflicting pedagogical philosophies in Spain between 1875 and 1975 shaped national identity. On this *fin de siglo* period Boyd notes: 'the recipes for pedagogical reform varied as widely as the definitions of regeneration; the disaster that progressives attributed to Spain's failure to modernize, conservatives interpreted as God's punishment for national apostasy. Partly because there was no coherent elite leadership on the issue, middle-class enthusiasm for educational reform eventually subsided. Nevertheless, political mobilization in favor of educational reform endured long enough to provoke a response among the dynastic politicians, who achieved consensus on a number of essential reforms that reflected their awareness of the potential power of state schooling to reinforce the existing order. From 1900 on, as challenges to the regime mounted, the dynastic parties sought to reassert their authority of the state over education. But as state activity intensified, the groups contesting

power correspondingly increased their efforts to influence, directly or indirectly, what children learned in the classroom' (p. 42).

6   'Entre 1903 y 1906, Unamuno recorrió precisamente toda la España liberal, dando conferencias – o "sermones laicos", como él decía – en apoyo de las nuevas leyes de Instrucción Pública. Algunos amigos le suplican que no se disperse así, pero Unamuno les contesta que sus "hermanos en lengua y patria" necesitan, más que sus "paradojas" literarias, lo que él llama "el pan de la cultura europea"' (Marichal, p. 25).

7   *Colección Unicaja Manuscritos de los Hermanos Machado*, Introduction, transcription and notes by Rafael Alarcón Sierra, Pablo del Barco and Antonio Rodríguez Almodóvar, 10 vols (Málaga: Servicio de Publicaciones de Unicaja, 2005), II, p. 39.

8   In the *Unicaja* workbooks we are given a glimpse of the person behind the mask: 'Gritó: carnaval se acaba. / Y se quitó la careta. / No tenía cara', *Poemas Sueltos*, p. 65.

9   Poem xxvii (*NC*).

10   Little did Machado know in 1905 that in a few years he would be destined for Soria. It was a frequent occurrence during his years in Soria that pine forests or evergreen oak groves were razed by farmers or torched by arsonists. In 'Por tierras de España', Machado sketches Soria's barren countryside by describing how farmers hasten its deforestation. Much like the madness of razing a tree to reach its fruit, the farmers destroy the pine groves to reap short-term rewards: 'El hombre de estos campos que incendia los pinares / y su despojo aguarda como botín de guerra, / antaño hubo raído los negros encinares, / talado los robustos robledos de la sierra'.

11   In the *Diccionario Larousse Ilustrado* (1978), the *cucaña* also includes a figurative meaning: 'Ganga, cosa que se consigue con poco trabajo o a costa ajena'. This is the meaning that Machado was perhaps alluding to in poem IV published in *Revista de Occidente* in September 1923: 'Siglo struggle-for-lifista, / cucañista, / boxeador más que guerrero, / del vapor del guerrero'.

12   We find a variation of this quote elsewhere in Mairena: '. . . si mañana un vendaval de cinismo, de elementalidad humana, sacude el árbol de la cultura y se lleva algo más que sus hojas secas, no os asustéis. Los árboles demasiado espesos necesitan perder algunas de sus ramas en beneficio de sus frutos. Y a falta de una poda sabia y consciente, pudiera ser bueno el huracán' (1986: p. 63).

13   Of interest is what Mairena says of Martín: 'Hay hombres que nunca se hartan de saber. Ningún día – dicen – se acuestan sin haber aprendido algo nuevo. Hay otros, en cambio, que nunca se hartan de ignorar. No se duermen tranquilos sin averiguar que ignoraban profundamente algo que creían saber. ¡A igual a A!, decía mi maestro, cuando el sueño eterno comenzaba a enturbiarle los ojos. Y añadía, con voz que no sonaba ya en este mundo: ¡Áteme usted esa mosca por el rabo!' (1971a: p. 69).

Conclusion

[1] In the prologue to the 1917 edition of *CC*, Machado tells us: 'Somos
víctimas – pensaba yo – de un doble espejismo. Si miramos afuera y
procuramos penetrar en las cosas, nuestro mundo externo pierde en
solidez, y acaba por disipársenos cuando llegamos a creer que no existe
por sí, sino por nosotros. Pero si, convencidos de la íntima realidad,
miramos adentro, entonces todo nos parece venir de fuera, y es nuestro
mundo interior, nosotros mismos, lo que se desvanece. ¿Qué hacer entonces? Tejer el hilo que nos dan, solar nuestro sueño, vivir; sólo así podremos
obrar el milagro de la generación' (2001a: p. 79).

Index